WITHDRAWN BY THE
UNIVERSITY OF MICHIGAN

Joni Mitchell

Joni Mitchell

New Critical Readings

Edited by

Ruth Charnock

BLOOMSBURY ACADEMIC
NEW YORK • LONDON • OXFORD • NEW DELHI • SYDNEY

BLOOMSBURY ACADEMIC
Bloomsbury Publishing Inc
1385 Broadway, New York, NY 10018, USA
50 Bedford Square, London, WC1B 3DP, UK

BLOOMSBURY, BLOOMSBURY ACADEMIC and the Diana logo are trademarks of
Bloomsbury Publishing Plc

First published in the United States of America 2019

Copyright © Ruth Charnock and Contributors, 2019

For legal purposes the Permissions on p. ix constitute an
extension of this copyright page.

Cover design: Louise Dugdale
Cover image: photo by Jeff Goode/*Toronto Star* via Getty Images

All rights reserved. No part of this publication may be reproduced or
transmitted in any form or by any means, electronic or mechanical,
including photocopying, recording, or any information storage or retrieval
system, without prior permission in writing from the publishers.

Bloomsbury Publishing Inc does not have any control over, or responsibility for, any
third-party websites referred to or in this book. All internet addresses given in this
book were correct at the time of going to press. The author and publisher regret any
inconvenience caused if addresses have changed or sites have ceased to exist,
but can accept no responsibility for any such changes.

Whilst every effort has been made to locate copyright holders the publishers would be
grateful to hear from any person(s) not here acknowledged.

Library of Congress Cataloging-in-Publication Data
Names: Charnock, Ruth.
Title: Joni Mitchell : new critical readings / edited by Ruth Charnock.
Description: New York : Bloomsbury Academic, 2019. | Includes bibliographical
references and index.
Identifiers: LCCN 2018040737| ISBN 9781501332098 (hardback : alk. paper) |
ISBN 9781501332104 (epdf)
Subjects: LCSH: Mitchell, Joni–Criticism and interpretation. |
Popular music–History and criticism.
Classification: LCC ML410.M6823 J68 2019 | DDC 782.42164092–dc23
LC record available at https://lccn.loc.gov/2018040737

ISBN: HB: 978-1-5013-3209-8
ePDF: 978-1-5013-3210-4
eBook: 978-1-5013-3211-1

Typeset by Newgen KnowledgeWorks Pvt. Ltd., Chennai, India
Printed and bound in the United States of America

To find out more about our authors and books visit www.bloomsbury.com
and sign up for our newsletters.

For Joe, who gave me Blue, *and for Adam, who has never asked me to turn it off.*

Contents

List of Permissions ... ix
Preface: Everything's Backwards, or Joni, Chase that Butterfly! *Ruth Charnock* ... x
Acknowledgments ... xiii

Introduction *Ruth Charnock* ... 1

Part 1 "The Breadth of Extremities": Voice, Instrument, Feeling

1 "The Hexagram of the Heavens, the Strings of My Guitar": Joni Mitchell's Crip Virtuosity *Matthew J. Jones* ... 21
2 "Oh Borderline": Joni Mitchell's Aging Voice as a Site of Queer Resistance *Emily Baker* ... 43
3 "Both Sides, Now": Voice, Affect, and Thirdness *Joanne Winning* ... 65
4 "Dreams and False Alarms": Melancholy in the Work of Joni Mitchell *Anne Hilker* ... 83

Part 2 "The Only (Black) Man in the Room?" Mitchell's Milieu

5 In Search of Lost Chords: Joni Mitchell, *The Last Waltz*, and the Refuge of the Road *Gustavus Stadler* ... 103
6 "Tar Baby and the Great White Wonder": Joni Mitchell's Pimp Game *Eric Lott* ... 121
7 Tangled up in *Blue*: The Shadow of Dylan and Stylistic Swerves in Early-Seventies Joni Mitchell *Howard Wilde* ... 141

Part 3 "Busy Being Free": Love, Time, Feminism

8 "Here's a Man and a Woman Sitting on a Rock": Joni Mitchell, Margaret Atwood, and Irritable Feminism *Pamela Thurschwell* ... 167

| 9 | Hollow: "Cactus Tree" and the Signs of Freedom *Peter Coviello* | 185 |
| 10 | "The Only Thing That's Never Going Away": Still Listening to *Blue* *Ruth Charnock* | 201 |

List of Contributors   221
Index   225

Permissions

The editor and publisher gratefully acknowledge the permission granted to reproduce the copyright material in this book:

Arc Iris, "The Last Time I Saw Richard," performance at Great Scott, May 2017. Lyrics used by permission of the artists.

"Of A Time." © A. Beckett, 2018. Permission granted by the artist.

Every effort has been made to trace copyright holders and to obtain their permission for the use of copyright material. The publisher apologizes for any errors or omissions in the above list and would be grateful if notified of any corrections that should be incorporated in future reprints or editions of this book.

Preface: Everything's Backwards, or Joni, Chase that Butterfly!

I go out, I'm misunderstood, I see a butterfly, I go for a swim.
                                        Joni Mitchell in conversation, 2013

"It's weird. Everything's backwards," says Jocie Adams, in a 2017 gig recording,[1] before launching into her band Arc Iris's cover of Joni Mitchell's "The Last Time I Saw Richard" (1971). And this cover *is* weird, if not immediately discernible as backwards. It starts with a series of looped samples of Mitchell's speaking voice saying things like "I see a butterfly," "You cannot say 'I like this tomato soup' without an ego. But I don't go around feeling misunderstood," "I go for a swim," "I go out," interspersed with a few sung responses from Jocie Adams, as if she's in conversation with Joni Mitchell or fantasizing about how she would reply to her, if she had the chance. "Mundanely misunderstood," Adams chimes in at points in the song's opening; and "Joni, chase that butterfly!" at others. Just before the song moves into something a little more recognizable (but not wholly so), it breaks down into strange, discombobulating, minor key synth-burbles, as if the listener has gone for that swim with Joni and is now sitting on the bottom of the pool, watching the bubbles rise and hearing the glassy noises from above.

By using samples of Mitchell's voice—all taken from a 2013 interview—to frame a song released in 1971, Arc Iris plays with time: creating a scenario where 2013 Joni talks to 2017 Jocie, who also brings 1971 Joni into the present (this time with synths and keyboards). Arc Iris's cover enacts a kind of temporal drag, to borrow Elizabeth Freeman's phrase, "a counter-genealogical practice of archiving culture's throwaway objects"—objects such as old interviews, let's say, or songs from the early 1970s (2010, xxiii). The important work of temporal drag, Freeman tells us, means revaluing and reevaluating "retrogression, delay, and the pull of the past on the present" (2010, 62), work, of course, that Joni Mitchell does in "The Last Time I Saw Richard," by looking back to an encounter with an ex-partner while also, in complex analeptic and proleptic figures, dreaming of a time when this encounter will be over and the past won't have such a pull, work that Arc Iris does in their cover of the song, and work that this book also engages in. Time does not necessarily just move forward, as Mitchell has told us a number of times.

These samples and Adams's responses free Joni Mitchell up from the strictures of linear time, and, relatedly, from an interview with a man who kept interrupting her. Arc Iris' interpretation reminds us of how boring it is to be misapprehended, whether you go around feeling it or not. "I don't go around feeling misunderstood," Mitchell says, to which Adams replies, almost parenthetically, "mundanely misunderstood." Mitchell, of course, *has*, at times, gone around feeling misunderstood—"The Last Time I Saw Richard" is one such example. But, rather than pull her up on this, perhaps realizing how much of a drag it must be to have so many things you've thought or felt or said out there in the ether, for interpretation and misinterpretation, Arc Iris registers sympathetically what Joni *doesn't* say—or not here, at least.

These samples also evoke Mitchell's mobility outside of the star-maker machinery: she goes out, she sees a butterfly, she goes for a swim. Sure, she has an ego—but she doesn't let it weigh her down. And Adams wills Mitchell on to even more movement—when Mitchell says, "I see a butterfly," Adams interjects "Joni, chase that butterfly!—in a line that simultaneously harks back to and reaches forward out of "Richard's" "dark cocoon."[2] In this, Arc Iris's cover imagines a Joni beyond the dreamer at the end of "The Last Time I Saw Richard," waiting "to get [her] gorgeous wings and fly away." It's a version of Joni Mitchell where she doesn't have to sit in boring interviews, or listen to boring ex-husbands, where she can swim, and look, and run, and be understood. It's a version where Arc Iris asks Mitchell to carry on seeking her joy, not to give up, to carry on after things that are fleeting, and not to let the pricks get her down.

As Lucy Robinson puts it, "[s]inging someone else's songs, like re-using someone else's interviews is [. . .] a way of having a conversation with the past that keeps track of how it has been valued and maintained over time" (McGeeney, Robinson, Thomson, and Thurschwell, 2018, n.p.). In the act of covering and sampling, Arc Iris also invites the listener to think about how they might, too, have valued and maintained an attachment to Joni Mitchell over time. Moreover, their performance invites us to reflect on how we make and make up Joni Mitchell, through scraps of things we've heard her say and pushed together, through other people's words about her, through fantasized conversations with her, through glimpses of her in documentaries, and through the songs—over 50 years of music, nineteen studio albums, two live albums, and nine compilations.

I open this book with what some might say is an esoteric object—in Arc Iris's cover—because, in some ways, this is an esoteric collection, which looks for ways in to Mitchell's music that feel weird and backwards, which samples from it here and there, which is interested in micro-moments, ephemera, as well as the more obvious objects, and in thinking about how listeners collaborate in making these objects. Covers are a way of brushing up against history while also making it present.[3] They remind us that the song was an object that was made and can be remade and reexperienced but also that, every time we listen to a song, we participate in its making by making it our own. Every time we sing along in our rooms or in a karaoke booth, every time we listen to a song in our head (my friend calls it "playing the psychic jukebox"), as well as every time we play or sample someone else's song, we are cover artists. And every time we write about a song, too: the critic is also a cover artist, constantly citing, interpreting, reworking.

I also open with Arc Iris's cover because it is gorgeous and surprising and reminds us that Joni Mitchell, all the Joni Mitchells, are very much *here*: moving, pissed-off, dreaming, loving, thoughtful, disruptive, innovative, restless.

Long may that be so. Joni, chase that butterfly.

Notes

1 Arc Iris, "The Last Time I Saw Richard" (Great Scott, May 2017). https://www.youtube.com/watch?v=BcwDrseG_VA (accessed: June 2, 2018).
2 Joni Mitchell, "The Last Time I Saw Richard," *Blue* (Hollywood: Reprise Records, 1971).
3 Thanks to Ian Balfour for this insight, and so many others. Balfour, "Opening Remarks for Critical Karaoke Covers," *Critical Karaoke 2014: Opening Remarks*. http://popmusicstudies.org/ck/?p=7 (accessed: June 2, 2018).

Works Cited

Arc Iris, "The Last Time I Saw Richard," Great Scott, May 2017. https://www.youtube.com/watch?v=BcwDrseG_VA (accessed: June 2, 2018).

Balfour, Ian. "Opening Remarks for Critical Karaoke Covers," *Critical Karaoke 2014: Opening Remarks*. http://popmusicstudies.org/ck/?p=7 (accessed: June 2, 2018).

Freeman, Elizabeth. *Time Binds: Queer Temporalities, Queer Histories*. Durham and London: Duke University Press, 2010.

McGeeney, E., Robinson, L., Thomson, R., and Thurschwell, P. "The Cover Version: Researching Sexuality Through Ventriloquism," in *Researching Sex and Sexualities*, ed. Charlotte Morris, Paul Boyce, Andrea Cornwall, Hannah Frith, Laura Harvey, and Yingying Huang. London: Zed Books, 2018. 150–72.

Mitchell, Joni. *Blue*. Hollywood: Reprise Records, 1971.

Acknowledgments

This book is very much a shared object, born not just out of my deep, deep (deep) love for Joni Mitchell but also out of the experience of talking about her with friends. One such love-in happened at the Experience Music Project Conference in Seattle, 2014, and it was there that the idea for a symposium and book on Joni Mitchell first appeared, over many drinks (thanks to the 5 Point Bar here, too). Several of the friends present then are also in these pages, and it is to them that I'd like to extend my first thanks: to Pete Coviello, Gus Stadler and Pamela Thurschwell who also kindly read and commented on sections of this book, as well as writing her own piece for it. You all continue to be very echt. And to Emily Baker, Anne Hilker, Matthew J. Jones, Eric Lott, Howard Wilde, and Joanne Winning—thank you, all, for producing such beautiful, varied, and smart work on Joni. Thanks too, to honorary 5-Pointer, Ian Balfour, whose enthusiasm for this project has been a great help and to Ally-Jane Grossan, who first showed an interest in publishing it. And to everybody who made the Court and Spark symposium at the University of Lincoln in 2015 such an absolute wonder and made the day (particular credit here to Andrew David and Deborah Wilson-David) and this book feel more possible.

Joni Mitchell: New Critical Readings was partly written on paid research leave from the School of English and Journalism at the University of Lincoln—thanks to them for that invaluable support and to all my great colleagues—particularly Siân Adiseshiah, Rupert Hildyard, and Chris Marlow. Andrew Elliott stepped in at the last minute to help with a referencing disaster and managed to be soothing, punny, and technologically proficient all at once. Unmeasurable thanks and boxes of Yogi Tea for eternity go to him. Love to my brilliant friends Christine Grandy, Adam Houlbrook, Seda Ilter, Tom Akehurst, Sam Shave, and Sam Richardson who were a tremendous support in a variety of ways. And thanks to the Mansions of the Future who provided a restful and creative space for indexing and proofing at the end of this project. Thanks, too, to everyone at Alfred Publishing, particularly to Amy Clarke. Bloomsbury have been brilliant to work for—patient (!), clear, and supportive. Particular thanks to Leah Babb-Rosenfeld, Katherine De Chant, and Susan Krogulski for all your help and encouragement. Thanks to Les Irvin, jonimitchell.com's webmaster, and an absolute font of knowledge, and to Ann Powers, Anne Karppinen, and Lloyd Whitesell. Without your fantastic work, this book would be much smaller. Arc Iris, particularly Jocie and Zach, provided invaluable information and some gorgeous covers in the final hours. Thank you!

Jen Clayton and Karen Ann Schaller both read and commented on sections of this book with huge alacrity and insight, and Michelle Whiteside helped things happen. They are my (un)holy trinity. My family continue to be excellent purveyors of things musical and written—I send them much love and gratitude. Adam O'Meara is magic and does not yet know how much Joni is in his future but will, soon. All my love, mega thanks and kisses to him.

And to Joni, of course, and always, my almost unlanguageable appreciation.

Introduction

Ruth Charnock

You know it never has been easy
Whether you do or you do not resign
Whether you travel the breadth of extremities
Or stick to some straighter line.

—Joni Mitchell, "Hejira," 1976.

Joni Mitchell is a great dancer, the kind of smoker you want to be, a ruthless and meticulous emotional surgeon (how many feelings has she pulled from you today?), a bedazzling agent of the surprising note and line, an exultant skater (think of *Hejira*'s gatefold images, the cover of the 2005 compilation *Songs of a Prairie Girl*, or "River's" dreams of frozen escape), a rightful declaimer of her own brilliance ("about as humble as Mussolini," David Crosby says—but why should she be?), sometimes a kind of Tiresias, picking her way through various wastelands, shaking her fist at culture's decline, but sometimes, too, a dreamer in a hotel room, watching Woodstock on the TV and wishing she was there. She's someone you'd want with you on a long car journey—she would drive—and next to you at the jukebox, jabbing the buttons before doing a slow twist in the Wurlitzer glow. She is, one wagers, a pool shark. She is and isn't the best authority on her own work: in a 2013 interview, she criticizes and minimizes her extraordinary back-catalog before absorbedly reciting at length a poem she wrote at school, as if its metaphoric flourishes somehow beat "Cold Blue Steel and Sweet Fire" or its cultural commentary rivals "The Hissing of Summer Lawns."[1] She has provided the most capacious and sustaining accompaniments to your adolescence, early adulthood, and middle age (and you're pretty sure she'll be good for your dotage too). Her songs are the best at detailing the traps of womanhood and heterosexuality and, sometimes, too, ways in which you might escape or step around these traps. Yet she refuses to align herself explicitly with a feminist politics and this feels maddening and intriguing and painful. She makes you want to wear a beret. She makes you want to drive out of your life and away from your loves, while wearing a beret. She has read more Nietzsche than you, but says she isn't an intellectual.[2] Unlike Nietzsche, she makes disappointment into a thing that you want to experience again and again. She makes you want to bake and paint and shout and jive and drink and kiss and wail and think about the Earth and think about yourself and think about yourself thinking about the Earth. She makes ambivalating feel like a fine use of a day. And inexplicably, of late, she has made you want to wear a mustard-yellow crocheted cardigan and paint your kitchen wall coral pink.

This is my Joni, of course—although some elements here may belong to your Joni, too. As this collection evidences, writing about Joni Mitchell often entails writing about oneself. We can see this in Sean Nelson's gorgeous 33 ⅓ book on *Court and Spark*, which opens with a story of Nelson as a child, in the car with his mom driving through Laurel Canyon, listening in delight as she sings along to "Help Me" (2007, 2). Or Katherine Monk's philosophy-imbued *Joni: The Creative Odyssey of Joni Mitchell*, which sees Monk, aged six, listening to *Song to a Seagull* with her sister, feeling how "it sent a prematurely existential shiver down my six-year-old spine" (2012, ix). Lloyd Whitesell's *The Music of Joni Mitchell* features an account of his attendance at a 1995 performance by Mitchell, listening with excitement to her new "unexpected aggressive electric sound" (2008, 15). In Malka Marom's 2014 collection of interviews with Mitchell, *Both Sides Now*[3] she writes of driving to a coffeehouse in 1966 and hearing Joni Mitchell for the first time. "Her song was like a kaleidoscope that splintered my perception [. . .] then refocused to illuminate a reality I had not dared to see" (2014, x). Meanwhile, David Yaffe's recent biography, *Reckless Daughter: A Portrait of Joni Mitchell* opens with Yaffe aged 15, in his girlfriend's room, listening with her to *Blue*, "falling in love with a girl and falling in love with this music" (2017, xi). "The people who get the most out of my music see themselves in it," Mitchell tells Michelle Mercer (2012, 3). *Joni Mitchell: New*

Critical Readings, features several "my Joni, myself" moments. Eric Lott recounts an (enviable!) moment of sneaking backstage and meeting Joni on the *Shadows and Light* tour, while Peter Coviello writes of teaching a stanza of "Cactus Tree" to explain the function of rhyme to his college students. And my chapter maps several scenes of adolescent listening to Joni Mitchell, one of them my own, to think about the complex work of desire that this listening entails, particularly when reflecting on it from adulthood.

What do we talk about when we talk about Joni Mitchell? Recent work, some of which has been just mentioned, has drawn our attention to Mitchell's brilliance and sometimes orneriness as an interview subject (Marom 2014; Hoskyns 2016); to the twists, turns, and sheer wealth of her creativity (Yaffe 2017); to the stories that make up her *Blue* Period (Mercer 2012); to her snapshot of love and Los Angeles in *Court and Spark* (Nelson 2007); to the multitude of her philosophical and artistic interlocutors (Monk 2012); to the ways in which her work is misunderstood (Daum 2014); and to how her songs are constructed (Whitesell 2008). While it draws on this great, existing work, *Joni Mitchell: New Critical Readings* provides new ways of thinking about Joni Mitchell's music: as queer, as literary, as embodied, and as complexly temporal, to name just a few of the interventions that the coming essays make. This book represents the first edited collection of essays on Mitchell's oeuvre. It brings together essays by musicologists, literary scholars and theorists of popular culture and features close reading, detailed listening, musicological analysis, literary comparison, historicization (macro and micro) and personal anecdotes. The pieces that follow talk to each other in many different ways but all share in common a sustained interest in listening, with intense thought and feeling, to Joni Mitchell.

There are lots of ways to listen to Joni Mitchell, of course. Several of the recent critical accounts, discussed earlier, open with the authors listening as a child or adolescent. Yet, for other writers on Mitchell, adolescent listening, particularly female adolescent listening, is a problem. Meghan Daum describes this feeling in her own "Joni and me" story, aptly titled "The Joni Mitchell Problem":

> I realize the clause "Joni and me" has been written upwards of 10 million times, mostly in diaries with flowers drawn in the margins and in sonnets

written in galloping pink cursive. I realize that there is nothing original about being a late twentieth-century-born female who feels that nearly every major life event (first love and heartbreak, leaving home, next love and heartbreak) was accompanied by a Joni that was custom-written for the occasion. (2014, 151)

In order for Daum to lay claim to "her" Joni, she pushes aside the 10 million teenage girls who also love her (their teenage status suggested here by the diary-doodling and poetry-writing which, Daum suggests—wrongly!—are purely the preserve of the teenage girl). There's a complex defensiveness in Daum's tone here that abuts her vow of love for Joni, and this love's particular and cherished coordinates. It's the tone of a woman feeling that she has to do the work of legitimizing what she loves, as if loving it isn't legitimacy enough, while also anticipating the ways in which this love will be trashed: as unoriginal, as romantic, as solipsistic, as immature, as too personal, as—let's just say it—too *feminine*: girl's stuff. Michelle Mercer does something similar in her book on *Blue*, noting that she is "roughly the eight-nine millionth teenage girl to have an existential transformation through *Blue*" and that Joni Mitchell has "already taken enough blame for being a muse to every flaxen-haired girl who picked up a guitar and mistook emotional turbulence for art" (2012, 3). In this dismissal, Daum and Mercer both presume that female listeners, particularly young female listeners, are a lumpen and knowable object. Doing so, they assume "a singularity of female spectatorship [listenership, in this instance] or subjecthood" as cultural theorist Lauren Berlant puts it (1988, 239). All teenage girls listen in the same way and we all know what that listening sounds like: it's emotional, it's personal, it's romantic and it's misinterpretive or uncritical—"wrong, wrong, wrong"—according to Meghan Daum (2014, 151). While Daum and Mercer's texts are otherwise insightful, impassioned, and engaging accounts of fandom and Mitchell's oeuvre, the fact that both authors similarly feel the need to navigate both the unoriginality and genderedness of an attachment to Joni Mitchell, and that they both target teenage girls as their bad object, is worth pausing upon. To borrow Daum's phrase, this commonality suggests that the real "Joni Mitchell Problem" might not be about listening to *Blue* rather than *Mingus* but, instead, about gender.[4]

In disparaging teenage girls who listen to Joni Mitchell, Daum and, to a lesser extent, Mercer, join a long roster of critics who denigrate female listening, and especially adolescent female listening. As musicologist Elizabeth Keenan puts it, with regard to the poptimism versus rockism debates of the last few years, "the tastes of 13-year-old girls are usually the most easily maligned, whether in pop music or in books or in films."[5] Keenan is replying here to music critic Saul Austerlitz's 2014 piece for the *New York Times Magazine* entitled "The Pernicious Rise of Poptimism."[6] In it, Austerlitz bemoans the extent to which a critical emphasis on pop music (over other "knottier music") means that music critics have begun to align their ears with those of teenagers (as Keenan points out, the "girls" part of Austerlitz's complaint is implied but not directly stated). "Should gainfully employed adults whose job is to listen to music thoughtfully really agree so regularly with the taste of 13-year-old girls?"[7] Austerlitz asks. This is a clear attempt, as Keenan identifies, to "bring back discourses of authenticity/quality/'good music' that privilege white dudes who make mediocre music above [the music of] women and people of color"[8]—an attempt that this collection, in tune with Keenan, is engaged in resisting.

Arguably, Joni Mitchell is no poptimist.[9] For example, in a 2015 piece for *New York Magazine*, she claims to never have heard Taylor Swift's music and, while she can be found expressing her appreciation for certain pop stars—Prince, The Police, even Journey![10]—one imagines that she would not want to be placed alongside them. Nor can we readily class her music as pop. But the poptimism versus rockism discourses are relevant to thinking about the reception of Mitchell's music, and its listeners, in so far as they reveal the gendered politics of listening, criticism, and ideas of value that continue to circulate in music writing. My argument here is that female critics' accounts of listening to Joni Mitchell, particularly those that limn the critical and the personal, often labor through convoluted justifications and distinctions ("I'm not *that* kind of female listener"[11]) even before coming to discuss the music. This tells us a lot about the anxieties that might attend female-authored music criticism, particularly when it addresses a female artist, and especially when, tonally, it resides on the borders of the critical and the personal. As a salve for this, as for many things, it is worth turning over to feminist music critic, Ann Powers.

In her reflective piece on National Public Radio's "The 150 Greatest Albums Made by Women," a list which, lest we forget, was topped by Joni Mitchell's *Blue*, Ann Powers writes, "the general history of popular music is told through the great works of men, [. . . and that] without a serious revision of the canon, women will always remain on the margins."[12] She also observes "the shelves weighed down with books about Jimi Hendrix and Nirvana, while only one or two about Aretha Franklin or Patti Smith [or Joni Mitchell, we might add] sit nearby."[13] (Regarding Joni Mitchell, while there have been plenty of biographies and collections of interviews published, there haven't been many critical treatments of her work and this is the first edited collection.) Powers goes on to specifically discuss Joni Mitchell's occupation of the margins, recounting a story told by screenwriter and Laurel Canyon regular, Carl Gottlieb, to music writer Barney Hoskyns[14] of the days in which David Crosby would bring Mitchell out to play for his friends: "Mitchell would emerge, play a few songs and retreat. 'She goes back upstairs, and we all sit around and look at each other and say, What was *that*? Did we hallucinate it?' Gottlieb said."[15] Commenting on the gender politics of this moment, Powers writes "there's [. . .] something off and sadly typical about this scene. In it, the female musician is a dream, a surprise and a disruptor. She can claim the center of attention, but her rightful point of origin, and the place to which she returns, is a margin."[16] (This collection, it goes without saying, does not put Joni Mitchell in the corner.)

While, inevitably (inevitable because she is female), Mitchell's work has always been gendered in ways that Powers identifies, recent criticism has increasingly interrogated the gender politics that surround and construct Mitchell's work. In particular, Anne Karppinen's recent monograph *The Songs of Joni Mitchell: Gender, Performance and Agency*, thinks in detail about how Mitchell has been marginalized within rock discourses, particularly within critical economies (2016, 1). Karppinen also examines Mitchell's own attitudes to gender, drawing, in part, on French feminist as well as musicological theory, to convincing effect. Sheila Whiteley contextualizes *Blue* as "forging a new world of possibilities for women" (2000, 78) in the early 1970s and draws comparisons between Mitchell's struggles with the misogynistic music industry and the broader concerns of second-wave feminism (whether Mitchell recognizes herself as a feminist or not) (1). Lloyd Whitesell's introduction also takes up the gender politics of Mitchell's work, acknowledging that "women's intellectual production has been historically undervalued" and that the critical treatment of Mitchell's music has, to some extent, been an example of this undervaluation (2008, 5).

While there is much to be said about Joni Mitchell and gender politics, Mitchell herself has often eschewed framings of her work in these terms. Of feminism, specifically, Mitchell has said that she hadn't heard of it until she went out for dinner with Warren Beatty and Jack Nicholson (I'm guessing in the early 1970s) and they enlightened her.[17] She has said, several times, bluntly "I am not a feminist."[18] We might feel, if we *do* identify as feminist and if Mitchell's music has been a crucial part of our education into this politics, that this disavowal is rather hard to take. But there's a lot to be said for not passing it over—it teaches us to interrogate the kinds of advocacy, as feminists, we might want from our female love objects, and how we might feel when we don't get this advocacy. It's also worthwhile registering the multitudinous ways in which Mitchell's music *does* sustain a feminist viewpoint, as pieces by Pamela Thurschwell, Peter Coviello, Emily Baker, and myself attest in this collection.

Relatedly, *Joni Mitchell: New Critical Readings* also features some of the first readings of Mitchell's work as queer. Performers—Arc Iris, for one, and John Kelly,[19] who performs as a convincing and moving drag Joni Mitchell, for another—have long realized the queerness of Mitchell's music. But, save for David Román's (2005) insightful and detailed discussion of Kelly's performances as Mitchell, and Ann Pellegrini's brief (but no less insightful) gloss on Román's reading (2007, 181), there has been little critical writing that has considered Joni Mitchell's music through a queer theoretical lens. In her work's challenges to heterosexual conventions, in its experiments with timing and experimentation, in its desire to dwell in "the open mesh of possibilities," to borrow the defining words of Eve Kosofsky Sedgwick (1993, 8), that come from *not* sticking "to some straighter line,"[20] this collection emphatically claims Mitchell's work as queer. Chapters by Matthew J. Jones, Emily Baker, Peter Coviello, and myself explore some of the possibilities of this claim.

* * *

It would not be going too far to say that Joni Mitchell's songs have been, thus far, the most capacious, sustaining, and clarifying cultural objects of my life. It has been a struggle sometimes, throughout the making of this book to put the contours of this feeling-for-Joni into words in a way that renders it cogent and interesting to others (and other contributors have expressed similar feelings). How do you write about the things you love? Sometimes, for me at least, words have slipped away, and it has seemed much more sensible to play "Harry's House/Centerpiece" on loop while inviting (ok, perhaps not inviting) unsuspecting loved ones to marvel with me at the volta that moves the listener from the snapshot of a man in the corporate 1970s yearningly fantasizing about his wife when she was a teenager, into the upswing surprise of a hopeful 1950s standard. Or to get caught, like Harry, in fantasies of the past—through imagined scenes glimpsed in the songs—Joni sitting with Sam Shepard in a diner in 1975, eating eggs and watching him watch other women; Joni waiting for the lights to change in 1994, furious with politicians, businessmen, record executives, quacks; Joni waiting for the lights to change in 1969, watching a musician play his heart out for nothing; Joni in love and pissed-off with her mum in 1998, pushing the bed against the window to look at the Christmas lights; Joni selfish and sad and wishing Christmas away in 1971; or Joni in 1973, playing *Court and Spark* to Bob Dylan as he pretends to fall asleep.[21] Such detours into deep listening and imaginings are, of course, the preserve of the ardent fan, not just the procrastinating scholar. But there's no need, really, to separate the two—as Lloyd Whitesell puts it, "the incisive knowledge of the scholar can go hand in hand with the intimate knowledge of the fervent fan" (2008, 10). All of the contributors in this collection are fans, as well as critics, and interested in what might be woven between and across these two modes of listening.

The chapters that follow are often exercises in the joys of deep and detailed listening. As Alexandra T. Vazquez has told us, "listening in detail ignores those accusations of going too far, of giving too much time to a recording" (2013, 4). This kind of listening might take the form of listening on loop, listening alone[22] or with others who like to listen as you do, obsessing over a song's particular turn of phrase, intake of breath, or bass line, reading things into track-sequencings, liner notes, or cover art, making arcanely themed playlists, or learning the chords so you can play along—to name but a few. The fan listens again and again, as a sign of caring for the song, and also with the desire to burrow deeper and deeper into a track. Listening in detail, too, is proof of your "worthiness" as a fan, evidence that you care *enough* about a song, and an artist, to attend to the labor that went into making a track, and to its minutiae as an object, rather than just consuming it quickly, then discarding it and moving on.

Listening in detail, in other words, is an act of love, of attachment—not something that one would immediately associate with the work of criticism, work that, in its title, this collection seems to foreground. Criticism has long been associated with *detachment*, distance, with holding an object at arm's length so as to scrutinize, interrogate, and dismantle it into its component parts. Critique is cool, unemotional, and cerebral rather than embodied. It disavows the personal attachment or aversion. Critique is often paranoid in its orientation, as the queer theorist Eve Kosofsky Sedgwick (2003) has identified; it is suspicious, always looking for cover-ups, secrets, what will happen next. Critique does not want to be absorbed by the object because to be absorbed might mean being at the object's mercy, taken in by it, and, maybe, surprised by it. The critic doesn't want to appear naive, or enamored, or too implicated by the object he is critiquing.

As is probably clear by now, *Joni Mitchell: New Critical Readings* doesn't play that way. This book is composed more of reparative readings (perhaps that would have been a better title), readings that, as Rita Felski puts it "[look] to a work of art for solace and replenishment rather than viewing it as something [. . .] to be indicted" (2015, 151). That's not to say that there *isn't* critique here—but it aims to redescribe Mitchell's work rather than dismantle it, leaving room in its reading for, as Felski puts it, "the aleatory and the unexpected, the chancy and the contingent" (152), in a mode that often employs "the language of enchantment, incandescence, and rapture without embarrassment" (175). The readings in this book display vulnerability, hope, epiphany, interest, recognition, surprise as well as, sometimes, disappointment, disenchantment, irritability, ambivalence, and frustration (shadows and light, after all). This book hopes to sit alongside other recent work in musicology that has turned toward ideas of care, nurture, first-person accounts, and reparative listening as vital tools in today's often eviscerating political, environmental, economic, and cultural scenes.[23]

There are numerous Joni Mitchell scenes left out of this book, of course, stones as yet unturned, songs not listened to or skipped over, period missed out. This collection does not listen to or watch everything that has made up Joni Mitchell's musical career so far. There's no "Dancin' Clown" in these pages, for example (although having just watched the video for this song for the first time, which sees Joni dancing around a kitchen with a ginger cat, playing a sweeping brush like a guitar, American Spirit dangling from her lips, this feels like a mistake and reason alone for a second volume).[24] There's very little here from her 1980s period and very little about her most recent collection of new material, *Shine* (2008). There's *Mingus* but not much *Taming the Tiger*. These omissions may irritate, please, or pass unnoticed, depending on the reader's predilections, but are not intended as any kind of comment on the works themselves.

This collection, unashamedly, delights in the Joni Mitchell that it delights in. Not because these are the "best" songs, or albums, or moments from her career (who knows what "best" means, anyway, and, frankly, conversations about value are only ever just conversations about personal taste that don't want to 'fess up to their attachments and aversions, in the opinion of this editor), but because these are the songs, albums, moments, that caught these writers' hearts, guts, ears, and imaginations. To put together a collection that *isn't* exhaustive or aiming to be, that, undoubtedly, is made up more of A- than it is of B-sides or rarities undoubtedly risks courting accusations of dilettantism, of being the kind of listener who goes for the greatest hits (such that they are), rather than the misses. Indeed, part of me has sometimes wished that I, or one of the other contributors to this collection, had advanced an arcane theory about "Funeral's" extra-diegetic noise or Alejandro Acuna's ankle bell technique on "Don Juan's Reckless Daughter." But these are thoughts yet to be unfolded and for another collection.

This book is profoundly interested in looking closely at specific moments in Mitchell's oeuvre, some already in full view, some only glimpsed so far, some that have, until now, occupied the vanishing spot, and in reflecting upon the ways in which we have constructed Mitchell: as an intimate, as a seer, as imprinted upon our life stories, and as revealing us to ourselves through her own acts of self-exposure. This book is concerned with mobility—how Mitchell's work moves through time and also moves us over time—and with the complexities and tricksiness of perspective. It thinks about how Mitchell sometimes runs behind the times, sometimes dwells at the side of the road (a hitcher? a prisoner?) watching the times go by, and sometimes races ahead, too fast for those listeners who want her to stay still for longer or forever.

These essays are also interested in thinking about objects from the past and how they might be much nearer to us than they first appear. Specifically, many of the essays in this book look at past moments in Mitchell's career and life— her appearance in *The Last Waltz*, her polio when aged 9—in ways that make these past moments vividly and instructively *present*. While Mitchell has said frequently that she doesn't like to look back,[25] this collection likes running behind the times, dragging things out, and dredging things up, always willing, as Elizabeth Freeman puts it, "to be bathed in the fading light of whatever has been declared useless" (2010, xiii)—whether by critics (personal or professional), or by Mitchell herself.

Although Mitchell has said that she doesn't like to look back, she has spent some time doing so, particularly but not only in recent years. Her most recent work, the 2014 quadruple-disc set *Love Has Many Faces: A Quartet, A Ballet, Waiting to Be Danced*, saw her selecting tracks from her back-catalog to make a new song sequence, intended originally for a ballet (which was made, featuring a smaller selection of songs as *The Fiddle and the Drum* in 2007 by the Alberta Ballet). Her last recording of original material, *Shine* (2007) features a revision of "Big Yellow Taxi." Prior to that, 2002's *Travelogue* (discussed by Emily Baker in her chapter for this collection) reorchestrated many Mitchell standards; while 2000's *Both Sides Now* reimagined a selection of jazz standards, "A Case of You" and the titular track (Joanne Winning talks about the latter in her chapter on Mitchell and thirdness). Despite her undeniable status as a musical innovator, Mitchell is a persistent (re)interpreter of her own work. She also inspires complicated cover versions, as my piece for this collection touches upon. Furthermore, as Mitchell identifies in the liner notes to *Love Has Many Faces*, her work has long been interested in retrospection. "I create back-flashes in my songs by cutting old songs into them,"[26] Mitchell comments, referring to songs like "Harry's House/Centerpiece" (from 1975's *The Hissing of Summer Lawns*) and "Chinese Café/Unchained Melody" (from 1982's *Wild Things Run*

Fast). As Lloyd Whitesell has astutely delineated, Mitchell's songs often cite themselves—something like "Blue," for example, contains "an almost exact quotation of a passage from [. . .] the introduction to "My Old Man" (2008, 136). And "Amelia" (from *Hejira*, 1976) sees Mitchell return for a one-night stay in the "Cactus Tree motel" ("Cactus Tree" from *Song to a Seagull*, 1968), as Peter Coviello discusses in his essay here.

In its orientation to Mitchell's music, which we know won't please everyone, this collection sometimes swoops, like a magpie or—why not?—a black crow, to pick up the ephemera and minutiae of Mitchell's career, lifting them up for a new look. For example, in his piece about Mitchell's *Don Juan*-era blackface alter ego, Art Nouveau, Eric Lott draws our attention to a long-forgotten curiosity: Mitchell's 1980 short film for Barry Levinson: *The Black Cat in the Black Mouse Socks*.[27] Gustavus Stadler zooms in on another moment that's easy to overlook: The Band's Rick Danko staring intently at Mitchell's left hand as she plays "Coyote" in *The Last Waltz*. And Emily Baker thinks about how certain albums, in the case of her chapter, *Travelogue*, come to seem ephemeral to critics: lacking substance, easily discardable and of little lasting worth.

Other conversations in this collection may sound, initially, more familiar but come with new twists. In his piece, Howard Wilde interrupts the decades' old Bob vs. Joni back-and-forth, by proposing that the two might not even be traveling in the same vehicle. Anne Hilker sheds new light on figures of melancholy in Mitchell's music, drawing parallels and distinctions with the work of renowned anthropologist, Mary Douglas. Meanwhile, Matthew J. Jones's chapter picks up the much discussed question of Joni's guitar technique and tweaks it.

Relatedly, this collection makes a series of new assemblages, putting Mitchell's work with other cultural objects. Some of Mitchell's interlocutors in this book are literary, reflecting both the training of several of our contributors and the literariness of Mitchell's music. For example, in her chapter, Pamela Thurschwell sets up a dialogue between Joni Mitchell and fellow Canadian author Margaret Atwood—both, Thurschwell argues, "irritable feminists." In his chapter, Peter Coviello draws lines between Mitchell, Henry James, and a

Paula Fox novel from 1970. And my chapter considers a series of set pieces in recent film and TV, where Mitchell appears to warn of trouble ahead.

This book is divided into three sections, although these groupings are not intended to be totalizing. Part One: "'The Breadth of Extremities': Voice, Instrument, Feeling," considers Mitchell's playing: across time, across borders, across restrictions, across contradictions. It opens with Matthew J. Jones's provocative and timely discussion of what he calls the "crip virtuosity" of Mitchell's musical style, honed, in part, because of her childhood polio. Jones draws our attention to the ways in which Mitchell's "queering of the fretboard" created a new idiom for the guitar. Emily Baker's chapter turns, with no less insight, to the "problem" (as it has been inaccurately perceived) of Mitchell's aging voice, particularly in the *Travelogue* era. Baker reframes this voice as one of experience, of defiant sensuality, a voice railing—queerly—against culture diktats that older women should be neither seen nor heard. Joanne Winning is also interested in Mitchell's later-career voice—this time, as it appears on her 2000 revisioning of "Both Sides, Now." Winning argues, convincingly, that we should view this as one of Mitchell's most affecting performances, bridging, as it does, innocence and experience. Finally in this section, Anne Hilker considers the multitudinous ways in which Mitchell's melodies and words have picked up themes and figures of melancholy. Ever the restless traveler, Mitchell's melancholic apex comes with "Amelia," in Hilker's lyrical reading.

Part Two: "'The Only [Black] Man in the Room?' Mitchell's Milieu," thinks about Joni's various roles, disruptions, disguises and swerves away from the music industry's boys' clubs. It opens with Gustavus Stadler's essay which considers a complex and charged moment in Mitchell's 1970s: her performance of "Coyote" as part of *The Last Waltz*. Stadler convincingly suggests that Mitchell disrupts the film's masculinist and mythologizing narrative by "embodying a dramatic unreadability" within the film. Next is Eric Lott's reading of Mitchell's "cross-cultural investigations" as Art Nouveau at the end of the 1970s. Appearing in blackface drag, Lott argues, was a way for Mitchell to move differently and more freely through the predominantly white, male LA scene. Closing this section, Howard Wilde picks up that old chestnut—Joni vs. Bob—and gives it new life, arguing that we should think of Mitchell as the "anti-Dylan," via a range of close comparisons between the two artists' work.

The final section of the collection, Part Three: "'Busy Being Free': Love, Time, Feminism," makes contact with Joni across time, through novels, films, and TV, thinking and feeling its way through her complex gender politics and the sometimes contradictory promises of her music. Pamela Thurschwell's chapter pairs Mitchell with a friend of spirit: Margaret Atwood. Mitchell and Atwood share a sensibility, according to Thurschwell, one which she names "irritable feminism." Relatedly, Peter Coviello thinks in his piece about what he calls "Mitchell's fierce and finely calibrated ambivalence," particularly toward the late 1960s counterculture's ideals and ideas of freedom. Finally, in conversation with both Coviello and Thurschwell's work, my own piece picks up *Blue* as an album that one is "supposed" to move on from but, for a range of complicated reasons, might not be able to. What might be at stake in still listening to *Blue*?

Mitchell has sometimes mercilessly speared the work of academics and critics. In her 2013 CBC interview, for example, she talks of "the academic poets [. . .] digging under my lines looking for hidden meaning and slapping themselves on the back going, "I think I'm onto something here!"[28] Ideally, the book to come will give far more pleasure than being at a gathering of "critics of all expression [. . .]/Saying it's wrong/Saying it's right."[29] We hope, ultimately, that these layered snapshots of Mitchell's work capture some of her shadows, and, especially, some of her light.

Notes

1. Joni Mitchell, *The Joni Mitchell Interview* (CBC Music, 2013). https://www.youtube.com/watch?v=pEJuiZN3jI8 (accessed: June 2, 2018).
2. David Wild, "Morrissey Meets Joni Mitchell: Melancholy and the Infinite Sadness," *Rolling Stone* (March 6, 1997). https://www.rollingstone.com/music/news/morrissey-melancholy-meets-the-infinite-sadness-19970306 (accessed: June 3, 2018).
3. Marom's book was published under two different titles: *Joni Mitchell: Both Sides Now—Conversations with Malka Marom*, and *Joni Mitchell: In Her Own*

Words—Conversations with Malka Marom. These are listed throughout according to which version the author has used.

4 Although, arguably, we could say that the question of whether you prefer *Mingus* or *Blue* is also a question about gender.

5 Elizabeth Keenan, "Gender Trouble: 'Poptimism' and the Male Critical Voice," (April 9, 2014). https://badcoverversion.wordpress.com/2014/04/09/gender-trouble-poptimism-and-the-male-critical-voice/ (accessed: June 1, 2018).

6 Saul Austerlitz, "The Pernicious Rise of Poptimism," *New York Times Magazine* (April 4, 2014). https://www.nytimes.com/2014/04/06/magazine/the-pernicious-rise-of-poptimism.html (accessed: June 1, 2018).

7 Ibid.

8 Keenan, "Gender Trouble."

9 Although, of course, there have been times when Mitchell has, tongue in cheek set out to create a pop record. See her account of "You Turn Me On, I'm A Radio" in Marom, 68.

10 See Vic Garbarini, "Joni Mitchell Is a Nervy Broad," *Musician Magazine* (January, 1983). http://jonimitchell.com/library/print.cfm?id=199 (accessed: June 2, 2018). Joni Mitchell also really likes The New Radical's "You Get What You Give." See David Wild, "Q&A: Joni Mitchell," *Rolling Stone* (April 13, 2000). https://www.rollingstone.com/music/features/joni-mitchell-q-a-20000413 (accessed: June 2, 2018).

11 The "vast majority" of female fans "are not fanning properly," declares Meghan Daum, *The Unspeakable and Other Subjects of Discussion* (New York: Picador, 2014), 151.

12 Ann Powers, "A New Canon: In Pop Music, Women Belong at the Center of the Story," *NPR Music* (July 24, 2017). https://www.npr.org/2017/07/24/538601651/a-new-canon-in-pop-music-women-belong-at-the-center-of-the-story (accessed: June 2, 2018).

13 Ibid.

14 You can read the account in full in Barney Hoskyn, *Hotel California: Singer-Songwriters and Cocaine Cowboys in the LA Canyons, 1967–1976* (London: Harper Perennial, 2006), 43.

15 Powers, "A New Canon."

16 Ibid.

17 David Wild, "Morrissey Meets Joni Mitchell: Melancholy and the Infinite Sadness."

18 In a Q&A with David Wild for *Rolling Stone* (October 15, 1992). https://www.rollingstone.com/music/features/joni-mitchell-19921015 (accessed: June 3, 2018);

in a 1998 conversation with Ani DiFranco for the *Los Angeles Times*: http://jonimitchell.com/library/view.cfm?id=150 (accessed: June 3, 2018); and in a 2013 interview with Jian Ghomeshi which you can watch, in its entirety, here: http://jonimitchell.com/library/video.cfm?id=391 (accessed: June 3, 2018).

19 There is much, much more to be said on Kelly's performances as Joni Mitchell than I have space for here, unfortunately. For a great example, see: https://www.youtube.com/watch?v=YGI_s7wsZXI (accessed: June 3, 2018).
20 Joni Mitchell, "Hejira," *Hejira* (Hollywood: Asylum Records, 1976).
21 Joni Mitchell, *Love Has Many Faces: A Quartet, A Ballet, Waiting to Be Danced* (Rhino Entertainment Company, 2014), liner notes, 10.
22 Author Zadie Smith has said this is the only way she can listen to Joni Mitchell. See Zadie Smith, "Some Notes on Attunement: A Voyage around Joni Mitchell," *New Yorker* (December 17, 2012). https://www.newyorker.com/magazine/2012/12/17/some-notes-on-attunement (accessed: June 2, 2018).
23 For example, William Cheng's *Just Vibrations: The Purpose of Sounding Good.* Michigan: University of Michigan Press, 2016.
24 Joni Mitchell, "Dancin' Clown," *Chalk Mark in a Rain Storm* (Hollywood: Geffen Records, 1998). See video here: https://www.youtube.com/watch?v=73IvazD2u6c (accessed: June 2, 2018).
25 Joni Mitchell, *The Joni Mitchell Interview* (CBC Music, 2013). https://www.youtube.com/watch?v=pEJuiZN3jI8 (accessed: June 2, 2018).
26 *Love Has Many Faces*, liner notes, 5.
27 Interested readers can watch this film here: http://jonimitchell.com/library/video.cfm?id=412.
28 Joni Mitchell, *The Joni Mitchell Interview* (CBC Music, 2013). https://www.youtube.com/watch?v=pEJuiZN3jI8 (accessed: June 2, 2018).
29 Joni Mitchell, "Shadows and Light," *The Hissing of Summer Lawns* (Hollywood: Asylum Records, 1975).

Works Cited

Austerlitz, Saul. "The Pernicious Rise of Poptimism," *New York Times Magazine*, April 4, 2014. https://www.nytimes.com/2014/04/06/magazine/the-pernicious-rise-of-poptimism.html (accessed: June 1, 2018).

Berlant, Lauren. "The Female Complaint," *Social Text*, 19.20 (Autumn, 1988). 237–259.

Cheng, William. *Just Vibrations: The Purpose of Sounding Good*. Michigan: University of Michigan Press, 2016.

Daum, Meghan. *The Unspeakable: And Other Subjects of Discussion*. New York: Picador, 2014.

DiFranco, Ani. "Ani DiFranco Chats with the Iconic Joni Mitchell," *Los Angeles Times*, September 20, 1998. http://jonimitchell.com/library/view.cfm?id=150 (accessed: June 3, 2018).

Felski, Rita. *The Limits of Critique*. Chicago: University of Chicago Press, 2015.

Freeman, Elizabeth. *Time Binds: Queer Temporalities, Queer Histories*. Durham and London: Duke University Press, 2010.

Garbarini, Vic. "Joni Mitchell Is a Nervy Broad," *Musician Magazine*, January, 1983. http://jonimitchell.com/library/print.cfm?id=199 (accessed: June 2, 2018).

Hoskyns, Barney. *Hotel California: Singer-Songwriters and Cocaine Cowboys in the LA Canyons, 1967–1976*. London: Harper Perennial, 2006.

Hoskyns, Barney. *Reckless Daughter: A Joni Mitchell Anthology*. London: Constable, 2016.

Karppinen, Anne. *The Songs of Joni Mitchell: Gender, Performance and Agency*. Oxon: Routledge, 2016.

Keenan, Elizabeth. "Gender Trouble: 'Poptimism' and the Male Critical Voice," April 9, 2014. https://badcoverversion.wordpress.com/2014/04/09/gender-trouble-poptimism-and-the-male-critical-voice/ (accessed: June 1, 2018).

Marom, Malka. *Joni Mitchell: Both Sides Now—Conversations with Malka Marom*. London: Omnibus Press, 2014.

Mercer, Michelle. *Will You Take Me as I Am: Joni Mitchell's Blue Period*. Milwaukee: Backbeat Books, 2012.

Mitchell, Joni. "Shadows and Light," *The Hissing of Summer Lawns*. Hollywood: Asylum Records, 1975.

Mitchell, Joni. *Hejira*. Hollywood: Asylum Records, 1976.

Mitchell, Joni. "Dancin' Clown," *Chalk Mark in a Rain Storm*. Hollywood: Geffen Records, 1998.

Mitchell, Joni. *The Joni Mitchell Interview*. CBC Music, 2013. https://www.youtube.com/watch?v=pEJuiZN3jI8 (accessed: June 2, 2018).

Mitchell, Joni. *Love Has Many Faces: A Quartet, A Ballet, Waiting to Be Danced*. LA: Rhino Entertainment, 2014.

Monk, Katherine. *Joni: The Creative Odyssey of Joni Mitchell*. Vancouver and Berkeley: Greystone Books, 2012.

Nelson, Sean. *Court and Spark 33 1/3*. London: Bloomsbury, 2007.

Pellegrini, Ann. "After Sontag: Future Notes on Camp," in *A Companion to Lesbian, Gay, Bisexual, Transgender, and Queer Studies*, ed. George E. Haggerty and Molly McGarry. Chichester: Wiley Blackwell, 2007. 168–193.

Powers, Ann. "A New Canon: In Pop Music, Women Belong at the Center of the Story," *NPR Music*, July 24, 2017. https://www.npr.org/2017/07/24/538601651/a-new-canon-in-pop-music-women-belong-at-the-center-of-the-story (accessed: June 2, 2018).

Román, David. *Performance in America: Contemporary U.S. Culture and the Performing Arts*. Durham and London: Duke University Press, 2005.

Sedgwick, Eve Kosofsky. *Tendencies*. Durham and London: Duke University Press, 1993.

Sedgwick, Eve Kosofsky. *Touching Feeling: Affect, Pedagogy, Performativity*. Durham and London: Duke University Press, 2003.

Smith, Zadie. "Some Notes on Attunement: A Voyage around Joni Mitchell," *New Yorker*, December 17, 2012. https://www.newyorker.com/magazine/2012/12/17/some-notes-on-attunement (accessed: June 2, 2018).

Vazquez, Alexandra T. *Listening in Detail: Performances of Cuban Music*. Durham and London: Duke University Press, 2013.

Whiteley, Sheila. *Women and Popular Music: Sexuality, Identity and Subjectivity*. London: Routledge, 2000.

Whitesell, Lloyd. *The Music of Joni Mitchell*. Oxford: Oxford University Press, 2008.

Wild, David. "Morrissey Meets Joni Mitchell: Melancholy and the Infinite Sadness," *Rolling Stone*, March 6, 1997. https://www.rollingstone.com/music/news/morrissey-melancholy-meets-the-infinite-sadness-19970306 (accessed: June 3, 2018).

Wild, David. "Q&A: Joni Mitchell," *Rolling Stone*, October 15, 1992. https://www.rollingstone.com/music/features/joni-mitchell-19921015 (accessed: June 3, 2018).

Wild, David. "Q&A: Joni Mitchell," *Rolling Stone*, April 13, 2000. https://www.rollingstone.com/music/features/joni-mitchell-q-a-20000413 (accessed: June 2, 2018).

Yaffe, David. *Reckless Daughter: A Portrait of Joni Mitchell*. New York: Sarah Crichton Books/Farrar, Straus and Giroux, 2017.

Part One

"The Breadth of Extremities": Voice, Instrument, Feeling

1

"The Hexagram of the Heavens, the Strings of My Guitar": Joni Mitchell's Crip Virtuosity

Matthew J. Jones

Joni Mitchell's musical "voice" has been described by critics and fans as idiosyncratic, innovative, and even visionary, but never as disabled. Mitchell (née Roberta Joan Anderson) is a survivor of childhood polio and has lived with post-polio syndrome (PPS) since the 1980s. A degenerative condition, PPS exacerbates the muscle weakness in her lower back, arms, and hands left by poliovirus; it also causes intermittent nerve inflammation that manifests as chronic pain. Polio and PPS directly impact Mitchell's musicianship in specific ways. When first she started to play baritone ukulele, then later the guitar, Mitchell lacked the dexterity necessary to produce complex chords and intricate fingerpicked accompaniment. Instead, she relied on "an adaptability and resourcefulness that is often underdeveloped in those whose bodies fit smoothly into the prevailing, sustaining environment" (Garland-Thomson 2011, 604). Mitchell cultivated a novel approach to the guitar comprising many alternate tunings; unorthodox chord voicings (the exact arrangement and register of pitches in a chord); chord sequences more like jazz and classical music than the folk genre with which she is so often (mis)identified; a repertoire of simplified left-hand chord shapes; and an idiosyncratic right-hand technique that incorporates a plectrum, detailed fingerpicking, rhythmic strumming, pizzicato, and other effects. By changing its physical properties, Mitchell adapted the guitar to her body, queering the fretboard and creating a new idiom which constitutes one form of what I call *crip virtuosity* (Straus 2006, 2008, 2011; Lerner and Straus 2006).

Crip virtuosity is a queer concept with necessarily stretchy boundaries that must be adapted to the bodies of individual musicians. In academic-activist parlance, crip/cripping is akin to queer/queering inasmuch as both function as more radical forms of the identities "disabled," "gay," or "lesbian," active processes of progressive social-political transformation, and strategies for interpreting a variety of cultural texts, including the "text" of instrumental techniques.[1] One happy result of all this cripping is the expansion of our notion of musical virtuosity. By closely attending to styles of musical expression and the role of the body in performance, composition, and listening, crip virtuosity reminds us that, in Tobin Siebers's memorable phrase, "situated knowledge adheres in embodiment" (2008, 23).

From an ablest perspective, crip virtuosity seems like an oxymoron. How could persons with disabilities (PWDs)—so often numbered among those bodies that do *not* matter—perform virtuosically?[2] How do we understand crip musicianship without resorting to cliché narratives of heroism (the Beethoven model), romanticized suffering (the Schubert model), or pejorative exceptionality (greatness *in spite of* disability) (Straus 2011)? A one-size-fits-all answer to these questions belies the intertwined political projects of disability activism and theory which attend to bodily specificity in nuanced ways. Therefore, this chapter focuses on a single case study—the guitar technique of singer-songwriter and multi-instrumentalist Joni Mitchell—in the hopes of initiating a broader discussion of crip virtuosities.

To date, there have been few critical analyses of Mitchell's music and none from a disability studies perspective. As Carl Wilson recently surmised, "the few books on Mitchell have been limited, either too hagiographic or subsuming her under second-wave feminism or California lifestyle-ism."[3] With a few exceptions, writing about Mitchell tends to plumb her work for autobiographical trivia, matching this song to that ex-lover or life event, without engaging with critical questions about her compositional, performance, or recording practices or issues like race, gender, sexuality, or politics.[4] My examination of Mitchell's guitar technique is, therefore, intended to move away from facile biography or uncritical diva worship. Nevertheless, certain events in her life remain important, so I begin with a brief "pathography" to contextualize my later comments about Mitchell's crip virtuosity.[5] Second, I examine the history of two seemingly antithetical terms: "crip" and "virtuoso." Third, I analyze one of the most striking elements of Mitchell's music—harmony—using the lens of crip virtuosity. Finally, I discuss Mitchell's novel guitar technique as a form of crip virtuosity that attends to the particularities of her disabled body.

Pathography: Joni Mitchell

Joni Mitchell contracted polio in October of 1952. Decades later, she recalled falling ill with a painterly eye to detail:

> I dressed myself that morning in pegged gray slacks, a red and white gingham blouse with a sailor collar, and a blue sweater. I looked in the mirror, and I don't know what I saw—dark circles under my eyes or a slight swelling in my face—but I said to myself, "You look like a woman today."
>
> After I got outside, I was walking along with a school friend, and at the third block, I sat down on this little lawn and said "I must have rheumatism," because I'd seen my grandmother aching and having to be lifted out of the bathtub. I complained a bit more but still went and spent the day in school. Next day, I woke and my mom said, "Get up, come!" I said, "I can't." She didn't believe me and yanked me out of bed, and I collapsed. (White 1995, 13–16)

Alone in North Castleford's children's polio ward, 100 miles from her home in Saskatoon, the self-described "broken doll" endured blistering compresses wrapped tight around her paralyzed legs to prevent muscular atrophy and fell asleep each night to the mechanical rhythms of iron lungs.[6] Her mother came to visit just once and wore "a mask over her face and a haunted look in her eye," and her father never came.[7]

Her mother left a small Christmas tree on a bedside table in the polio ward, which young Joan was allowed to keep illuminated for an hour after the official lights-out. To the consternation of her nurses, she entertained herself by singing Christmas carols, loudly. When her doctor, himself a polio survivor who used a wheelchair, told Joan that she would be unable to return home for Christmas because she could not walk, the precocious child resisted. One night, Mitchell told the angel atop her Christmas tree, "'I am not a cripple,' and [she] said a little prayer, some kind of pact, a barter with God for [her] legs, [her] singing."[8] With a determination that shocked and surprised her doctors, the young girl regained use of her legs through grueling physical therapy and eventually returned to her home and family. However, her body bore the stigmata of polio. Her spine was "twisted severely forward in a curvature called lordosis, and then back to the right in a lateral curve called scoliosis [...] One leg was impaired, but the muscles didn't atrophy, so there was no withering," and the muscles of both hands, especially the left, were weakened (White 1995, 15–16).

Although Mitchell was "born too soon [...] to benefit from the imminent introduction of [polio] vaccines, [she was] born at just the right time to feel the beat of the rock and pop worlds of youth music, the counterculture, and beyond" (McKay 2013, 23). As a teenager, she caught the rock-and-roll bug, excelled at various dance fads, and scandalized her conservative peers by sneaking off to the "wrong" side of town where the music was better for dancing. If polio and rock and roll "shaped (misshaped) [her]; the 60s shaped [her] again" (McKay 2013, 31). During her brief stint at the Alberta College of Art, Mitchell bought a copy of Peter Seeger's *How to Play Folk-Style Guitar* and "went straight to the [Elizabeth] Cotten picking. Your thumb went from the sixth string, fifth string, sixth string, fifth string."[9] However, polio-related muscle weakness made her clumsy on the fretboard. Her left hand could not move between chord shapes easily, and her right hand "ended up playing mostly the sixth string but banging it into the fifth string."[10] A few years later, friend and singer-songwriter Eric Andersen introduced Mitchell to open-chord guitar tunings which proved to be the catalyst that launched decades of musical exploration and innovation.

Mitchell seldom writes songs about her own disability. In fact, the only such reference occurs in a relatively late song, "Come in from the Cold" (1991). The evocative line, "I feel disabled by these bonfires in my spine," could index either a physiological experience or describe being overwhelmed by emotional intensity. She makes passing references to physical disabilities in other songs: an "aging cripple selling Superman balloons" ("Nathan La Franeer," 1968), and bluesman Furry Lewis, "propped up in his bed with his dentures and his leg removed" ("Furry Sings the Blues," 1976). "A Chair in the Sky" (1979) captures jazz bassist Charles Mingus's paralysis from amyotrophic lateral sclerosis (ALS). In other songs, like "Big Yellow Taxi" (1970), "Sex Kills" (1994), and "This Place" (2007), illness and disability serve as conceits for ecological, political, and cultural conditions while, in the song "Dog Eat Dog"

(1985), Mitchell paraphrases Nietzsche to anthropomorphize corruption, singing "Money is the road to justice, and power walks it on crooked legs."[11] While disability is not a substantial trope in Mitchell's lyrics, it is the defining characteristic of her guitar technique.

Cripping virtuosity

In the late twentieth century, a remarkable era of disability activism culminated with the passing of the Americans with Disabilities Act of 1990. Following the tradition of feminist, queer, and antiracist activism, some disability activist-intellectuals resignified terms like "crip" (a variant of "cripple" that functions as both verb and adjective) and "cripping" (gerund). According to Carrie Sandahl, "cripping spins mainstream representations or practices to reveal able-bodied assumptions and exclusionary effects [and exposes] the arbitrary delineation between normal and defective and the negative social ramifications of attempts to homogenize humanity" (2003, 37). Both Alison Kafer and Robert McRuer place "crip" at the fulcrum of feminist, critical race, and queer theories (Kafer 2013; McRuer 2006). "To crip" is to resist what McRuer calls "compulsory able-bodiedness" (2006, 2). In expanding Adrienne Rich's influential notion of "compulsory heterosexuality" (which sets up straightness, binary gender, and reproductive sex as "normal" and serves, therefore, to police expressions of "deviant" gender and sexuality) (Rich 1980, 631–660), McRuer posits that systemic compulsory able-bodiedness establishes the absence of disability (broadly defined) as "normal" embodiment. Rosemarie Garland-Thomson assigns to this privileged subject position the neologism "normate."[12] A tool of compulsory able-bodiedness, the *medical* model of disability supposes that intervention, treatment, and ultimately cure are desirable to "correct" a disabling condition. By contrast, the *social* model of disability arose from the activist culture of the 1980s and 1990s and proffers that compulsory able-bodiedness "produces disability" using a cultural logic similar to "the system of compulsory heterosexuality that produces queerness" (McRuer 2006, 2). The straight and able-bodied rely on the queer and the disabled for their intelligibility.

Likewise, the virtuoso and the crip can be cast as doppelgängers, opposites whose respective value is embedded in the terms used to describe each category. Virtuosity is a prized attribute in most musical traditions. Extraordinary musical prowess matters; spectator-listeners thrill at the seemingly effortless execution of technical feats. According to the *Oxford English Dictionary*, a specifically musical virtuosity came into existence during the seventeenth century.[13] However, as James Deaville points out, such

> general dictionary definitions do not address the diversity and complexity of [virtuosity] or the host of contradictory meanings and interpretations that not only cut across centuries of music-making and virtually every style type, but also play out in other disciplines and professions, ranging from dance and theater to jurisprudence and theology. (Deaville 2014, 277)

Things grow more complicated "in the habitus of Western civilization [because] we use ['virtuosity'] to describe artistic or sport performances, the public presentations of teachers, clerics, and other speakers, accomplishments in work contexts, and even love-making" (Deaville 2014, 276). There also exist older, more arcane meanings; a secondary definition describes the virtuoso as one "with special knowledge of or interest in the work of art or curios."[14] Finally, virtuosity shares a common etiology with "virtue" and all of its moralizing implications. A virtuoso, then, may be a scholar, musician, artist, connoisseur, or other such person of *great worth* whose esteem is measured by the value of their contributions to culture, society, or history. Ghosts of these older definitions haunt modern usages of the terms, for virtuosos are prized, revered, rewarded, and removed from run-of-the-mill folk.

Historically, too, People with Disabilities (PWDs) have been set apart, though in ways that have none of the cultural cache and glamour of the virtuoso. Terms like "crippled," "retarded," "lame," "gimp," "slow," "queer," and "freak" exclude PWDs from the category of "the human." Throughout the nineteenth century and the first half of the twentieth century, sequestration in asylums or institutions banished PWDs from daily life, and so-called ugly laws made it illegal for "unseemly" or "unsightly" persons to be seen in public (see Schweik 2009). One venue in which PWDs could achieve some success was entertainment, but it came at a cost. PWDs with visible disabilities were put on display (sometimes posthumously) in circus sideshows, freak shows, and carnivals. Perhaps the most (in)famous exhibition was that of Sarah Baartman, the so-called Hottentot Venus. An African woman of the Khoi people, Baartman became a spectacle due to steatopygia, a genetic characteristic of some sub-Saharan African women, including the Knoisans. The condition leads to substantial deposits of tissue around the buttocks and thighs and gives individuals a distinctive callipygian shape. Throughout England and continental Europe, spectators paid to gawk at Baartman's body. After her death, her preserved skeleton and a cast of her body were put on display until the late-1970s. Savants and prodigies (some of whom we might now identify on the autism spectrum) shocked audiences with their musical accomplishment *in spite of* their "pitiable" conditions. Remnants of the freak show are very much part of twenty-first-century popular culture. The *Got Talent* franchise spectacularizes PWDs like Susan Boyle for the seeming incongruence between their status as "freaks" and their ability to perform beautiful music.[15] Because her pain condition and muscle weakness are forms of invisible disability (unlike guitarist Django Reinhardt, whose hands sustained damage in a fire) Mitchell could pass as "normate." Yet her music has been frequently Othered when fellow musicians and journalists describe her "weird" chords or her unusual style of playing the guitar.

Music remains rooted in assumptions about the normate body (*Extraordinary Bodies*, Garland-Thomson 1996, 8). For instance, most musical instruments, when played traditionally, require two arms, two hands, and ten functional fingers while others, including organs and modern pianos, require two legs and two feet as well to manipulate their pedals. According to Alex Lubet, professional-level classical music performance "requires physical technique that is at once highly developed and highly standardized" (2011, 3). However, "the protocols of jazz [and here, one might add, other forms of popular music] provide better opportunities for musicians with disabilities not only to perform, but to perform in ways that are actually expressions of lives with disabilities" (Lubet 2011, 42). To an extent, Lubet romanticizes popular music practices, which are governed by rules and conventions, albethey different ones from concert music. The rock guitar or jazz saxophone virtuoso improvises (rather than reads from a score) rapid, complex passages with precision and agility but also practices those licks with diligence and regularity. Likewise, the virtuoso gospel or R&B singer makes difficult vocal runs seem effortless, even if she eschews the bel canto aesthetic of classical singing. Even great punk musicians have to perform "badly" in the *right* way (Fabbri 1981, 52–81). However, Lubet's core insight is valuable. Broadly speaking, popular music is more hospitable to idiosyncratic performance techniques, including those of PWDs.

Crip virtuosity, then, refers to forms of exceptional music-making that are rooted in disability; they would not exist as such without particular disabling conditions. Thus, it may be more appropriate to speak of *crip virtuosities*, as no two crip virtuosos will travel the same path to artistic creation. Some use prosthetics (Def Leppard drummer Rick Allen); others develop techniques to exploit the unique possibilities of their extraordinary bodies (Django Reinhardt). Further, crip virtuosities can be learned by the able-bodied or differently disabled PWDs. Anyone willing to experiment with the techniques can crip their own musicality in ways that align with a vision of a world where the "fluidity of [the term crip] makes it likely that [its] boundaries will dissolve" (Sandahl 2003, 27).

Cripping harmony

Joni Mitchell is often (mis)cast as a folk musician, but she is a musical misfit, a stylistic wanderer, and an innovative technician who eschews labels—especially those of genre (with all their attendant ideological baggage).[16] In its harmonic complexity, melodic inventiveness, and formal experimentation, Mitchell's music has more in common with jazz, some classical music, and the edgier corners of progressive pop than with folk. Speaking broadly, harmony in much popular music can be inconsequential in and of itself. Regarding basic pop music harmonic idioms, Middleton suggests that, "If you can construct a song over a single riff, or a repeating 12-bar blues chord-sequence, then you can use the same riff or sequence to create a somewhat different song tomorrow; so can someone else" (Middleton 2000, 72; see also Middleton 1990, esp. chapter 7). What performers do within the harmonic framework matters, on the whole, more than the chords as such. However, harmony is one of the most interesting aspects of Mitchell's musical "misfitting."

In 2005, Mitchell candidly told the California Commonwealth Club that "all of the chords in standard tuning sounded hackneyed to me [. . .] I craved chords you couldn't get off the guitar."[17] Critical of the Western penchant to equate happy feelings with major harmonies and sad emotions with minor chords, Mitchell's "chords of inquiry" balance the dissonance and consonance of her own physiological and psycho-emotional experiences.[18] "My whole life was full of questions," she writes. "Will I survive this disease? Will I ever walk again? Where is my daughter? Is she alright? Will we nuke them? Will they nuke us? Is there a mate for me?" (Mitchell 2014, 14). Childhood polio, the emotional trauma of giving up a child for adoption, the stresses of being a woman in a misogynistic culture, the disappointments of failed romances, the lingering effects of PPS, environmental degradation, and right-wing political agendas created a persistent dissonant buzz in the background of daily life. Mitchell's chords reflect these tensions. She began to use harmony to express the complexity of human feeling, not just her own emotions. For example, she describes minor chords as

> pure tragedy; in order to infuse [them] with a thread of optimism, you add an odd string to the chord to carry the voice of hope. Then perhaps you add a dissonant because in the stressful society we live in dissonance is aggressing against us at every moment. So, there's an inquiry to the chords comparable to the unresolved quality of much poetry. (Whitesell 2008, 119)

Her exploration of alternate tunings began with simple open chords like those used by blues guitar and banjo players, for example open-D [D A D F# A D] and open G [D G D G B D]. In time, the restless musical misfit craved more nuanced sounds, and she expanded her repertoire of tunings to include harmonic extensions beyond the seventh, biting dissonances, and jarring suspensions. Tuning "down" (decreasing tension on the strings) extended the range of the guitar considerably below that of standard tuning, which has as its bass limit a low E2. There are passages throughout Mitchell's oeuvre that are impossible to play in standard tuning because the instrument simply cannot produce the necessary notes, especially bass notes as low as Bb or A. As her tunings grew increasingly complex, Mitchell developed her own system to keep track of the patterns: letter names indicate the pitch class of the sixth (lowest) string and numbers indicate the fret at which adjacent strings are tuned. Standard (or Spanish) tuning (E A D G B D) would be written as E-5-5-5-4-5, a pattern familiar to anyone who has ever tuned a guitar; open-D tuning becomes D-7-5-4-3-5. For non-musically literate players, this system is rather intuitive. You don't need to know specific pitches, but you do need a sensitive ear and perhaps a few extra sets of guitar strings.

Mitchell's more complex tunings can be easily explained using this method. She gave one such tuning the fanciful moniker "California Kitchen."[19] The open strings are tuned to C G D F C E, or a "C11 sus2" chord. In "Joni Notation," the tuning would look like this: C-7-7-3-7-4. It's not necessary to know what type of chord it is, only how it sounds. This exact chord voicing is impossible in standard tuning because the guitar cannot produce the lowest pitch in that register. While a guitarist can produce this chord in a different voicing, to do so requires difficult hand positions, and the resulting chord lacks the unique timbre and movement between notes in the chord of Mitchell's. Finally, some tuning patterns can be used with a variety of different bass notes; others push the instrument's capabilities so far that they cannot be transposed because such drastic reduction of string tension prevents a pitch from sounding, while increasing the tension snaps the higher strings.

Most of Mitchell's tunings use open strings as the tonic, and bar chords at each fret place the building blocks of harmony literally at her fingertips; barring at frets V and VII respectively produces subdominant and dominant harmonies.[20] In many of the "more radical tunings, the ringing open strings take on a different sort of drone quality—[which she uses] between chords as a sort of connecting thread" (Rodgers 1996, 19). Mitchell thinks of this as a basic wash applied to the canvas of a song.

> If I start a canvas now, to get rid of the vertigo of the blank page, I cover the whole thing in olive green then start working the color into it. So every color is permeated with that green. It doesn't really green the colors out but antiques them, burnishes them. The drone kind of burnishes the chord in the same way. The color remains as a wash. These other colors then drop in, but always against the wash. (Rodgers 1996, 19)

Still, Mitchell's "'modern chords' [. . .] have an overall softness to them, with consonances and dissonances gently playing off each other" (Rodgers 1996, 18). Her complex, dissonant chord structures and unusual harmonic sequences pique our ears, which have grown accustomed to a fairly limited number of harmonic patterns in popular music. The unique sound of these harmonies results from a combination of alternate tunings and Mitchell's right-hand technique, which I discuss in more detail later.

Cripping technique

While "an interesting tuning can be fertile ground for writing a song," Mitchell cautions that "it's how you work the tuning with your hands and compositional sense that counts" (Rodgers 1996, 20). Recall that the "social model" demands changes in the built world that respond to the bodies of PWDs. Likewise, crip virtuosity alters both instruments and techniques to match the bodies of musicians with disabilities. Standard tuning can be understood as the "normate" guitar environment, created around the assumption that players possess two hands and ten dexterous fingers to travel along the fretboard and the coordination to strum or to fingerpick. Mitchell's tunings constitute an intervention, a change to that environment in response to the particular capabilities of her body. Accordingly, the patterns of standard tuning no longer work—like rearranging the letters on a keyboard each time you sit down to type. Traversing the neck of her cripped guitar feels, looks, and sounds very different than playing in standard tuning because the physical and auditory coordinates have changed. Each tuning has "its own little universe of sounds and possibilities," so Mitchell has to learn anew where to put her left-hand fingers (Rodgers 1996, 20), though there are "certain things that you'll try from tuning to tuning that will apply" or carry over into others, resulting in a degree of technical consistency (Rodgers 1996, 18). Her style also requires a keen internal sense of rhythm to execute complex syncopations, cross-rhythms, and contrapuntal lines beneath vocal melodies that twist and turn in unpredictable ways over surprising harmonic progressions. Although Mitchell's crip virtuoso style doesn't require the kind of dexterity needed for a

Brian May or a Bonnie Raitt guitar solo, it takes patience, time, and diligence to master. And it ain't easy!

Because she could never "begin to learn the neck like a standard player, linearly and orderly [Mitchell had] to think in a different way," which she often describes as *"moving blocks"* (Rodgers 1996, 18, emphasis added). For weakened, less dexterous, and immobilized fingers, moving a block may be a more accessible task than fine motor skills or intricate finger work typically associated with guitar virtuosity. "Rather than forming her hand into complex chord shapes like a standard guitar would," Les Irvin (webmaster of the official Joni Mitchell homepage) says, "[she] was able to play bar chords, for example lay down just one finger across all six strings [. . .] That allowed her left hand to do less work and at the same time get interesting chord combinations" (Ingles 2007). Because Mitchell keeps her fingers in relatively static positions as they glide up and down the neck, chords sound in exactly parallel voicing, a guitar transposition of the impressionist musical technique known as "harmonic planing." For example, using only open strings and bar chords at V and VII produces the exact arrangement of intervals between different notes in the chord, at different pitch levels. She frequently uses hammer-ons/offs to break up the monotony of exact parallel voicing in a single song.

Like the impressionist composers she admires, Mitchell makes timbre (tone color) an essential component of her style, and she achieves a myriad of novel sounds because of the "slackness" (the decreased tension on the strings) of her tunings. Strings buzz, rattle, and pop as they vibrate along the neck, and Mitchell incorporates these extra-musical elements into her strumming, sometimes using a pick, her fingernails, or her hand to click and slap the strings to exaggerate the effect, as in the opening riff of "Cold Blue Steel and Sweet Fire" (1972). She sometimes snaps single strings (in classical music known as a "Bartók" or "snap pizzicato") which adds both a strong rhythmic accent and a percussive effect that is especially audible in "The Wolf that Lives in Lindsay" (1979). Her light touch also results in frequent high harmonics more often than most guitarists regularly employ.

To facilitate movement between different tunings, Mitchell groups them into closely related families which allows her to "twiddle" only a knob or two at a time rather than risk breaking a string or causing extreme instability in the overall intonation. Family resemblances between tunings become clear when they are written in Mitchell's notation style. Table 1.1 contains several such "relatives." Most feature strings five and four tuned at the seventh fret while the upper three strings exhibit some variations. Following Mitchell's lead, I have grouped some of the most common left-hand "blocks" into families. Those in Table 1.2 use open and bar chords with slight variations, for instance, the addition of two or three fingers at higher adjacent frets. Table 1.3 consists of chord shapes anchored by the index finger on the third string. Mitchell discovered these shapes through a process of trial and error, and the shapes here represent only the most common among her songs. Diagrams read left (sixth string) to right (first string); numbers indicate the fret at which a particular string is pressed. However, these shapes produce chords with varying degrees of consonance and dissonance at any fret.

The song "Cactus Tree" (1968) features an open major chord turning E-7-5-4-3-5 with a capo at the second fret so that the studio recording sounds in F#-Major with a persistent tonic pedal point (Table 1.4).[21] Using only a few

Table 1.1 Guitar tunings

Joni Notation/ Tuning	Chord Type	Open Chord Voicing	Example Songs
X-7-5-4-3-5	Major, root position	R-5th-R-3rd-5th-R	Amelia, Both Sides, Now
X-5-7-5-4-3	Major, second inversion	5th-R-5th-R-3rd-5th	The Circle Game, Little Green
X-7-7-5-4-3	Major Sus 4	4th-R-5th-R-3rd-5th	Otis and Marlena, Underneath the Streetlight
X-7-7-2-3-5	Major add 9	R-5th-9th-3rd-5th-5th	Cherokee Louise, Night Ride Home
X-7-7-3-7-4	Major add 9, add 11	R-5th-9th-11th-R-3rd	Coyote, Just Like This Train
X-7-7-3-2-5	Sus add 9 (no 3rd)	R-5th-9th-4th-5th-R	Hejira, Slouching Towards Bethlehem
X-7-3-5-2-5	Minor 11th	R-5th-7th-3rd-11th-7th	Moon at the Window, Sex Kills

X indicates the variable pitch of string 6.

Source: From author's data.

Table 1.2 Shapes based on an open or bar chord

Chord Shape Name	Left-Hand Fingering
A: The Six Open Strings	0-0-0-0-0-0
B: Open + 2	0-0-0-11-0-11; 0-0-0-3-3-0; 0-0-0-2-2-0; 0-0-4-3-0
C: Full Bar	5-5-5-5-5-5;; 10-10-10-10-10-10
D: Partial Bar	0-0-7-7-7-7; 4-4-4-4-0-0
E: Full Bar + 2	5-5-7-5-6-5; 7-7-7-9-9-7

*0 indicates an open string. Numbers indicate the fret at which each string is depressed.
Source: From author's data.

Table 1.3 Shapes anchored by index finger on String 3

A: 0-2-0-1-0-0
B: 0-0-2-1-0-0
C: 0-2-0-1-0-3
D: 2-3-4-1-0-0

Source: From author's data.

closely related left-hand shapes, Mitchell creates flowing contrapuntal lines against the resonant open strings by fingerpicking with her right hand, using her thumb to consistently pluck the sixth string to create a tonic drone in the bass. In this case, the moving blocks consist of the same two- or three-finger shapes, oscillated between two frets.

Open and alternate tunings facilitate the execution of precise fingerpicked figures in songs like "The Dawntreader" (1968), "The Priest" (1970), "Sunny Sunday" (1994), and "The Wolf that Lives in Lindsay" (1979) (the latter also a fascinating study in guitar timbres). According to Joel Bernstein, Mitchell's early albums contain

> some very fine, detailed fingerpicking—note for note, there are very specific figures. As time goes on, she gets into more of a strumming thing until it becomes more like a brush stroke—it's a real expressive rhythmic thing. Her early stuff doesn't really swing, there's not jazz stuff going on in it, and she's not implying a rhythm section as much, whereas now she obviously has a lot going on in the right hand. It's at the same time simpler and deeper. (Rodgers 1996, 21)

Her sense of rhythm and accent creates complex contrapuntal accompaniments as she deftly maneuvers around an unwavering underlying beat. Open tunings

Table 1.4 Moving blocks in "Cactus Tree"

0 6 0 5 0 0	0 4 0 3 0 0
0 6 0 5 0 3	0 4 0 3 0 4

Source: From author's data.

also facilitate movement around the entire neck of the guitar, and Mitchell's songs often require playing well above the twelfth fret and harmonics. Another common technique involves the juxtaposition of fretted strings high on the neck with ringing open strings below them, as heard in the opening riff of "Chelsea Morning" (1969), and in songs like "Barangrill" (1972), "Just Like This Train" (1974) and "Harlem in Havana" (1998). Mitchell conceives of her guitar as an orchestra in which "the treble strings become a cooljazz [sic] horn section, the bass snaps out syncopations like a snare drum, the notes ring out in clusters that simply don't come out of a normal six string" (Rodgers 1996, 18).

Playing in alternate tunings is dangerous. All that "twiddling around isn't good for the instrument, generally speaking. It's not good for the neck"—which is calibrated for standard tuning. In adapting her guitar to match her body's capabilities, Mitchell risks real damage to her instrument. Strings break under the strain, and necks twist, warp, and bend in ways that mirror the impact of polio on her own spine. Consequently, Mitchell has been very selective about the guitars she uses, opting for instruments whose necks can withstand the differing levels of tension. Mitchell's slack tunings also unsettle the intonation, and she admits to being frequently frustrated by such tuning problems. To compensate, she cultivated a nimble left-hand touch to bed the strings as little as possible while also facilitating fluid movement up and down the entire length of the neck. This, in turn, helps keep her instrument in tune, but even her light left-hand touch is sometimes "defeated by the extreme slackness of some of her tunings" (Rodgers 1996, 21).

By the end of the mid-1990s, PPS and other health problems made it impossible for Mitchell to perform. As she told Jody Denberg in 1998:

> I was diagnosed as having [PPS], which they said was inevitable [. . .] that forty years after you had the disease [. . .] the wires that animate certain muscles are taken out by the disease and the body in its ingenious way. The

filaments of the adjacent muscles send out branches and try to animate that muscle, so it's kind of like the [Energizer] bunny. The muscles all around the muscles that are gone begin to go also because they've been trying to drive this muscle for so long [. . .] the weight of the guitar became unbearable. Also, the acoustic guitar requires that you extend your shoulder out in an abnormal way. [. . .] Some of the damage to my back, in combination with that position, was very painful.[22]

In the 1990s, "genius luthier" Fred Walecki of Westwood Music built for Mitchell a custom-made, "thin as a wafer [. . .] two-and-a-half pound" guitar out of German spruce that "fit [her] hip and even kinda cups up like a bra."[23] Walecki equipped it with a Roland VG-8 processor that could digitally manipulate the sound coming out of an amplifier to virtually create her tunings while leaving the guitar itself in standard tuning. For the first time in her career, Mitchell could play her songs with precise intonation and without pain. The instrument facilitated a return to the stage in the late-1990s and inspired a new album, *Taming the Tiger*.

Conclusion

Both critical studies of the music of Joni Mitchell and crip studies of music are emergent, interdisciplinary subfields. Accordingly, this chapter intends to contribute to ongoing conversations among scholars across both groups, by facilitating a move away from hagiography and toward a more rigorous analysis of musical technique and performance. To that end, I put forth the concept of "crip virtuosity" as one way to think about the extraordinary body in performance. In this case, it can account for the idiosyncrasies of Mitchell's playing that result directly from the lingering effects of childhood polio and PPS. Just as disability activists sought to change the built environment to facilitate access by the broadest number, thereby interpellating more people into the category of "human," Mitchell adapted the guitar to suit her bodily specificity by queering the fretboard and finding a new way to traverse and make musical sense (as knowledge and sensation) of it, thereby expanding the category of "virtuoso." Hers is not the only form of "crip virtuosity," but an instructive first case study, one remarkable form of disablist music-making that can go unnoticed in a culture of compulsory able-bodiedness.

Notes

1 Transgender activist and author Kate Bornstein advances a similar argument around the terms "tranny" and "transgender" in her book *Kate Bornstein Is a Queer and Pleasant Danger* (Boston: Beacon Press, 2012) and in the 2014 documentary of the same name. According to Bernstein, "I understand 'tranny' to be a radical, sex-positive gender identity. Tranny is to trans person as fag is to gay man or dyke is to lesbian." Bornstein also writes about this in a blog post which can be found here: http://katebornstein.typepad.com/kate_bornsteins_blog/2014/05/tranny-revisited-by-auntie-kate.html (accessed: June 3, 2018).
2 In *Bodies That Matter: On the Discursive Limits of Sex* (New York: Routledge, 1993), Judith Butler excludes any reference to disability.
3 Carl Wilson, "Chords of Inquiry," *Bookforum* (September 2017). https://www.bookforum.com/inprint/024_03/18474 (accessed: June 3, 2018).
4 Notable exceptions include Lloyd Whitesell's *The Music of Joni Mitchell* (New York: Oxford University, 2008); Eric Lott's *Black Mirror: Cultural Contradictions of American Racism* (Cambridge: Harvard University, 2017); Amy Kintner's "Back to the Garden Again: Joni Mitchell's 'Woodstock' and Utopianism in Song," *Popular Music*, 35.1 (2016): 1–22; and Matthew Jones, "Back to the Garden: Socio-Ecological Critique and the Music of Joni Mitchell," a paper presented at the 2008 meeting of Feminist Theory and Music in Greensboro, NC.
5 Pathography is "the study of the effects of an illness on the writer's (or other artist's) life or art, and the effects of an artist's life and personality development on [their] creative work," Robert J. Campbell, *Psychiatric Dictionary*, 6th edn (Oxford: Oxford University, 1989).
6 Rene Montagne, "The Music Midnight Makes: In Conversation with Joni Mitchell," *NPR* (December 9, 2014). http://www.npr.org/templates/transcript/transcript.php?storyId=369386571 (accessed: June 3, 2018).
7 Ibid. It was not uncommon for polio wards to prohibit family visits due to the risk of contagion.
8 Timothy White, "Joni Mitchell," 14. Mitchell regularly recounts this story. For a detailed account, see Lucy O'Brien, *Shadows and Light: Joni Mitchell, The Definitive Biography* (London: Virgin Publishing, 2002), 24–27.

9 Jeffrey Pepper Rodgers, "My Secret Place: The Guitar Odyssey of Joni Mitchell," *Acoustic Guitar* (August, 1996). Reprinted in *The Complete Joni Mitchell: So Far* (Los Angeles: Alfred Publishing, 2014), 17–21.
10 Ibid.
11 Joni Mitchell, "Come in from the Cold," *Night Ride Home* (Hollywood: Geffen Records, 1991); "Nathan La Franeer," *Joni Mitchell* (Hollywood: Reprise Records, 1967); "Furry Sings the Blues," *Hejira* (Asylum Records, 1976); *Mingus* (Asylum Records, 1979); "Dog Eat Dog," *Dog Eat Dog* (Hollywood: Geffen Records, 1985).
12 In *Extraordinary Bodies: Figuring Physical Disability in American Culture* (New York: Columbia University, 1996), Rosemarie Garland-Thomson defines the normate as the "veiled subject position of cultural self, the figure outlined by the array of deviant others whose marked bodies shore up the normate's boundaries [and] through which people can represent themselves as definitive human beings" (8).
13 *Oxford English Dictionary*, "virtuosity." http://www.oed.com/view/Entry/223847?redirectedFrom=VIRTUOSITY#eid (accessed: June 3, 2018).
14 *Oxford English Dictionary*, "virtuoso." http://www.oed.com/view/Entry/223848?redirectedFrom=virtuoso#eid (accessed: June 3, 2018).
15 Rosemarie Garland-Thomson, ed., *Freakery: Cultural Spectacles of the Extraordinary Body* (New York: New York University Press, 1996). In nineteenth-century Europe, around the time Ludwig van Beethoven was losing his hearing, rudimentary schools for the deaf and blind were established on the periphery of cities like Vienna. For more information, see Joseph Straus, *Extraordinary Measures: Disability in Music* (New York: Oxford University Press, 2012), especially chapters one and two.
16 I intentionally borrow Rosemarie Garland-Thomson's notion of the misfit as it relates to disability studies in her "Misfits: A Feminist Materialist Disability Concept," *Hypatia*, 26.3 (2011): 591–609.
17 Joni Mitchell, "Earth Day Speech" to the California Commonwealth Club (April 22, 2005). http://www.commonwealthclub.org/events/archive/podcast/joni-mitchell-earth-day-speech-42205 (accessed: June 3, 2018).
18 Mitchell began using this term at some point in the 1970s. She describes her descriptive language for harmony in an interview with Malka Marom in Marom's *Joni Mitchell: In Her Own Words* (Ontario: EWC Press, 2014), 74–75.
19 It's unclear when Mitchell first derived this whimsical name, but in a 1967 radio interview with Gene Shay, she describes this specific tuning using the "California Kitchen" moniker. When asked by Shay why she chose that specific name, Mitchell flatly responded "That's what I called it." Clips of this interview can be heard in Paul Ingles, "The Emergence of Joni Mitchell," *Public*

Radio International (September 24, 2007). http://www.prx.org/playlists/6475 (accessed: June 3, 2018).
20 I use these terms to refer to the chords built on the fourth and fifth scale degrees, respectively, not to describe harmonic function as in Western classical music. Mitchell incorporates a variety of harmonic idioms ranging from so-called functional harmony to modal progressions and mixtures of the two. For a thorough description of Mitchell's harmonic palette see Whitesell, chapter 5.
21 Mitchell sometimes performs "Cactus Tree" in Open-D (D-7-5-4-3-5) with a capo at the fourth fret. In a 1974 broadcast of the BBC's *Old Grey Whistle Test*, she performs the song in Open-D with the capo on the second fret, creating a tonal center. Whitesell's work on Mitchell's harmonic palette has been rather helpful here; see 120–125.
22 Jody Denberg, "A Conversation with Joni Mitchell," *KGSR-FM* (September 9, 1998).
23 Ibid.

Works Cited

Bornstein, Kate. *Kate Bornstein Is a Queer and Pleasant Danger*. Boston: Beacon Press, 2012.

Butler, Judith. *Bodies That Matter: On the Discursive Limits of Sex*. New York: Routledge, 1993.

Campbell, Robert J. *Psychiatric Dictionary*, 6th edn. Oxford: Oxford University Press, 1989.

Deaville, James. "Virtuosity and the Virtuoso," in *Aesthetics of Music: Musicological Perspectives*, ed. Stephen Downes. New York and London: Routledge, 2014.

Denberg, Jody. "A Conversation with Joni Mitchell," KGSR-FM Radio, September 9, 1998.

Fabbri, Franco. "A Theory of Musical Genres—Two Applications," in *Popular Music Perspectives*, ed. Daniel Horn and Phil Tagg. Göteborg and Exeter: International Association for the Study of Popular Music, 1981, 52–81.

Garland-Thomson, Rosemarie. *Extraordinary Bodies: Figuring Physical Disability in American Culture*. New York: Columbia University Press, 1996.

Garland-Thomson, Rosemarie, ed. *Freakery: Cultural Spectacles of the Extraordinary Body*. New York: New York University Press, 1996.

Garland-Thomson, Rosemarie. "Misfits: A Feminist Materialist Disability Concept," *Hypatia*, 26.3 (2011): 591–609.

Ingles, Paul. "The Emergence of Joni Mitchell," *Public Radio International*. September 24, 2007. https://exchange.prx.org/playlists/6475 (accessed: June 3, 2018).

Jones, Matthew. "Back to the Garden: Socio-Ecological Critique and the Music of Joni Mitchell." Paper presented at Feminist Theory and Music 9, 2008, Greensboro, NC.

Kafer, Alison. *Feminist Crip Queer*. Bloomington: Indiana University Press, 2013.

Kintner, Amy. "Back to the Garden Again: Joni Mitchell's 'Woodstock' and Utopianism in Song," *Popular Music*, 35.1 (2016): 1–22.

Lerner, Neil, and Joseph Straus, eds. *Sounding Off: Theorizing Disability in Music*. New York: Routledge, 2006.

Lott, Eric. *Black Mirror: Cultural Contradictions of American Racism*. Cambridge: Harvard University Press, 2017.

Lubet, Alex. *Music, Disability, Society*. Philadelphia: Temple University Press, 2011.

Marom, Malka. *Joni Mitchell: In Her Own Words—Conversations with Malka Marom*. Ontario: ECW Press, 2014.

McKay, George. *Shakin' All Over: Popular Music and Disability*. Ann Arbor: University of Michigan Press, 2013.

McRuer, Robert. *Crip Theory: Cultural Signs of Queerness and Disability*. New York: New York University Press, 2006.

Middleton, Richard. *Studying Popular Music*. London: Open University Press, 1990.

Middleton, Richard. "Work-in-(g) Practice: Configuration of the Popular Music Intertext," in *The Musical Work: Reality or Invention?* ed. Michael Talbot, Liverpool: Liverpool University Press, 2000, 59–88.

Mitchell, Joni. *Song to a Seagull*. Hollywood: Reprise Records, 1968.

Mitchell, Joni. *Clouds*. Hollywood: Reprise Records, 1969.

Mitchell, Joni. *Ladies of the Canyon*. Hollywood: Reprise Records, 1971.

Mitchell, Joni. *For The Roses*. Hollywood: Asylum Records, 1972.

Mitchell, Joni. *Court and Spark*. Hollywood: Asylum Records, 1973.

Mitchell, Joni. *Hejira*. Hollywood: Asylum Records, 1976.

Mitchell, Joni. *Mingus*. Hollywood: Asylum Records, 1979.

Mitchell, Joni. *Dog Eat Dog*. Hollywood: Geffen Records, 1985.

Mitchell, Joni. *Night Ride Home*. Hollywood: Geffen Records, 1991.

Mitchell, Joni. *Turbulent Indigo*. Hollywood: Reprise Records, 1994.

Mitchell, Joni. *Taming the Tiger*. Hollywood: Reprise Records, 1998.

Mitchell, Joni. "Earth Day Speech." The California Commonwealth Club, April 22, 2005.
Mitchell, Joni. *Shine*. Santa Monica: Hear Music/Universal, 2007.
Mitchell, Joni. *Love Has Many Faces: A Quartet, A Ballet, Waiting to Be Danced*. Liner Notes. Burbank: Rhino Records, 2014.
Montagne, Rene. "The Music Midnight Makes: In Conversation with Joni Mitchell," *NPR*. December 9, 2014. https://www.npr.org/2014/12/09/369386571/the-music-midnight-makes-in-conversation-with-joni-mitchell (accessed: June 3, 2018).
O'Brien, Lucy. *Shadows and Light: Joni Mitchell, the Definitive Biography*. London: Virgin Publishing, 2002.
Oxford English Dictionary, "virtuosity." http://www.oed.com/view/Entry/223847?redirectedFrom=VIRTUOSITY#eid (accessed: June 3, 2018).
Oxford English Dictionary, "virtuoso." http://www.oed.com/view/Entry/223848?redirectedFrom=virtuoso#eid (accessed: June 3, 2018).
Rich, Adrienne. "Compulsory Heterosexuality and Lesbian Existence," *Signs*, 5.4 (1980): 631–660.
Rodgers, Jeffrey Pepper. "My Secret Place: The Guitar Odyssey of Joni Mitchell," *Acoustic Guitar*. August, 1996. Reprinted in *The Complete Joni Mitchell: So Far*. Los Angeles: Alfred Publishing, 2014, 17–21.
Sandahl, Carrie. "Queering the Crip or Cripping the Queer?: Intersections of Queer and Crip Identities in Solo Autobiographical Performance," *GLQ*, 9.1–2 (2003): 25–56.
Schweik, Susan. *The Ugly Laws: Disability in Public*. New York: New York University Press, 2009.
Siebers, Tobin. *Disability Theory*. Ann Arbor: University of Michigan Press, 2008.
Straus, Joseph. "Normalizing the Abnormal: Disability in Music and Music theory," *Journal of the American Musicological Society*, 59.1 (2006): 113–184.
Straus, Joseph. "Disability and 'Late Style' in Music," *The Journal of Musicology*, 25.1 (2008): 3–45.
Straus, Joseph. *Extraordinary Measures: Disability in Music*. New York: Oxford University Press, 2011.
White, Timothy. "Joni Mitchell: A Portrait of the Artist," *Billboard*. December 8, 1995, 13–16.
Whitesell, Lloyd. *The Music of Joni Mitchell*. New York: Oxford University Press, 2008.
Wilson, Carl. "Chords of Inquiry," *Bookforum*. September 2017. https://www.bookforum.com/inprint/024_03/18474 (accessed: June 3, 2018).

2

"Oh Borderline": Joni Mitchell's Aging Voice as a Site of Queer Resistance

Emily Baker

In late 2002, aged 59 years old, Joni Mitchell released *Travelogue*,[1] a double album of self-penned songs from her three decades of music-making. Before we hear a note, we see Mitchell's latest self-portrait: half-smiling, she peers out of a mottled shadow through curls of smoke that look as though they could twist out of the frame altogether. Presented in a thick-rimmed gold frame, the self-portrait is set against a yellow background—implying a picture in an exhibition, a past master of popular music. As the name suggests, *Travelogue*'s visual promise concerns the passing of time, a reflective and nostalgic take on Mitchell's musical journey across the decades. In her musical realization of that promise, Mitchell set down her alternatively tuned guitar and picked up a collaborative relationship with arranger Vince Mendoza. Backed by a swooning 71-piece orchestra playing in a grand, symphonic jazz style, *Travelogue* and its predecessor *Both Sides Now*[2] are part of a swathe of millennium-era pop/jazz crossover albums (Parsonage 2004, 60–80). *Both Sides Now* was a carefully curated collection of jazz standards and torch songs. It also included renditions of two of her most popular songs "A Case of You" and (of course) "Both Sides, Now." It was a commercial hit, simultaneously casting Mitchell as a jazz diva/crooner and aligning her self-penned songs with the Great American Songbook. And yet, when Mitchell and Mendoza turned their attention solely to her back-catalog, *Travelogue* was considered too risky a release by her long-serving label, Reprise Records.

The problem for Reprise was that the repertoire operated only in part as a greatest hits record—the songs that featured on *Travelogue* had had varying success in the first place. Ultimately unconvinced of the premise, they refused to release it and, as they handed distribution and marketing duties over to sister company Nonesuch Records, Mitchell was furious:

> I'm quitting after this because the business has made itself so repugnant to me [. . .] they're not looking for talent, they're looking for a look and a willingness to cooperate. And a woman my age, no matter how well preserved, no longer has the look. And I've never had a willingness to cooperate.[3]

As she saw it, *Travelogue* was as musically adept as anything else she had previously released; part of her continuing artistic journey. But some critics heard it as the end of the creative line—bemoaning the palpable *pastness* of a record so saturated with memory that it "sagged under the weight of its own reflection,"[4] while others wrote with faint praise that *Travelogue* was "terminally civilized."[5] Put bluntly, at best, Mitchell and Mendoza's collaboration was heard as coproduced eulogy. At worst, it was lambasted for being an "overdressed [. . .] vanity project."[6] In the *New York Times*, John Rockwell wrote, frustratedly, that the willful experimentation that characterized Mitchell's back-catalog had been exchanged for a saccharine nostalgia in *Travelogue*. For Rockwell, the album might well appeal to the most loyal fans as a means of clinging to the memories of a shared musical past. But he describes and explains her diminished vocal range and softer, more muted tone as evidence that Mitchell had capitulated to the kind of conservatism which is unproblematically perceived as synonymous with aging. Matthew Gilbert supports this view, describing the performative effects of *Travelogue*: "It's Joni somewhere between Broadway and Bach [. . .] It's theatrical, it's grandiose, and it's not the Joni Mitchell I want to hear unless I'm looking for distraction in a dentist's waiting room."[7] Gilbert's scorn gestures toward the repeated leaps of faith that Mitchell has encouraged and engendered in her fans across the course of her career but suggests that *Travelogue* marks the end of his confidence in her creative innovation. For both critics, Mitchell's early catalog is the place to hear the *real* Mitchell, by which they mean a suitably inventive one. Indeed, Rockwell goes as far as to suggest that we abandon the twenty-first-century aging star altogether and head to downtown Manhattan for an all-the-queerer (and ostensibly more *authentic*) experience: drag artist John Kelly's countertenor performances of Mitchell's career-defining albums, *Ladies of the Canyon*, *Blue*, *Court and Spark*, and *Hejira*.[8]

In this chapter, I argue against the idea that Mitchell's subversive streak can only be detected in her youthful soprano, suggesting that this misses both the point and potential of her twenty-first-century musical output. While others have closely analyzed the nuances and effects of Mitchell's voice as it carries the textures of age, time, and experience (Apolloni 2016; Elliott 2015), I suggest that these affective textures challenge sociocultural assumptions about the perceived norms and capabilities of older people. I argue that *Travelogue*'s broad premise is a queer one: to rearrange, reframe, and reimagine the constituent elements of popular music. Mitchell's aging (and therefore non-normative) voice challenges an ageist status quo that says that she should retreat and retire from public view as she ages. Further still, I assert that the very act of singing constitutes a mode of queerness: with Mitchell's voice expressing a still-active sensuality, a desire deemed highly inappropriate for a woman her age.

My attention is particularly caught by *Travelogue*'s "Borderline," a song that appeared originally only eight years before *Travelogue*, on the Grammy award-winning pop/rock album *Turbulent Indigo*.[9] Mitchell has explained that it is a song which is concerned with "roads, fences," adding that "they're like cholesterol in the arteries [. . .] everybody seems to love to draw these lines. So, as we come to this millennium, everyone's a divisionist in some way."[10] "Borderline" is a musical meditation on the way we generate categories to define ourselves. Partitioning along differences in gender, nation, class, race, and age, Mitchell sings about how these boundaries are silently, routinely, and problematically inculcated within culture. In this way, it is a song which arrives readymade as a call to arms for the queer project: to critique and interrogate identity categories (Jagose 1996; Sullivan 2003).

The chapter follows a two-part structure: first, I argue that the *Travelogue* version of "Borderline," which switches from mid-90s rock to millennium-jazz, draws attention to the mechanics and rules of genre. In this way, I argue that Mitchell's queerness comes through her systematic undoing of vocal, musical, and cultural norms. In the second part, I tune in to the specifics of Mitchell's vocal performance and examine how interplaying vocal colors often compete with and contradict each other. I pay particular attention to the way that, in

"Borderline," a flighty "featheriness" contrasts with a guttural "cragginess" and argue that both sounds communicate the kind of desire that destabilizes the idea that the aging female body is a sexless body.

From *Turbulent Indigo* to *Travelogue*

Upon its release in 1994, *Rolling Stone* magazine celebrated *Turbulent Indigo* as Mitchell's best album since the mid-1970s and made the connection between its intense sadness, Mitchell's history as the pin-up "confessional" singer-songwriter and her disintegrating marriage to *Turbulent Indigo*'s coproducer, Larry Klein.[11] On the record, Mitchell looks in from the outside: at love, sociocultural hierarchies, politics, power structures, and the quotidian. Writing in *Time* magazine, Guy Garcia remarked that *Turbulent Indigo* was drenched in Mitchell's musical idiolect, with "crystalline arrangements; unorthodox guitar tunings; the fluid, bittersweet melodies"[12] and celebrated her return to commercial form.

On the *Turbulent Indigo* version of "Borderline," the elements of the song broadly adhere to the norms of rock music, but with Mitchell's musical quirks intact. She communicates a sense of loneliness through a jittery guitar groove, while a yearning pedal steel reaches up and out to a rumbling bass guitar. Later, an otherworldly synthesizer enters the fray, howling from the stratosphere. It is an arrangement which leaves space for her biting lyrics. To be sure, Mitchell's brand of rocky authenticity is characterized by these musical signifiers—where the parameters of the genres are broadly adhered to but actively stretched. In an interview, she describes *Turbulent Indigo*'s to-ing, fro-ing, pushing and pulling of musical categories as part of her larger feeling of musical homelessness; of being without a musical lineage and of being repeatedly pushed out of proliferating genres.[13] Of course, the irony here is that, for all her talk of being repeatedly and routinely (self-) cast as the outsider, *Turbulent Indigo* was celebrated by precisely those industry insider voices that Mitchell claims to have been rejected by. In other words, for all its peculiarities, *Turbulent Indigo* was the mark of Mitchell being assimilated *back* into a musical mainstream that she had both resisted and been excluded from since the 1970s.

Four years later, change was afoot again as she sought to distance herself from the established orthodoxies of popular music.[14] Now aged 55, the question of stopping work was repeatedly put to Mitchell, especially given the context of her Grammy success. For some, her chronological age represented a timely opportunity to gracefully bow out on a commercial and critical career high. With her orchestral phase on the horizon, Mitchell refused the idea of quitting altogether but intimated that certain fetishized musical idiosyncrasies from her past were to fall by the wayside. In an interview from this period, she snaps: her voice had changed significantly, her old guitar style was now "completely foreign to [her and she had] no idea how [she] did it."[15] Further still, she explains a relationship with her songs which is entirely anti-nostalgic. Instead of rose-tinted reflection, Mitchell treats her repertoire as a place for constant (re)interpretation and experimentation. She says: "I never wanted to be a human jukebox [. . .] I think more like a film or dramatic actress and a playwright. Those plays are more suitable to me. I feel miscast in my early songs. They are ingénue roles."[16] Mitchell's notion of her "miscasting" subverts the popular association of authenticity and "rightness" with the younger, rather than the older performance (think of the common accusation that "heritage acts" have "lost it"—a phrase that suggests that the earlier performance by the younger self is more "real"—and the aging performer little more than a faded facsimile).

Travelogue is a collection of handpicked and perhaps unlikely songs to get the orchestral treatment. With the repertoire set, a wholesale alteration of the arrangement of each song enabled Mitchell to enact an entirely different kind of vocal performance. The dramatic reworkings convey similar cultural work as a cover version but instead of passing the song between artists (with different identity markers impressed on the song in the process), Mitchell's self-cover highlights the change in her body and voice (Griffiths 2002, 51–64; Plasketes 2013, 11–39). Some of the songs are entirely transformed in terms of vocal pitch and phrasing. But what is interesting about "Borderline" is that the key remains the same, which suggests little deterioration to Mitchell's range in the short time between the two releases. And yet, "Borderline" is transformed in its newly orchestrated state. The process behind this reframing warrants further investigation.

The Mendoza effect

Vince Mendoza's ambitious and expansive arrangements are central to *Travelogue's* sound. He draws inspiration from a diverse and eclectic range of stylistic references: from master jazz orchestrator Gil Evans to the Romantic grandeur of Johannes Brahms; from the complex and varied musical forms of Igor Stravinsky to the avant-garde rhythmic and harmonic complexity of György Ligeti.[17] The resulting aesthetic is rich and celebrated by some for being "impeccably tasteful"[18] and nothing short of "a miracle."[19] But, as noted earlier, others were less convinced. Writing in the *Los Angeles Times*, Robert Hilburn says that although "the overall effect is liberating and revealing"[20] the album feels rather "strained"[21]—suggesting that Mitchell's (in)famous subversive streak was being tamed by Mendoza's maneuvering of the orchestra and that Mendoza was, in effect, straightening up Mitchell's tempestuous musical history. An adjustment like Mendoza's could well be perceived as a negation of Mitchell's willful and persistent challenges to pop music trends, norms, and expectations. On *Travelogue*, she may well appear to surrender her agency as songwriter, arranger, and guitarist in exchange for Mendoza's touch. Indeed, it is easy to read Mitchell's metamorphosis between *Turbulent Indigo* and *Travelogue* from rock to jazz; from an electric band to "acoustic" orchestra; from the more masculine rock star to feminine jazz diva as an indicator of her impending withdrawal from the music scene. After all, as Catharine Parsonage notes in her exploration of singers who swing into jazz from pop "[it offers a] ... neutralizing, cleansing function as the musical material is specifically located away from the rock world" (2004, 5–6).

Certain critics perceived *Travelogue* as Mitchell's swan song, that ostensibly "seem[ed] to wave goodbye with every visual and aural offering" (Smith 2004, 97). Mendoza's orchestration casts a moody grandeur, seeming to neutralize Mitchell's capricious life-journey and preparing her for a dignified death. Indeed, for all her protestations of being "unwilling to cooperate," this shift could easily be perceived as Mitchell's finally yielding to the sociocultural requirement to age appropriately according to her gender, adhering to a normative narrative of growing old gracefully and quietening with age (Dolan and Tincknell 2012; Dolan 2014, 342–351).

But what I want to suggest is that Mitchell is overtly aware of the kind of gravitas, maturity and "certain sort of musical artistic purity" that orchestral instruments carry in contemporary culture, and she looks to invert their connotations (Redhead in Moore 2012, 263). Chris Jones writes that *Travelogue* is representative of Mitchell's belief that "older forms such as jazz or classical [music] equate to more serious vehicles for her dissections of modern America."[22] And though Jones deems this a "specious philosophy,"[23] Mitchell's carefully curated and unusual track-listing troubles the normative constituent elements of repertoire and performance style. As I hear it, dissidence is her intention. This is especially clear on "Borderline," where the song's tooling of symphonic jazz offers an additional means of spotlighting precisely the boundaries that lyrically preoccupy Mitchell.

"Like a barbed wire fence": the gradual transgression of rhythmic borderlines

The rhythmical reconfiguration of "Borderline" for *Travelogue* is dramatic, with Mitchell's idiomatic, driving, percussive guitar exchanged for a jazz-inflected *paso doble*. The *paso doble*'s groove has a distinctly macho history with its roots in bullfighting. By slowing the song's tempo from the original recording, Mendoza and Mitchell assert this overtly masculine rhythmical framework to represent a particular kind of Eurocentric, flamboyant, and hegemonically masculine showmanship. The *paso doble*'s neat and strict boundary provides space for Mitchell to be free with her vocal phrasing—playing cat and mouse with the orchestra with each passing bar—through and between the lines which carve up and delineate time.

In 2014, Mitchell outlined how her creative philosophy "always contained the question of how far the pop song could go. What themes it could hold without collapsing."[24] And so, it is significant that, over the course of "Borderline," the rigidity of the *paso doble* is pushed to the point of disintegration. Toward the end, a series of drum kit flourishes twist around descending flute chirrups while snarling brass—bolstered by double bass and cello—provide a springboard for violins to soar and swoop out toward the horizon. All the while, Mitchell's voice acts as the matador, with every breath and vocal melody teasing the symphonic jazz orchestra.

The (queer) mechanics of the voice

Roland Barthes's famous theory of the "grain" of the voice is a useful tool to try and pin down the nuances of vocal performance. He argued that musicologists were overly obsessed with the idea of good vocal performance being bound up in the singer's adherence to both the musical text and the historical conventions of singing. For Barthes, musicologists had failed to recognize the embodied element of singing. He offers the grain as a solution. "The 'grain,'" he explains, "is the body in the voice as it sings, the hand as it writes, the limb as it performs" (Barthes 1977). It is a mode of listening that encourages us to go deeper. For Barthes, the meaning of a vocal performance lies in the enunciation and diction of the performer; teeth that clatter and whistle as lyrics spill from the singer's mouth; vocal sounds that resonate through the skull or that seem to emanate from the gut. What the grain offers the listener is a means of describing the visceral response we might have to a vocal performance.

On "Borderline," it is as if Mitchell and Barthes are in conversation. Mendoza's orchestrations provide not just a musical *context*—but the sonic *space* to focus the listener on Mitchell's grain. Barthes claims that the voice has the capacity to move the listener: it "sways us to *jouissance*."[25] As I listen, I am wooed by a palette of vocal colors that evoke Mitchell's body. In an age-phobic society, this is a subversive move: gesturing to the older Mitchell's still-active desires, wants and needs expressed lyrically, materially and performatively. "Borderline" is a particularly disorientating listening experience, with Mitchell's lyrical sniping delivered through a grain that simultaneously sashays and shivers. Her vocal performance speaks of, for and from bodies ordinarily excluded from the youthful, sensual expressions of popular music.

The relationship between body and voice is explored by Steven Connor in his idea of the "vocalic body" (2000). While his theory mostly concerns the practice of ventriloquism, Connor's work is a useful tool to examine the singing voice. He writes that, of course, bodies produce voices, but that the reverse is true too: when we hear a voice, it creates the shape of the body it has come from:

> the vocalic body is the idea—which can take the form of a dream, fantasy, ideal, theological doctrine, or hallucination—of a surrogate or secondary body, a projection of a new way of having or being a body, formed and sustained out of the autonomous operations of the voice. (Connor 2000, 34)

And so, the vocalic body speaks of the shape, size, ability, class, gender, race, ethnicity, and age of the speaker or singer. On "Borderline," Mitchell's vocalic body is the Other to pop music's dominant industry processes and youth-soaked popular sounds. As I will explore, hers is a voice of competing and contradictory vocal timbres: where notes sometimes hang heavily only to be transformed and countered by a melodic fragility. I suggest this is a deliberate strategy, that Mitchell is queering cultural expectations of the pop star by amplifying her aging (and therefore non-normative) vocalic body.

When a not-quite-but-almost 60-year-old woman steps in front of a microphone, the body which is routinely encoded as being both conceptually and materially abject, is caught in the sensual act of singing. Mitchell's voice evokes a complex sexuality through a queer sound; her ambiguous vocal timbre (which I will discuss in more detail, shortly) confuses perceptions of the voice as a fixed identity marker (Jarman-Ivens 2011). It is, I suggest, this vocal ambiguity that produces the intrigue in Mitchell's performance of "Borderline." In it, Mitchell *undoes* the conventions of popular music. What characterizes Mitchell's queer grain is a paradoxical composite of effects and techniques, where Mitchell's voice is as "craggy" as it is "breathy."

"The craggy alto"

The majority of the reviews of *Both Sides Now* and *Travelogue* foregrounded Mitchell's age, with a particular emphasis on the decreased mobility of that once-elastic soprano. For example, *The Scotsman* described her delivery as an "inert" performance that seemed to "iron out the idiosyncrasies"[26] of her voice. However, fans were more forgiving—one writes that although her "range is somewhat diminished [. . .], her voice remains a fine instrument for carrying the burden of her songs."²⁷ Either way, Mitchell's vocal delivery in *Both Sides Now* and *Travelogue* was a jolt to many. Writing in the *New York Times*, Stephen Holden reflects on a live performance of "Both Sides, Now," saying that:

> Few contemporary voices have aged more shockingly than Joni Mitchell's. The craggy alto [. . .] is so changed from the sweetly yodeling folk soprano of her earliest albums that it hardly seems possible that the two sounds could have come from the same body.²⁸

Such *cragginess* provides a challenge for Holden, who positions Mitchell's "ingénue" voice as her "real" voice and her older voice as the imposter. The ambiguities of Mitchell's voice are especially pertinent here: youthful vocalizations, so often posited as the epitome of whimsical femininity, haunt their opposite—the "craggy alto"—a deeper, and therefore more masculine voice. These vying vocalic bodies trouble the neat, collective cultural memory of "Joni Mitchell." This, perhaps, provides an explanation for Reprise Records' anxiety about marketing *Travelogue* and its consequent lukewarm critical reception. Mitchell's cragginess draws our attention to the voice's gendered performativity, with her lowered range and a brushed timbre signifying the sonic markers of age.

The notion of "cragginess" is, in part at least, to do with vocal range. Listening to Joni Mitchell's performance of "Borderline," one might recall and attempt to reconstruct the famous soprano chirruping of the early 1970s, through the craggy lines. But Mitchell has repeatedly denied *being* a soprano and described her early-career voice as a performative trick—nothing more than the calculated mimicry of vocal inflections that would afford her cigarettes and movie tickets, little luxuries that supplemented her thrifty life as an art student (Henderson 2005; Monk 2012). In an interview with National Public Radio, she disparagingly calls her 1970s voice her "little helium voice"²⁹ and explains a symbiotic relationship between repertoire and voice. She describes how songs were crafted to foreground her high-pitched voice but that, over time, "things conspired to rob [her] of it."³⁰ In Mitchell's typically cryptic and contradictory style, just what those "things" are: whether the realities of age gradually creeping up on the body, or hedonism, is left unsaid. In the context of a quasi-greatest hits album like *Travelogue*, songs taken from Mitchell's 1990s output are not primarily haunted by Mitchell's "helium voice"—they arrive already "robbed" of that—but her performance is certainly *craggier* than even its slightly earlier iterations. Yet the cragginess of her performance is counterbalanced by another quality which foregrounds the affective power of the breath.

"Feathery lines"

Throughout her singing career, Mitchell has experimented with the affective qualities of breath. Talking to Malka Marom, she discusses her signature vibrato sound—where the note just "disintegrate[s], just peter[s] out." Mitchell depicts these sounds as the aural expression of her visual artistic practice, calling them her "feathery lines" (Marom 2014, 228). In this way, we can think of her "feathery lines" as the sonic equivalent of the brush being pulled over the canvas as she paints (Marom 2014, 4).

Reviews of *Travelogue* called the intentionality of these "feathery lines" into question, with critics suggesting that Mitchell's ailing health was responsible for her apparent diminished levels of vocal control. A committed smoker, Mitchell's voice is routinely discussed in reference to the habit's effect on her voice. But where it is noted for having "taken on a smoky flavor"[31] and therefore a sense of rocky authenticity on *Turbulent Indigo*, Mitchell's voice and repertoire on *Travelogue* left critics astonished. In the *Guardian*, Betty Clarke writes that the album could function as a health warning on account of the "nicotine-ravaged vocals of the once angelic, now gasping Joni Mitchell."[32]

Even the most positive of reviews alludes to Mitchell's smoking. Writing about *Travelogue* in the *Jazz Times*, Christopher Loudon says:

> Tough as it is to rationalize, Joni Mitchell's pack-a-day habit seems only to have enriched that exquisite voice of hers. On this, her first album for Nonesuch and second, after the jazz-infused *Both Sides Now*, with the London Symphony Orchestra, Mitchell's nicotine-stained throatiness shapes a vaguely melancholy sagacity that is stunningly beautiful.[33]

In the time between the two recordings of "Borderline," there was an apparent shift in Mitchell's attitude toward her own voice in relation to smoking. Back in 1994, she poured tea during an interview with *Rolling Stone* and described her smoking as a "bad habit."[34] In early interviews for *Travelogue* she admitted to still not taking good care of her voice—blaming a combination of smoking and excessive talking for her vocal changes.[35] But increasingly, Mitchell became defensive around those who criticized her voice, who implied that those "feathery lines" demonstrated a lack of vocal control, and ultimately called into question her artistry. When journalist Neil McCormick suggested that her years of smoking had finally caught up with her Mitchell retorted: "I have smoked since I was nine, so obviously it didn't affect my early work that much."[36] Elsewhere, she has suggested that her altered voice is simply the "natural" result of the processes of aging (Monk 2012; Marom 2014). In 2007, Mitchell reflected on *Travelogue* in a promotional interview for what really would be her final release of new material (to date), *Shine*.[37] In it, she sidesteps the question of smoking in favor of a discourse on vocal health, claiming that a diagnosis of vocal cord lesions, nodules, and a compressed larynx was actually the cause of such a breathy tone on *Travelogue*,[38] symptoms which caused the "feathery lines" to appear more frayed than ever. It is difficult, if not impossible, to prove the extent to which these medical problems demonstrate the universal, "natural," material realities of aging and what may have functioned as a symptom accelerator. Regardless, what *is* interesting is the sociocultural effects generated by the breathy, aging singer. As Susan Fast notes, "breathiness is associated with sexual availability or arousal, or with submissiveness [. . .] and so often with the feminine" (Fast in Jennex 2013, 355). In this way, Mitchell's "feathery lines" produce an active, aging sensuality and therefore a queer sensuality—a sensuality being produced from a body outside of the socially sanctioned norm.

As I have noted, Mendoza's *paso doble* gradually unravels, hinting at Mitchell's aging sexuality as it rocks and rolls. But it is through the featheriness of her voice that this sexuality is truly felt. "Feathery lines" are problematic in a culture where sexuality, femininity, and expressions of desire are deemed to be exclusively for the young. In refusing to adhere to the sociocultural requirement to quieten with age, Mitchell rattles the bars of the heterosexual matrix of sex, gender, and sexuality that silently maintain the power of the patriarchy (Butler 1993, 1999; Carrera, DePalma, and Lameiras 2012; Swinnen and Port 2012; Tretheway 2001). "Feathery lines" operate as a queer, naughty disturbance, with Mitchell's aging voice lightly brushing, caressing, and softly touching the listener (Barthes 1977, 179; Bonenfant 2010, 74–80).

On *Travelogue*, through a mix of both orchestral arrangement and recording processes, the listeners' attention is drawn to the corporeal processes that generate the singing voice. As Alexandra Apolloni notes, "Mitchell's voice is miked so that it integrates seamlessly into the lush orchestration. Her singing is rich and smooth, and the way she leans into notes sounds wistful and nostalgic" (2016). As I hear it, Mitchell's vocal performance on *Travelogue* utilizes the technologies of the crooner so that both her "craggy alto" and her "feathery lines" are front and center.

Crooner technologies

Developed in the 1920s, the crooning style was a result of engineers and studio technicians developing microphones that would help popular singers fill a concert hall over and above the accompanying orchestra. The sensitivity of these newly-invented gadgets was remarkable, with the voice heard up-close and more personally than ever before (Baade 2012; Jarman-Ivens 2011; McCracken 2001). It was a style that made stars of Bing Crosby, Rudy Vallee, Frank Sinatra, and Perry Como, singers who learnt to foreground the grain of the voice, whispering in the listener's ear, with the microphone magnifying every intimate croak and crackle. Crooners wooed the listener with sentimental songs about love and longing—velvet voices that "promised the odours, textures and warmth of another body" (Connor 2000, 38). While crooning was not exclusively a male mode of performance (like its female equivalent "torch singing"), the style of performance, its repertoire, and cultural effects are often received along gendered lines. As Christina Baade outlines in "Victory through Harmony" (2012), the arousing qualities of the crooner's voice led to the BBC banning their records from the airwaves during the Second World War. The crooner was considered a dangerous distraction for women who, whether in the munitions factory or at home caring for the family, might be seduced by the fleshy tones of the singer. The BBC felt that the crooner threatened the concentration of the Allied war effort, armed with a voice that wooed, and sonically troubled the stability of the family unit. Over time, the crooner's subversive power has been erased, replaced by a cultural sense of the crooner's voice as conveying a rather naff mawkishness. The crooner's voice has come to be associated with a soft effeminacy, at odds with culturally sanctioned masculinity.

It is significant then, that Mitchell singles out the songs and style of the crooner era as a key source of inspiration for her later work.[39] Performing in this style, she subverts the gendered conventions of the genre and suggests that the crooner's dulcet tones contain something far more radical than first meets the ear. In deliberately harnessing the crooner's non-normative masculinity, Mitchell pulls on a history which stars one of the most improbably subversive figures in popular music. By crooning, Mitchell employs vocal techniques and technologies which sonically magnify her "feathery cragginess." Every melodic sigh, croak, stumble, and rhythmic crackle functions as a signifier of her aging, sensual body, so often marked as abject in a youth-obsessed culture. Mitchell queerly and boldly embodies this Otherness. "Borderline" is thematically antithetical to the kind of lovelorn whimsy of the crooner and yet it jumps into the style with both feet.

Conclusion

Between *Turbulent Indigo* and *Travelogue*, the transformation of Mitchell's vocal style and timbre is remarkable. In collaboration with Vince Mendoza, she abandons her iconic guitar playing in order to sonically fix the listener's ear to the nuances of her vocal performance. A cloak of conservativism might appear to drape itself over her orchestral phase but as I hear it, on "Borderline" especially, the message of the record is clear. This is not a musical taming. Rather it is a way of highlighting the enormity of the normalized processes, practices, bodies, and voices that govern us all. The later "Borderline" undoes norms through the subversive complexities of Mitchell's vocal technique and its surprising reframing of the earlier version. Mendoza puts well-established musical histories to work, using the trope of the *paso doble* to emphasize the rigidity of the organized structures that control Western culture. Then Mitchell's voice enters the frame—rough and ragged—a carefully timed performance which gradually builds in intensity and begins to obfuscate the clarity of this trope. It is in this way that her performance invites a queer reading, especially on a song like "Borderline," which is concerned with the way difference is used as a tool for division. Mitchell's inconsistent vocal timbres speak of and for bodies which are ordinarily excluded from the youth-focused parameters of popular music. Armed with the qualities of age, time, and experience, her voice demonstrates how aging processes contain extraordinary queer potential: still-active; out there in the world; bold and whispering; and full of wants and needs.

In 1994, Mitchell was asked about her feelings on getting older, about the material realities of aging and how it might have an effect on future music-making. She responded by pointing toward the vagaries of it all, "[it's] like Neil [Young] says, 'it's better to burn out than to rust.' Well, I don't want to burn out, and I don't want to rust! There must be a third choice."[40] Looking back at the cover of *Travelogue*, Mitchell's smoky and enigmatic self-portrait points toward her alternative to Young's dichotomy, a queer method that undoes the taken-for-grantedness of age and its processes.

Notes

1 Joni Mitchell, *Travelogue* (New York: Nonesuch, 2002).
2 Joni Mitchell, *Both Sides Now* (Hollywood: Reprise Records, 2000).
3 James Reginato, "The Diva's Last Stand," *W Magazine* (December 2002). http://jonimitchell.com/library/view.cfm?id=1025 (accessed: January 6, 2017).
4 Jim Fusilli, "Review: *Travelogue*, All Things Considered" (December 26, 2002). http://jonimitchell.com/library/print.cfm?id=1080 (accessed: January 6, 2017).
5 "Rock and Pop: A Dream Falls Flat," *The Scotsman* (November 22, 2002). https://www.scotsman.com/lifestyle/culture/music/rock-and-pop-a-dream-falls-flat-1-629680 (accessed: January 6, 2017).
6 John Rockwell, "Joni Mitchell's Long and Restless Journey," *New York Times* (January 5, 2003). http://www.nytimes.com/2003/01/05/arts/music-joni-mitchell-s-long-and-restless-journey.html (accessed: January 10, 2017).

7. Matthew Gilbert, "Joni Mitchell: *Travelogue*," *The Boston Globe* (November 19, 2002). http://jonimitchell.com/library/view.cfm?id=984 (accessed: January 10, 2017).
8. Rockwell, "Joni Mitchell's Long and Restless Journey."
9. Joni Mitchell, *Turbulent Indigo* (Hollywood: Reprise Records, 1994).
10. Jancee Dunn, "Question and Answer: Joni Mitchell," *Rolling Stone* (December 15, 1994). http://jonimitchell.com/library/view.cfm?id=19 (accessed: January 6, 2017).
11. John Millward, "Joni Mitchell: *Turbulent Indigo*," *Rolling Stone* (December 15, 1994). https://www.rollingstone.com/music/albumreviews/turbulent-indigo-19941215 (accessed: January 6, 2017).
12. Guy Garcia, "A Deeper Shade of *Blue*," *Time* Magazine (December 19, 1994). http://jonimitchell.com/library/view.cfm?id=380 (accessed: January 6, 2017).
13. Nathan Delphini, "Joni Mitchell—Midday Interview: Turbulent Indigo and Her Art" (October 17, 1994). https://vimeo.com/22500245 (accessed: January 10, 2017).
14. Cited in Roger Catlin, "One Side Now," *Hartford Courant* (May 25, 2000). http://jonimitchell.com/library/view.cfm?id=585 (accessed: January 10, 2017).
15. Catlin, "One Side Now."
16. Ibid.
17. Vince Mendoza, "About Vince," http://vincemendoza.net/about-vince (accessed: January 6, 2017).
18. Tim Perlich, "Travelogue," *Now Toronto* (November 21, 2002). http://jonimitchell.com/library/view.cfm?id=1006 (accessed: January 10, 2017).
19. "Travelogue," *Entertainment Weekly* (November 22, 2002). http://jonimitchell.com/library/view.cfm?id=972 (accessed: January 10, 2017).
20. Robert Hilburn, "Travelogue," *Los Angeles Times* (November 24, 2002). http://jonimitchell.com/library/view.cfm?id=1010 (accessed: 20 June 2017).
21. Hilburn, "Travelogue."
22. Chris Jones, "Joni Mitchell: Travelogue Review," *BBC Music* (November 19, 2002). http://www.bbc.co.uk/music/reviews/z2vr (accessed: May 30, 2016).
23. Jones, "Joni Mitchell: Travelogue Review."
24. Sean O'Hagan, "Joni Mitchell: The sophistication of her music sets her apart from her peers—even Dylan," *Guardian* (October 26, 2014). https://www.theguardian.com/music/2014/oct/26/joni-mitchell-blue-hissing-summer-lawns-court-spark-hejira-dylan (accessed: May 20, 2016).
25. The term "jouissance" toys with a double meaning, where a sense of enjoyment verges on the sexually gratifying. Across the chapters of *Image, Music, Text*, Barthes differentiates between *plaisir* and *jouissance*. He describes the former as a sense of pleasure that operates within culturally sanctioned parameters.

Jouissance, is described in more transgressive terms—a sense of ecstasy which overwhelms, and therefore troubles cultural norms.

26 "Rock and Pop: A Dream Falls Flat."
27 Joseph Duemer, "Travelogue," *BlogsCritics.org* (December 8, 2002). http://jonimitchell.com/library/view.cfm?id=1035 (accessed: May 20, 2016).
28 Stephen Holden, "Something's Lost and Something's Gained," *New York Times* (February 13, 2000). http://www.nytimes.com/2000/02/13/arts/music-something-s-lost-and-something-s-gained.html?src=pm (accessed: December 9, 2016).
29 Renee Montagne, "The Music Midnight Makes: In Conversation with Joni Mitchell," *National Public Radio* (December 9, 2014). [Last accessed: May 20, 2017], https://www.npr.org/2014/12/09/369386571/the-music-midnight-makes-in-conversation-with-joni-mitchell (accessed: May 20, 2017).
30 Montagne, "The Music Midnight Makes: In Conversation with Joni Mitchell."
31 Dunn, "Question and Answer: Joni Mitchell."
32 Betty Clarke, "Joni Mitchell: Travelogue," *Guardian* (November 22, 2002). https://www.theguardian.com/music/2002/nov/22/popandrock.artsfeatures2 (accessed: December 20, 2017).
33 Christopher Loudon, "Joni Mitchell: Travelogue," *Jazz Times* (January 3 2003). https://jazztimes.com/reviews/albums/joni-mitchell-travelogue/ (accessed: December 20, 2017).
34 Dunn, "Question and Answer: Joni Mitchell."
35 Reginato, "The Diva's Last Stand."
36 Neil McCormick, "Joni Mitchell: My Life Came Down to Being a Granny," *The Telegraph* (April 1, 2015). https://www.telegraph.co.uk/culture/music/rockandjazzmusic/3668299/Joni-Mitchell-still-smoking.html (accessed: December, 20 2017).
37 Joni Mitchell, *Shine* (Santa Monica: Hear Music/Universal).
38 Aidan Dunne, "Saint Joni," *Irish Times* (July 19, 2008). http://jonimitchell.com/library/view.cfm?id=1894 (accessed: December 20, 2017).
39 O'Hagan, "Joni Mitchell"; Malka Marom, *Joni Mitchell: In Her Own Words Words—Conversations with Malka Marom* (Toronto: ECW Press, 2014).
40 Dunn, "Question and Answer: Joni Mitchell."

Works Cited

Apolloni, Alexandra. "Authority, Ability, and the Aging Ingénue's Voice," in *Voicing Girlhood in Popular Music: Performance, Authority, Authenticity*, ed. Jacqueline Warwick and Allison Adrian. London: Bloomsbury, 2016, 143–170.

Baade, Christina. *Victory through Harmony: The BBC and Popular Music in World War II*. New York: Oxford University Press, 2012.

Barthes, Roland. *Image Music Text*. Trans. Simon Heath. London: Harper Collins, 1977.

Bonenfant, Yvon. "Queer Listening to Queer Vocal Timbres," *Performance Research*, 15.3 (2010): 74–80.

Butler, Judith. *Bodies That Matter: On the Discursive Limits of Sex*. New York: Routledge, 1993.

Butler, Judith. *Gender Trouble*. 2nd edn. New York: Routledge, 1999.

Carrera, Maria Victoria, Renée DePalma, and Maria Lameiras. "Sex/Gender Identity: Moving Beyond Fixed and Natural Categories," *Sexualities*, 15.8 (2012): 995–1016.

Catlin, Roger. "One Side Now," *Hartford Courant*, May 25, 2000. http://jonimitchell.com/library/view.cfm?id=585 (accessed: June 2, 2018).

Clarke, Betty. "Joni Mitchell: Travelogue," *Guardian*, November 22, 2002. https://www.theguardian.com/music/2002/nov/22/popandrock.artsfeatures2 (accessed: June 2, 2018).

Connor, Steven. *Dumbstruck: A Cultural History of Ventriloquism*. Oxford: Oxford University Press, 2000.

Delphini, Nathan. "Joni Mitchell—Midday Interview Turbulent Indigo and Her Art," October 17, 1994. https://vimeo.com/22500245 (accessed: June 2, 2018).

Dolan, Josephine. "Smoothing the Wrinkles: Hollywood, 'Successful Aging,' and the New Visibility of Older Female Stars," in *The Routledge Companion to Media and Gender*, ed. Cynthia Carter, Linda Steiner, and Lisa Mclaughlin. Abingdon: Routledge, 2014, 342–351.

Dolan, Josephine, and Estella Tincknell. *Aging Femininities: Troubling Representations*. Newcastle-Upon-Tyne: Cambridge Scholars, 2012.

Duemer, Joseph. "Travelogue," *BlogsCritics.org*, December 8, 2002. http://jonimitchell.com/library/view.cfm?id=1035 (accessed: June 2, 2018).

Dunn, Jancee. "Question and Answer: Joni Mitchell," *Rolling Stone*, December 15, 1994. http://jonimitchell.com/library/view.cfm?id=19 (accessed: June 2, 2018).

Elliott, Richard. *The Late Voice: Time, Age and Experience in Popular Music*. London: Bloomsbury, 2015.

Entertainment Weekly. "Travelogue," November 22, 2002. http://jonimitchell.com/library/view.cfm?id=972 (accessed: June 2, 2018).

Fusilli, Jim. "Review: Travelogue, All Things Considered," December 26, 2002. http://jonimitchell.com/library/print.cfm?id=1080 (accessed: June 2, 2018).

Garcia, Guy. "A Deeper Shade of *Blue*," *Time* Magazine, December 19, 1994. http://jonimitchell.com/library/view.cfm?id=380 (accessed: June 2, 2018).

Gilbert, Matthew. "Joni Mitchell: Travelogue," *The Boston Globe*, November 19, 2002. http://jonimitchell.com/library/view.cfm?id=984 (accessed: June 2, 2018).

Griffiths, Dai. "Cover Versions and the Sound of Identity in Motion," in *Popular Music Studies*, ed. David Hesmondalgh and Keith Negus. London: Hodder Arnold, 2002, 51–64.

Henderson, Stuart. "'All Pink and Clean and Full of Wonder': Gendering 'Joni Mitchell,' 1966–1974," *Left History*, 10.2 (Fall 2005): 83–109.

Hilburn, Robert. "Travelogue," *Los Angeles Times*, November 24, 2002. http://jonimitchell.com/library/view.cfm?id=1010 (accessed: June 2, 2018).

Holden, Stephen. "Music: Something's Lost and Something's Gained," *New York Times*, February 13, 2000. http://www.nytimes.com/2000/02/13/arts/music-something-s-lost-and-something-s-gained.html?src=pm (accessed: June 2, 2018).

Jagose, Annamarie. *Queer Theory: An Introduction*. New York: New York University Press, 1996.

Jarman-Ivens, Freya. *Queer Voices: Technologies, Vocalities and the Musical Flaw*. New York: Palgrave Macmillan, 2011.

Jennex, Craig. "Diva Worship and the Sonic Search for Queer Utopia," *Popular Music and Society*, 36.3 (2013): 343–359.

Jones, Chris. "Joni Mitchell: Travelogue Review," *BBC Music*, November 19, 2002. http://www.bbc.co.uk/music/reviews/z2vr (accessed: June 2, 2018).

Loudon, Christopher. "Joni Mitchell: Travelogue," *Jazz Times*, January 3, 2003. https://jazztimes.com/reviews/albums/joni-mitchell-travelogue/ (accessed: June 2, 2018).

Marom, Malka. *Joni Mitchell: In Her Own Words—Conversations with Malka Marom*. Toronto: ECW Press, 2014.

McCormick, Neil. "Joni Mitchell: My Life Came Down to Being a Granny," *The Telegraph*, April 1, 2015. https://www.telegraph.co.uk/culture/music/rockandjazzmusic/3668299/Joni-Mitchell-still-smoking.html (accessed: June 2, 2018).

McCracken, Allison. "Real Men Don't Sing Ballads: The Radio Crooner in Hollywood, 1929–1933," in *Soundtrack Available: Essays on Film and Popular Music*, ed. Arthur Knight and Pamela Robertson-Wojcik. Durham and London: Duke University Press, 2001, 105–134.

Mendoza, Vince. "About Vince," 2017. http://vincemendoza.net/about-vince (accessed: June 2, 2018).

Millward, John. "Joni Mitchell: Turbulent Indigo," *Rolling Stone*, December 15, 1994. https://www.rollingstone.com/music/albumreviews/turbulent-indigo-19941215 (accessed: June 2, 2018).

Mitchell, Joni. *Both Sides Now*. Hollywood: Reprise Records, 2000.

Mitchell, Joni. *Shine*. Santa Monica: Hear Music/Universal, 2007.

Mitchell, Joni. *Travelogue*. New York: Nonesuch, 2002.

Monk, Katherine. *Joni: The Creative Odyssey of Joni Mitchell*. Vancouver: Greystone Books 2012.

Montagne, Renee. "The Music Midnight Makes: In Conversation with Joni Mitchell," *National Public Radio*, December 9, 2014. https://www.npr.org/2014/12/09/369386571/the-music-midnight-makes-in-conversation-with-joni-mitchell (accessed: June 3, 2018).

Moore, Allan. *Song Means: Analysing and Interpreting Recorded Popular Song*. Farnham: Ashgate, 2012.

O'Hagan, Sean. "Joni Mitchell: The sophistication of her music sets her apart from her peers—even Dylan," *Guardian*, October 26, 2014. https://www.theguardian.com/music/2014/oct/26/joni-mitchell-blue-hissing-summer-lawns-court-spark-hejira-dylan (accessed: May 20, 2016).

Parsonage, Catherine. "The Popularity of Jazz—an Unpopular Problem: The Significance of 'Swing When You're Winning,'" *The Source: Challenging Jazz Criticism*, 1 (2004): 60–80.

Perlich, Tim. "Travelogue," *Now Toronto*, November 21, 2002. http://jonimitchell.com/library/view.cfm?id=1006 (accessed: January 10, 2017).

Plasketes, George. "Introduction: Like a Version," in *Play It Again: Cover Versions in Popular Music*, ed. Derek Scott and Stan Hawkins. Farnham: Ashgate, 2013, 11–39.

Reginato, James. "The Diva's Last Stand," *W* Magazine. December, 2002. http://jonimitchell.com/library/view.cfm?id=1025 (accessed: January 6, 2017).

Rockwell, John. "Joni Mitchell's Long and Restless Journey," *New York Times*, January 5, 2003. http://www.nytimes.com/2003/01/05/arts/music-joni-mitchell-s-long-and-restless-journey.html (accessed: January 10, 2017).

The Scotsman. "Rock and Pop: A Dream Falls Flat," November 22, 2002. https://www.scotsman.com/lifestyle/culture/music/rock-and-pop-a-dream-falls-flat-1-629680 (accessed: January 6, 2017).

Smith, Larry David. *Elvis Costello, Joni Mitchell and the Torch Song Tradition*. Westport: Praeger, 2004.

Sullivan, Nikki. *A Critical Introduction to Queer Theory*. Edinburgh: Edinburgh University Press, 2003.

Swinnen, Aagje, and Cynthia Port. "Aging, Narrative, and Performance: Essays from the Humanities," *International Journal of Ageing and Later Life*, 7.2 (2012): 9–15.

Tretheway, Angela. "Reproducing and Resisting the Master Narrative of Decline: Midlife Professional Women's Experiences of Aging," *Management Communication Quarterly*, 15.2 (2001): 183–226.

3

"Both Sides, Now": Voice, Affect, and Thirdness

Joanne Winning

In his endnotes to the novel *An Equal Music*, in which he records the musical experiences of his violinist protagonist Michael Holme in remarkable, exquisitely fine-grained detail, Vikram Seth writes: "Music to me is dearer even than speech. When I realized that I would be writing about it I was gripped with anxiety. Only slowly did I reconcile myself to the thought of it" (Seth 1999, n.p.). Despite his strong misgivings, Seth produces nuanced, captivatingly accurate descriptions of the experience of listening to and playing chamber music in the novel, proving, in fact, that it is possible to write about that seemingly most untouchable of mediums. Without doubt, the task of writing about music is fraught with certain challenges in trying to capture both its sonic and affective elements through written language, which is seemingly such a codified system of meaning-making and so far removed from the music's visceral, nonverbal terrain.

Seth's anxiety is in my mind as I turn to analyze one of Joni Mitchell's most notable and treasured songs, "Both Sides, Now."[1] What I want to address in this chapter is how this particular song presents a compelling example of the power of the human voice to trigger strong affective responses in listeners, so much so that it can become emblematic of their own histories and experiences. This song, perhaps uniquely in Mitchell's canon because of its history, offers a highly productive case for considering the ways in which the singing voice occupies the space between singer and listener, enfolding the subjectivities of both. This kind of intersubjectivity I will explore through the concept of "thirdness" in this chapter. I will also think about how Mitchell's voice embodies time passing (when we hear the song sung at different stages in a life) in the change to timbre and tessitura (its texture and range) as it ages. While speaking and singing voices are generally considered to be two mutually exclusive categories, I will explore the early twentieth-century experimental practices of *Sprechstimme*—in which the binary of speaking and singing breaks down to convey deep emotion—as an instructive parallel to Mitchell's somewhat raw and ragged vocal production in her later version of "Both Sides, Now." This chapter will also consider the changes "Both Sides, Now" itself goes through, in terms of its musical setting and instrumentation, since these too undoubtedly contribute to the sheer power of the song to generate deeply felt emotions in its listeners.

An iconic song, "Both Sides, Now," whose history is long and whose place in the popular cultural fabric is assured, was written by Mitchell in March 1967. First recorded by Judy Collins on her 1967 album *Wildflowers*, the song has two incarnations by Mitchell herself. She recorded it in 1969, as the concluding track on the album *Clouds* (whose title lifts one of the song's main lyrical symbols), and then again in 2000, as the concluding track on the concept album *Both Sides Now*.[2] In this later incarnation, "Both Sides, Now" stands alongside "A Case of You" as one of two revisions an older Mitchell makes to seminal songs from her youthful oeuvre.[3]

"Both Sides, Now" is one of Mitchell's most covered tracks; at a recent count, over eighty artists between the late 1960s and the present day have interpreted and recorded the song. Its appeal surely lies in its ability to make us *feel*, but how do we find terms in which to talk about the song's power to move? Which critical tools will help us understand the ways in which the song is saturated with Mitchell's affect, but is also astoundingly capable of drawing out our own? Metaphorical and melancholic, the song's lyrics speak of a life long lived and a state of profound understanding about the indeterminacy of human experience. The song seems to embody a preternaturally astute awareness of life and its losses, its arc toward diminishment and alienation.

Yet one of the remarkable things about "Both Sides, Now" is that it was written by a 23-year-old Mitchell at a very early point in her musical career. In 1996, in an interview with Robert Hilburn, Mitchell describes the inspiration for the song as her reading of Saul Bellow's 1959 novel *Henderson the Rain King*.[4] Sitting reading on a flight herself, Mitchell finds its protagonist's observation that humanity has only recently been able to view clouds from both sides in the wake of the advances in aviation technology to be a philosophical stimulus. However, in a later interview in 2012, Mitchell gives a much fuller account of the traumatic circumstances that underpin the song's genesis, the aftermath of giving her daughter up for adoption at 21: " 'Both Sides, Now' was triggered by a broken heart, the loss of my child. In this three-year period of childhood's end, I'd come through such a rough, tormented period as a destitute, unwed mother. It was like you killed somebody, in those times" (Marom 2014, 25). This life-changing loss shaped Mitchell's early adulthood, bringing early profound pain, as she explains: "I had some serious battles for a twenty-one-year-old" (2014, 25). Mitchell's retrospective analysis of the song is both insightful and helpful for the sense it gives of the song's considerable potential to act as an affective container for the emotions of its listeners. She notes that "in its generalness, there was much that people could read into it [. . .] I know one guy played it for his parents, then sat them down and announced, 'I'm gay.' *It found utility in people's lives*" (2014, 25, emphasis mine). This notion of the song's "utility" is one I want to pursue through this chapter, asking what it is about "Both Sides, Now" that makes it *useful* as a conduit for one's own affects and thus ensures it occupies a cherished place in many people's emotional histories.

Thirdness

In its lyric cycle, "Both Sides, Now" articulates a list of binary oppositions through its three objects of focus: clouds, love, and life. In the course of the life lived in the song, these three immaterial things are viewed from radically different locations: up and down/give and take/win and lose. Clouds can be seen as "ice-cream castles in the air" but also "block the sun." Love is epitomized by "Moons and Junes and Ferris wheels" but is also "just another show" which inevitably ends. Life is captured in "dreams and schemes and circus crowds" but also "something's lost but something's gained/in living every day."[5] Most importantly though, "Both Sides, Now" proceeds to overturn these oppositional stances. Such binaries only serve to teach the narrator of their insufficiency and in the attempt to pin these elusive abstract things down, concrete meanings dissolve into "illusions." The song invokes the refusal of the binary and in its place, Mitchell espouses "both sides," seen and understood. In this strong sense, the song is an invocation of the in-between, of a kind of thirdness in the form of the third option of *both sides* (rather than one or the other)—of the failure and limitations of neat categories that define themselves against each other.

This might be a place to start to understand the affecting nature of this version of "Both Sides, Now." In order to illuminate the affective terrain of the song, I will consider its lyrical content, the specifics of Mitchell's voice and vocal production, and the structures of its later orchestration through the theoretical concept of thirdness, as articulated by the psychoanalyst Jessica Benjamin in her work on the psychodynamics of interpersonal relations between human subjects and the co-construction of feeling and identity.

If we frame the notion of the "in-between" in Benjaminian terms, we come to the figure of the third, the experience beyond the binary of self and other, and the notion of co-construction. In Benjamin's construction, human communication is fraught, threatening and, in complex emotional situations, confusing. The most common way of trying to control this confusion, often unconsciously, is to enforce "the one-way street," in which one person is the "doer," and the other person is the "done-to." This turns one person into the "subject" and the other into the "object." By contrast, healthier, more productive encounters are relational and acknowledge the connectedness of our subjectivities, our intersubjectivity. The metaphor of music, particularly musical improvisation, is useful for Benjamin, as it helps her to denote the complex transmission of affect that can, in the best circumstances, take place between two human beings, the subtle "two-way traffic" through which affect is jointly created and channeled:

> The *thirdness* of attuned play resembles musical improvisation, in which both partners follow a structure or pattern that both of them simultaneously create and surrender to, a structure enhanced by our capacity to receive and transmit at the same time in nonverbal interaction. The co-created third has the transitional quality of being both invented and discovered. To the question of "Who created this pattern, you or I?." the paradoxical answer is "Both and neither." (Benjamin 2018, 31, emphasis added)

For Benjamin, this is both a paradigm for good, effective analytic practice and more broadly, in the public sphere, a model for political action and restorative engagement between warring states and factions. The third is, to quote Benjamin, "the vantage point outside the two," the triangulated space that affords us the necessary reflective distance to comprehend the shape of our own identity and experience, at the same time as those of the other (Benjamin 2007). This may seem a very long way indeed from the frame of late twentieth-century popular music and Mitchell's oeuvre, but I would like to suggest that utilizing the concept of the third will allow us to get beneath the complex surface of musical form and its textures in order to understand its deep impact upon our felt experience, particularly thinking here about "Both Sides, Now."

Love Actually: a case study

As a shortcut, a cultural case study, I want to use a notable deployment of "Both Sides, Now"—and indeed of Mitchell herself as a cultural figure—by Richard Curtis in his popular (if much-debated) 2003 film, *Love Actually*. In among the broad sweep of the soundtrack, which ranges across popular music from the 1960s to the 2000s, and includes three original scores by Scottish composer Craig Armstrong, Mitchell's revisited "Both Sides, Now" acts as the film's affective core. Mitchell, indeed, has central structural relevance within *Love Actually*, appearing first in a mid-film scene in which the middle-aged couple Karen and Harry, played by Emma Thompson and Alan Rickman, sit together while she wraps family Christmas presents. Mitchell's 1971 song "River" plays in the background, well-placed because of its own Christmas narrative but also because, in its plaintive description of a love lost through lack of care, it scaffolds the storyline in which Harry will come to jeopardize his marriage and family life by getting drawn into an office affair. Harry questions Karen disdainfully about the music she is playing:

HARRY: What is this we are listening to?
KAREN: Joni Mitchell.
HARRY: I can't believe you still listen to Joni Mitchell.

KAREN: I love her. And true love lasts a lifetime. Joni Mitchell is the woman who taught your cold English wife how to feel.

HARRY: Did she? Oh well, I must write to her sometime and say thanks.

(Curtis 2003)

If Mitchell teaches Karen to feel earlier in her life, she also charts the emotional trajectory through which Karen must move in the course of the film, from the tired domesticity of a loveless marriage to the wreckage of the discovery of Harry's affair on the eve of Christmas, just before their children's school nativity play. This discovery turns on Harry's Christmas gift of the boxed edition of *Both Sides Now* which is not, after all, the expensive gold necklace Karen has accidentally found in his coat pocket days before Christmas and delightedly assumed is for her. Realizing that the gift must have another intended recipient (his secretary, in fact), "Both Sides, Now" swells in volume and Karen removes herself to the marital bedroom to absorb the revelation, to cry in desperation and then to swallow down the agony enough to rejoin the family and bustle them out of the front door. The wrenching scene's emotional charge depends upon catching together the acoustic backdrop of the song—a collage of Mitchell's voice and the richly textured orchestration of the song's later version—with Thompson's masterly performance of emotional disintegration, followed by an anguished repression.

Mitchell's necessity to the scene is neatly evidenced by Curtis's wife Emma Freud, live-tweeting about the film in a recent 2015 screening in New York: "Joni Mitchell. Help. Still hurts. Sat on the floor watching her do that scene—7 takes. Crying every time. Goddess. #LoveActually [6:29 AM—13 Dec 2015]." In an overdubbed commentary on the film, Curtis and cast members discuss the scene and Curtis explains how the song and plot are intertwined:

This is a version of "Both Sides, Now" that Joni Mitchell recorded 30 years after she originally wrote it. And I can't remember what came first but I think when I heard the song I thought it was so powerful that it was the thing that made me write this plot really. The thing is when Joni Mitchell wrote the song originally it was sort of precocious, you know, talking about what life and love and all those things add up to, when she was 25 or something but revisiting it to [sic] this sort of voice that smoked 10,000 cigarettes looking back on the whole of life, I think it's a great song.[6]

Curtis's description of the way in which the power of the later version of the song suggests a whole plotline of middle-aged marital infidelity to him indicates the generative potential of its emotional range. Echoing something of Mitchell's own account of the journey from youth to experience, Curtis focuses on the nature of the shift from "precocious" youthful philosophizing without the sufficient grounds of maturity to a revisiting 30 years later with "the voice that [has] smoked ten thousand cigarettes." I am particularly interested in his identification of Mitchell's voice as the locus of pain, experience, and authenticity; it is the voice profoundly affected by life, age, and the ravages of heavy smoking that most powerfully conveys Karen's wordless expression of pain and loss which quickly cedes to repression.

To return to the concept of thirdness with which I began the chapter, we might think about subject positions and locations here to understand something of how our own affective responses are mobilized. Watching the scene, located literally as selves outside its action, we witness Karen as the Other, disintegrating in the privacy of her bedroom. Mitchell's voice occupies the space of the third, the space in between us, as spectators, and Karen as jilted, middle-aged wife. The transmission of affect via Mitchell's voice triggers our processes of identification, taking us into the realm of our own experiences and personal histories, which chime with the pain we watch unfold on the screen.

Life, voice

How can a singing voice do this to its listeners? And indeed, what is it that we hear in the different voices of the two versions of "Both Sides, Now"? Let us consider the 25-year-old voice in the first recording. Untrained but supported by good breath work, it incorporates unique vocal phrasing with a sense of suppleness and depth. The song is delivered mostly in Mitchell's head voice, though it dips down through the mix into chest voice in the drop on the phrase "I recall," from C# to F#. In this incarnation, the voice is backed only by a guitar part that cycles through chords and a simple—though it has to be said signature, by which I mean nonstandard—strum pattern. In terms of structure, the song has a relatively common verse/verse/chorus pattern repeated three times.

The first striking difference in the rerecording of "Both Sides, Now" is, of course, the radically transformed voice that sings in a dramatically lower key. Where the song sits in F# major on *Clouds*, it has dived down to D major on *Both Sides Now*, lingering around D3, which is to say the D below Middle C—a location which the female voice, even an alto voice, usually cannot reach. Thus the 57-year-old voice exists in a radically different place from its youthful equivalent; the tessitura has dropped radically, from head to chest and, in its drop, embodies the timbre of age. For those familiar with the earlier recording, there is a strong emotional charge in listening to this aged voice. Like a kind of ghosting, the youthful voice of the 1969 recording is evoked by the dropped vocal register; the two versions sit in relation to each other in a way that creates a kind of third space for us as listeners, our own experience of age and time passing stitched into the act of listening.

As title track and last track on the album *Both Sides Now*, it is also important to consider the key role the song is ascribed in the cycle. As in *Clouds*, it is located as the concluding track. *Both Sides Now*'s construction was carefully considered and built to reflect a philosophical premise about the trajectory of emotions in the time frame of a human life story. Its coproducer Larry Klein describes it as "a programmatic suite documenting a relationship from initial flirtation through optimistic consummation, metamorphosing into disillusionment, ironic despair, and finally resolving in *the philosophical overview of acceptance and the probability of the cycle repeating itself*" (emphasis mine).[7] Klein goes on to describe the success of the recording in relation to Mitchell's vocal performance and its affective charge in strikingly embodied terms "the results have surpassed our expectations. In singing these songs, I believe that Joni has achieved something quite extraordinary in that *she has truly sung them as if, as Nietzsche would say, she had written them in her own blood*" (emphasis mine).[8]

Klein's description of *Both Sides Now* is instructive, first, for the way it describes the affective state of the last track as a "philosophical acceptance," but also because of this highly charged description of Mitchell's singing in Nietzschean terms as an expression of her own corporeal authenticity. Klein refers here to Mitchell's versions of various jazz standards, but also, by implication, he infers that this profoundly embodied vocalization also occurs in Mitchell's own songs on the album. In this context, it is notable where Mitchell's voice has been placed in the mix. Sound engineer Allen Sides brings this aged, affecting voice right forward, in front of the lush orchestration, so that our encounter with it is full, intimate and utterly inescapable. Undoubtedly, by comparison with its 25-year-old equivalent, there is much less vocal production and a loss of vocal suppleness such that the words, at times, appear almost spoken. The voice departs from traditional modes of singing and our encounter with it becomes something like being part of an intimate conversation, privately addressed by Mitchell who is attempting to impart her hard-won wisdom to us.

Voice, spokenness

In a seemingly random sidestep, I would like to consider this move toward spokenness through the early twentieth-century vocal technique of the Viennese vocalist Albertine Zehme. Working with the Austrian composer Arnold Schoenberg, Zehme commissioned the piece *Pierrot Lunaire*, a melodrama setting for a 21-poem cycle by the German poet Otto Erich Hartleben. A musical universe away from Mitchell's later twentieth-century folk in "Both Sides, Now," there are, nevertheless, some productive comparative points to be made about voice, affect, and communication. Zehme regarded the traditionally trained singing voice as an inadequate tool for expressing deep, primal emotion, writing that "the singing voice, bound in otherworldly chastity, fixed in its ascetic bondage as an ideal, exquisite instrument—even a strong exhale dulls its inaccessible beauty—is not suitable for intense emotional outbursts" (1911). Zehme went further in arguing that "to communicate, our poets and our composers need both singing as well as the spoken tone [. . .]. The words that we speak should not solely lead to mental concepts, but instead their sound should allow us to partake of their inner experience" (1911). In an attempt to disentangle the enmeshment of thought—circumvented at all times by language—and feeling—the experience of affect—Zehme advocated the *Sprechstimme* style. *Sprechstimme*, which translates from German, as "speech-voice," is a musical term that describes a vocal technique in the singing voice that hovers between spoken and sung sound. For Zehme, this hybridic sound is the most effective for conveying deep, affective meaning. As Clara Latham describes:

> [Zehme] characterized the trained singing voice as ascetic and ideal, writing that as an instrument it was not suitable for the production of raw emotion. It is this sense of "real feeling" or emotion that Zehme wanted to achieve. [. . .] She believed that the sound of the voice, unharnessed by technique, could produce affect and emotion, and this capability was independent from the function of the voice as a producer of meaningful expression. (2013, 106)

Zehme and Schoenberg's collaboration on *Pierrot Lunaire* produced a groundbreaking unconventional musical work which was received by the early twentieth-century musical establishment and educated European audiences as a redefinition of the terrain of both composition and vocal style. Alongside the innovations of atonality and in the allocation of instrumental voicings, Zehme's *Sprechstimme* technique recalibrated existing paradigms of the relationship between vocal production and meaning-making, a reinvention described even with regards contemporary twenty-first century performances as having "decisively changed our understanding of pitch and the relationship between words and music."[9]

Sitting in the audience at its premier at the Choralien Saal in Berlin in October 1912, the influential, revolutionary composer Igor Stravinsky came to describe *Pierrot Lunaire* as "the solar plexus as well as the mind of early 20th century music."[10] Stravinsky's allusion to the complex mesh of nerves in the abdomen as a signifier for this radical piece is an instructively embodied metaphor, which returns us to the body and the visceral impact of the voice which hovers somewhere between speaking and singing. Both in Western biomedical terms and the esoteric discourses of Ayurvedic teaching, the solar plexus constitutes one of the core locations of human bodily constitution. In colloquial terms, in the English language, we identify the solar plexus as the place where deep knowledge and felt experience become enmeshed; we talk of "gut feeling."[11]

This deep embodied effect upon the listener, who encounters the soundings of the voice that speaks as it sings in *Sprechstimme*, anticipates the formulation of the transformative potential of the embodied voice in the later twentieth century. Roland Barthes's theory of the "grain" in the human singing voice is particularly instructive here. An organic metaphor, we might think of the grain of wood as a way of understanding Barthes's concept; wood's grain describes the specific arrangement of the cellulose fibers out of which it is constituted. Similarly, Barthes's grain describes something both structural and organic, it alludes to the embodied production of sound: "the 'grain' is the body in the voice as it sings" (1977, 188). What we encounter then, when we hear the *grain* of the voice, is the close proximity of the body of the singer and the body of the listener (Barthes describes this as being "given" the body of the singer), taking them to the place (in the right circumstances and with the right singer) that Zehme identifies above as "inner experience" (Barthes 1977, 189). Accessing the body in this way depends upon *Sprechstimme* demonstrating its own kind of thirdness, as it breaks down the traditional binary between speaking and singing.

Undoubtedly, I am bringing discordant materials together here. Mitchell is certainly not vocalizing in *Sprechstimme* style in the later version of "Both Sides, Now"—however ravaged her voice she is singing and not speaking. But in the example of *Sprechstimme*, I want to capture some of Zehme's ideas about the transmission of affect possible in altered vocal style. Just as *Sprechstimme* blurs the boundaries between speech and song, in the rawness and almost unsung timbre of the untrained voice that has smoked 10,000 cigarettes but also lived 57 years, Mitchell also eschews what Zehme terms "otherworldly chastity" in favor of broken vocal phrasing, snatched breaths, riffing on her own 25-year-old melody reflectively, laconically, and with a melancholic evocation of loss. In this sense, Mitchell's voice becomes a third to itself; it articulates both sides—innocence and experience—in the present moment, the "now" of its performance.

Orchestration, chance

There is, however, another third to consider. The affective power of "Both Sides, Now" exists in the in-between that lies between Mitchell's aged timbre and the striking orchestration which is so radically different from its early guitar accompaniment. It is impossible to analyze Mitchell's later voice and the valences of the second incarnation of "Both Sides, Now" without considering the soundscape in which they exist. If the voice is changed in 2000, so too is the musical backing; from the sparse guitar backing has grown the thick, multilayered texture of full orchestral arrangement.

The third in the trinity of hands upon *Both Sides Now*'s conceptualization and realization was the American composer, arranger, conductor Vince Mendoza, who signed to Blue Note Records at the start of his career and has worked with a diverse range of artists from Robbie Williams, Björk, and Elvis Costello through to seminal jazz figures like Pat Metheny and Charlie Haden. Talking about his collaboration with Klein and Mitchell on *Both Sides Now* and the album that comes after it, *Travelogue* (2002), Mendoza describes his arrangement in the following way:

> For the first one [*Both Sides Now*], as you know, most of them were standards. We did a couple of Joni's tunes. And the experience was so nice that we immediately went into plans to do another one, which consisted of all her music this time. *I think it was partly because we thought that on the first record, her songs were the most effective in an orchestral setting, treated as tone poems.*
>
> Her poetry is so wonderful, and deep, and interesting, that to write poetry in music was the natural thing to do. So the second record was really all about writing tone poems with her music. Of course, there were a lot of challenges involved in that—when to use guitars and when not to, when to use her parts and when not to use her parts, *what is composed and what isn't*. All the problems inherent in redoing such staples in the American popular culture.
>
> That was a challenge. But just *the thought of doing orchestral tone poems to her music was natural; the words are vibrant and deep that was a natural thing to want to dive into that pool.* [emphases mine][12]

In particular, there are two key insights in Mendoza's description of the creative process of orchestrating the two Mitchell songs on *Both Sides Now* which help to explain the profound affective charge of both voice and the rerecording. Mendoza describes the choice of orchestral tone poems as "natural" settings for Mitchell's poetic lyrics. In musical terms, a tone poem is a "romantic work in one movement that is intended to portray extra-musical ideas in sound" (Bowman 2002, 170). In the same way as Klein's descriptions of Mitchell's Nietzschean singing from the body and notions of philosophical acceptance suggest, the musical tone poems Mendoza writes as containers for the voice function as more than just settings, evoking the arc of life and experience embodied in the voice, the journey of one movement which symbolizes the life course, from beginning to end. Mendoza also describes the complex process of navigating Mitchell herself as songwriter and musician in deciding "when to use her parts and when not to use her parts," in other words what to retain of the original song structure and what to lose. Notably he talks of "what is composed and what isn't." (Mendoza, 2007) What is certainly striking about the orchestration of "Both Sides, Now" is the way it constitutes a wash of sound behind Mitchell's vocals. At the outset of the song, the orchestra produces a swirling sound mass, a soundscape in which pitch is only occasionally clearly articulated and in which strings seem to segue into and out of each other in a sumptuously random way.

This soundscape might well be described in musical terms as "aleatoric." The term "aleatoric music," also known as Chance music, derives from the Latin *alea*, for dice, connoting the throw of the dice that is open to chance. It is defined as a "synonym for indeterminacy, i.e. music that cannot be predicted before performance or music which was composed through chance procedures" (Kennedy and Kennedy 2007). As the following extract from an aleatoric score demonstrates (Figure 3.1), many of the elements are left to chance and rely upon individual musician's choices about how to realize and perform the score. The boxed sections allow a musician to choose the duration of notes and rests; the headless beam notes allow the musician to choose pitch. If we were to think about this form through the concept of thirdness, we would of course note that any realization of the music relies upon every musician's attuned co-construction of the work.

If Mendoza's orchestral scaffolding for Mitchell's voice is an aleatoric tone poem, this is entirely in keeping with the philosophical premise of the song; that clouds, love, and life are unknowable, open to chance, that the most profound state of human subjectivity and experience is structured around illusion. "Both Sides, Now's" orchestration is strongly affective, it pulls and tugs at our

Figure 3.1 "Of A Time"

© A. Beckett, 2018.

emotions. It builds, it swells. As we reach the most intense phase of the lyrical journey, the point at which life itself defeats the endeavor of understanding and only its illusions remain, Wayne Shorter's soprano saxophone screeches and tears across the landscape of orchestration, keeping company with the angst and pain which Mitchell's voice embodies.

Voice, culture

In conclusion, I return to the case study of Curtis's *Love Actually*, and the early scene in which Karen wraps Christmas presents and Harry disparages her choice of music for the evening. Karen's comment that it is Mitchell who teaches her, as a "cold English wife," how to feel, of course refers to Mitchell's status as an iconic singer-songwriter of the 1960s and onward, and the ways in which her music educates her own generation and those beyond. But it also gestures toward something more specifically cultural. Joni Mitchell, Karen tells us, helps her to overcome the reticence and emotional repression that are associated with Englishness, to trade coldness for warmth. This teaching begets a lifelong love affair which may, the spectator speculates, outlive the failing marriage between Karen and Harry. Beneath the ironic, faintly comedic delivery of these lines, there is a message being conveyed about the power of music, and voice, to transform the coordinates of our emotional lives and histories. There is also a proleptic acknowledgment of the teaching Mitchell will deliver to us, as viewers, within the frame of this film's narrative. I bring this back to Mitchell's aged, ravaged, authentic voice, singing through the later bedroom scene and providing a crucial third space between the horror of marital infidelity and our own witnessing of it.

In his analysis of the relationship between the human voice and culture, the sound artist Yvon Bonenfant defines the way cultures teach us to either allow or withhold the breath depending on the amount of emotional and psychic repression structured into that culture's ideology. He writes that "we [. . .] end up embodying a culture of these choices, and invent together a cultural body that regulates vocal sound."[13] The regulation of vocal sound "[represses] this thing we might call emotional flow" and thus, by extension, "represses the *voice*."[14] Karen does not, indeed cannot, speak of her realization about Harry's betrayal; she cries silently so as not to alert either the children, or Harry himself, to her tears. The voice we hear in this scene is Mitchell's, ably conveying the depth of pain and loss that Karen cannot. Bonenfant notes that "the voice is an evident, key relational tool."[15] We might use this insight on two levels in relation to this filmic moment. On the one hand, Mitchell does the emotional work that Karen cannot, representing the passionate and evocative liberation of deep feeling through the voice. On the other hand, representing a kind of relational third, Mitchell's voice does this work for us too, allowing us (English or not!) to overcome our own respective repressions and to enter into an identificatory relationship with a character's abject fragmentation.

Richard Curtis concludes that "Both Sides, Now" is "a great song" for the formidable palette of affective depth it gives him in writing and realizing a script about love, loss, and human relationships. It is a song that also seems to possess its own tangible identity, independent even of Mitchell herself. She notes: "It was a song that I think I had to grow into. I don't think I performed it well until I was in my fifties" (Marom 2014, 25). In an uncanny sense, then, it is a song that arrives before its time in Mitchell's life and which cannot reach its full, magnificent potential until her voice and her experience have caught up with it. This journey, in the most moving of ways, is one we take with her.

Notes

1 Mitchell first published the song with the title "Both Sides, Now" in 1969 (*Clouds*). The title then comes to be used for the concept album *Both Sides Now*, sans comma, in 2000. This album includes the rerecorded and transformed version of the song as "Both Sides, Now" which forms the focus of this chapter.
2 The album *Both Sides Now* is mostly a collection of jazz standards, coproduced with Mitchell's ex-husband Larry Klein and orchestrated by Vince Mendoza. Larry Klein is, of course, notable as a musician in his own right—as bassist, songwriter, and producer, he has worked with many of the major names in late twentieth-century jazz. A generation younger than Klein and Mitchell, Vince Mendoza is an American composer, conductor and music arranger who has worked with a wide range of musicians across jazz, classical and soul genres.
3 "A Case of You" was first recorded in 1971, the penultimate track on Mitchell's forth studio album *Blue* (Hollywood: Reprise Records, 1971).
4 See Robert Hilburn, "Both Sides, Later," *Los Angeles Times* (December 8, 1996). Bellow's 1959 novel *Henderson the Rain King* details the escape of its protagonist Eugene Henderson from his middle-aged affluent existence in America to the remote villages of Africa.
5 Joni Mitchell, "Both Sides, Now," *Clouds* (Hollywood: Reprise Records, 1969).
6 Richard Curtis, Audio Commentary with Hugh Grant, Bill Nighy, and Thomas Sangster, *Love Actually* (Working Title Films, 2003).
7 Larry Klein, *Both Sides Now* liner notes, *Both Sides Now* (Hollywood: Reprise Records, 2000).
8 Klein, *Both Sides Now*, liner notes.
9 Program notes, Arnold Schoenberg "Pierrot Lunaire. Op. 21" Chicago Symphony Orchestra, February 25–28, 2012, 4.

10 Quoted in Virginia Sublett, "*Pierrot Lunaire* at 95: Arnold Schoenberg's Musical Hybrid and Twentieth-Century Vocal Chamber Music," *College Music Symposium*, 49.50 (2009/2010): 451–458. The Russian composer Igor Stravinsky is regarded as one of the most influential and innovative composers in transforming the landscape of twentieth-century classical music.
11 Further discussions of the complex relationship between the gut and feeling, and its expressions in forms of everyday speech, can be found in the work of the psychiatrist and psychoanalyst Alexis Brook. See Brook, "Bowel distress and emotional conflict," *Journal of the Royal Society of Medicine*, 84 (1991): 39–42.
12 Vince Mendoza, quoted in Paul Olson, "Vince Mendoza: Color, Counterpoint and Open Ears," *All About Jazz*, September 10, 2007. https://www.allaboutjazz.com/vince-mendoza-color-counterpoint-and-open-ears-vince-mendoza-by-paul-olson.php?pg=5 (accessed: March 31, 2018). *Travelogue* is a double album, which comprises twenty-two reworkings of Mitchell classics, all orchestrated by Mendoza.
13 Yvon Bonenfant, "On Sound and Pleasure: Meditations on the Human Voice," *Sounding Out!* (June 30, 2014). https://soundstudiesblog.com/2014/06/30/on-sound-and-pleasure-meditations-on-the-human-voice/ (accessed: June 2, 2018).
14 Ibid.
15 Ibid.

Works Cited

Barthes, Roland. "The Grain of the Voice," in *Image, Music, Text*. London: Fontana, 1977, 179–189.

Benjamin, Jessica. "Intersubjectivity, Thirdness, and Mutual Recognition," 2007. http://icpla.edu/wp-content/uploads/2013/03/Benjamin-J.-2007-ICP-Presentation-Thirdness-present-send.pdf (accessed: April 1, 2018).

Benjamin, Jessica. *Beyond Doer and Done to: Recognition Theory, Intersubjectivity and the Third*. Oxford: Routledge, 2018.

Bonenfant, Yvon. "On Sound and Pleasure: Meditations on the Human Voice." *Sounding Out!*, June 30, 2014. https://soundstudiesblog.com/2014/06/30/on-sound-and-pleasure-meditations-on-the-human-voice/ (accessed: March 31, 2018).

Bowman, David. *Rhinegold Dictionary of Music and Sound*. London: Rhinegold Publishing Ltd, 2002.

Brook, Alexis. "Bowel Distress and Emotional Conflict," *Journal of the Royal Society of Medicine*, 84 (1991): 39–42.
Curtis, Richard. Dir. *Love Actually*. Universal Pictures, 2003.
Hilburn, Robert. "Both Sides, Later," *Los Angeles Times*, December 8, 1996.
Kennedy, Michael, and Joyce Bourne Kennedy, eds., *The Concise Oxford Dictionary of Music*, 5th edn. Oxford: Oxford University Press, 2007.
Klein, Larry. Liner notes to *Both Sides Now*, Joni Mitchell. Hollywood: Reprise Records, 2000.
Latham, Clara. "Listening to the Talking Cure: Sprechstimme, Hypnosis, and the Sonic Organization of Affect," in *Sound, Music, Affect*, ed. Marie Thompson and Ian Biddle. London: Bloomsbury, 2013, 101–117.
Marom, Malka. *Both Sides Now: Conversations with Malka Marom*. London: Omnibus Press, 2014.
Mitchell, Joni. *Song to a Seagull*. Hollywood: Reprise Records, 1968.
Mitchell, Joni. *Clouds*. Hollywood: Reprise Records, 1969.
Mitchell, Joni. *Ladies of the Canyon*. Hollywood: Reprise Records, 1971.
Mitchell, Joni. *For The Roses*. Hollywood: Asylum Records, 1972.
Mitchell, Joni. *Hejira*. Hollywood: Asylum Records, 1976.
Mitchell, Joni. *Mingus*. Hollywood: Asylum Records, 1979.
Mitchell, Joni. *Dog Eat Dog*. Hollywood: Geffen Records, 1985.
Mitchell, Joni. *Night Ride Home*. Hollywood: Geffen Records, 1991.
Mitchell, Joni. *Turbulent Indigo*. Hollywood: Reprise Records, 1994.
Mitchell, Joni. *Taming the Tiger*. Hollywood: Reprise Records, 1998.
Mitchell, Joni. *Both Sides Now*. Hollywood: Reprise Records, 2000.
Mitchell, Joni. *Shine*. Santa Monica: Hear Music/Universal, 2007.
Olson, Paul. "Vince Mendoza: Color, Counterpoint and Open Ears," *All About Jazz*, September 10, 2007. https://www.allaboutjazz.com/vince-mendoza-color-counterpoint-and-open-ears-vince-mendoza-by-paul-olson.php?pg=5 (accessed: March 31, 2018).
Sublett, Virginia. "Pierrot Lunaire at 95: Arnold Schoenberg's Musical Hybrid and Twentieth-Century Vocal Chamber Music," *College Music Symposium*, 49.50 (2009/2010): 451–458.
Zehme, Albertine. "Why I Must Speak These Songs," 1911, quoted in Latham, 2013 [original source unknown].

4

"Dreams and False Alarms": Melancholy in the Work of Joni Mitchell

Anne Hilker

The twenty-first century opened with a renewed interest in melancholy that has continued well into its second decade (Radden 2000, 2009, 2013; Burton 2001; Réunion des musées nationaux 2005; Schwenger 2006; Bowring 2008; Wilson 2008; Holly 2013). Melancholy suggests "a turbulence of heart that results in an active questioning of the status quo, a perpetual longing to create new ways of being and seeing" (Wilson 2008, 8). Joni Mitchell's music frequently depicts melancholy in its swings of narrative theme and emotional expression. However, this chapter is interested in identifying additional musical strategies that produce a subtler register of melancholy in Mitchell's work. This register specifically comprises oppositions of lyric and tonality; the figure of the lone traveler in an isolated landscape and a persistent and audible undertone of restlessness. Such melancholic elements are often in tension with other emotional registers within Mitchell's music. Using "Amelia" (1976) as a case study, the final segment of this chapter shows how Mitchell deploys all three tropes (opposition, travel, and restlessness) to build a layered meditation on the lived experience of melancholy.

Contemporary definitions of melancholy associate it broadly with sorrow, rather than the more limited and Freudian notion of loss, which attributes melancholy's unrest only to the conflation of the self with a lost love object (Freud 1957, 159). Sorrow is not to be confused with mere sadness, which looks back, regretful and defeated. Although Mitchell's music indeed captures moments of sadness, to call it "sad" as a whole overlooks the range of its expression.[1] The melancholic shares with the Daoist concept of yin and yang a tendency to see life events in oppositional pairs, each carrying the seeds of the other—a philosophy Mitchell has herself referenced.[2] But resolution of those oppositions eludes the melancholic, yielding ongoing emotional turmoil rather than any lasting balance.

Mitchell's work often describes the melancholic's unease and, particularly, the artist's specifically melancholic torments: "You're in that continual conflict with yourself, you know. You can express these really high and beautiful thoughts but your life may not back them up" (Marom 2014, 87). Her own life has been marked dramatically by uncertainty and death.[3] And like the melancholic, she requires solitude: "I need a lot of time, solitary time. Ideally, I would like to be able to withdraw into a corner in a room full of people and work."[4] Furthermore, critics have often depicted Mitchell as a melancholic. For example, Eric G. Wilson places Mitchell alongside Samuel Taylor Coleridge. Each "endures the limbo. Each grasps the secret marriage of sorrow and joy. Each creates out of this insight original products" (Wilson 2008, 101).

The color blue

Mitchell's most critically acclaimed album, *Blue* (1971), references the color associated with the mood of melancholy since medieval times (Bowring 2008, 141–206). As an album, *Blue* performs the melancholic's search for resolution across its wide canvas, where experiences range from joy amid moments of hurt and anger ("All I Want"), a paean to a carefree Mediterranean frolic ("Carey"), to the depths of drug addiction ("Blue"), and the loss of a child ("Little Green"—generally accepted as a reference to Mitchell's daughter, Kelly, whom she gave up for adoption).[5] The final track ("The Last Time I Saw Richard") conjures despair, frustration, and loss, describing two lives that have moved apart—the story told from the shadowy space of an unnamed café. *Blue* has also frequently been read as the product of an intense period of melancholy in Mitchell's personal life (Yaffe 2017, 40, 142).

Mitchell has also specifically invoked or described melancholy in her lyrics. In the later "Hejira," from the album of the same name, its narrator makes vivid references to the harsher physical artifacts of life and death (1976). "Nothing

Can Be Done" (1991) is both desperate and resigned in its description of aging; "Chinese Café/Unchained Melody" (1982) despairs of life's changeability, and its final lines ask where time goes. "The Sire of Sorrow (Job's Sad Song)" (1994) elects "sorrow" for its chorus. But to hear these songs merely as singular expressions of melancholy obscures the musical strategies that make up its presence in more layered combinations of tone, melody, and lyric.

"Chords of Inquiry"

While *Blue*'s tonalities arguably match their lyric message, throughout Mitchell's other work particular combinations of chord and lyric, as well as the decoupling of their emotional coloring, produce keener expressions of melancholy. Mitchell employs a range of tonal strategies to alter or challenge lyrical assertions. Her tonalities express mood through the harmonics of chord and melody, the relative continuity and repetition of melodic line between verses, and the presence or lack of resolution in individual chords. At points in Mitchell's compositions, tonality enhances the uncertainty of the accompanying lyric, its meaning at once hopeful and despairing; at other times, songs contain rich harmonies and simple melodies that contradict their dark lyrical content. Certain scholars of Mitchell's music have called the effect that of duality or uncertainty (Whitesell 2008, 218; Bennighof 2010, 178) but they also recognize in it an overarching strategy, in terms that themselves invoke melancholy.[6]

Most frequent within this strategy is Mitchell's use of suspended chords.[7] Sometimes describing these as "chords of inquiry,"[8] Mitchell has said that "using them a lot is like keeping you in the state of no resolution," and she frequently pairs them with lyrics that convey uncertainty, delay, and futility (Marom 2014, 166). In its basic form, the suspended chord omits its third tone, one way in which the ear identifies the tonality of that chord, for example, as major or minor (Whitesell 2008, 18–19). That omission creates audible uncertainty that reinforces the lyrics' figuring of suspended, ambivalent states (Marom 2014; Whitesell 2008, 134–135). For example, in "The Last Time I Saw Richard" (*Blue*), the narrator dwells on her past encounter with Richard, while he has moved on to a marriage that has brought him boredom and alcoholism. Ending with the words "café days," describing the liminal space of darkness and anonymity, a sustained suspended chord adds to this phrase deliberately uncertain sound, moving in its final bars from Gsus2 to B minor.[9] Tonality here deepens the lyrics' suggestion of a phase of painful indecision.

Mitchell's opposition of lyric and tonality further express a sense of melancholy. Like melancholy itself, suspended chords load questions onto otherwise seemingly forthright lyrics. In particular, suspended seventh chords add an extra dissonance to uncertainty: the ear hears the jarring note below the root's octave, while lacking the confirmation of the tonal third. Mitchell has noted that she uses tonality to change the meaning of lyrics, and suspended sevenths do just that (Marom 2014, 166). Frequently and effectively, Mitchell pairs suspended sevenths with regular rhyming verse to destabilize the verse's meaning. One of her most well-known compositions, "Both Sides, Now" (*Clouds*), uses this strategy to infuse the song with the melancholic's questioning, using the figure of illusion versus reality to muse upon the quandaries of space, affection, and time. The suspended seventh lingers behind each point of uncertainty: Mitchell's spare studio recording ends each verse with the voice sustained against two measures of guitar at B7sus that finally resolve to E.[10] "Woodstock" (*Ladies of the Canyon*, 1970) employs a similar technique.[11] The song's chorus is predominantly A7sus, resolving only to E minor.[12] The use of the suspended seventh makes audible the song's hopeful, but as yet unrealized, dreams.

Other artists dropped the tonal challenge of the suspended sevenths in covering these works. Judy Collins omitted Mitchell's message of melancholy in her fast-paced hit cover of "Both Sides, Now" in 1967, her high clear voice briskly upbeat, the musical production overwhelming the suspended sevenths with skipping harpsichord, lush strings in major tonalities, and, in the last verse, the entry of a playful chime.[13] When Crosby, Stills, Nash & Young released their version of "Woodstock" in 1970, major chords replaced Mitchell's suspended sevenths.[14] Scholar Jon Andersen, noting this difference between the two versions, uses the language of melancholy—if not the term itself: the notion of paradise in Mitchell's original "is spun with a serpent tongue" with the message that "we'll just have to do the best we can [. . .] It won't be sufficient" (Andersen 2013, 48). Perhaps in pursuit of a simpler musical message, Collins and Crosby, Stills, Nash & Young left Mitchell's signature melancholy behind.

Mitchell's expression of melancholy lies not just in specific tonalities that alter the meaning of the lyrics they accompany, but also in more sustained oppositions of melody and lyric. In Mitchell's music, melody, and lyric often destabilize each other—for example, major tonalities and regular rhythms are paired with narratives of despair. One instance of this is the "The Circle Game" (*Ladies of the Canyon*) where the singsong repetitive melody is set against a lyric that relates the melancholic's contemplation of folly: time is the ultimate trap, humans forced to live—and age—in the face of its scarcity. "Cold Blue Steel and Sweet Fire" (*For The Roses*) suggests that suicide—or just another hit—beckons a destitute addict, describing looming self-destruction in graphic terms. But the accompanying saxophone riffs seduce, and the guitar is richly concordant, marked with the teasing whine of slides in the introduction and chorus.[15] The song's playfulness of melody subverts the gravity and grim stakes of its lyrics. "The Beat of Black Wings" (*Chalk Mark in a Rain Storm*), released in 1988, might have been familiar to the ear grounded in pre-Beatles rock, sampling from "Johnny Angel," made popular by a Shelley Fabares recording in 1962.[16] Its even dance beat and smooth harmonies enclose the story of a Vietnam-era soldier who has endured both deployment and his girlfriend's abortion of their child, deaths packed so tightly in the lyric that they seem to unfold relentlessly in a life ill-equipped to register their pain—while the ominous black wings in the chorus flap incessantly.[17] Its multiple tragedies are persistent and inevitable but, musically, it is almost cheery.[18] Of similar effect is the upbeat pacing of Mitchell's musical setting of William Butler Yeats's poem, "The Second Coming" ("Slouching Towards Bethlehem," *Night Ride Home*). Yeats's lyric emphasizes the instability of a humanity that faces destruction, a center that "cannot hold" (2008, 200). But in Mitchell's version, its apocalyptic references are set to frenzied pop-rock choruses, multiple overdubbings that belie their reference to the coming beast and its shape, seeming to celebrate its arrival. In "Love" (*Wild Things Run Fast*), voice and sax jazz riffs disrupt First Corinthian's reverential meditations on love. "Magdalene Laundries" (*Turbulent Indigo*) has the tone of a ballad, with a muted bass and an accessible melody, but its lyrics speak of the captivity of young women working in a convent laundry, one impregnated by the local priest, and all ultimately destined for unmarked graves. Biblical in theme and epic in scale, these narratives are also potentially moralizing, but instead they teeter off-balance when set to music that leers and lures. Simpler and starker, is Mitchell's use of hymn-like choral voices in "Shadows and Light" (*The Hissing of Summer Lawns*) to sacralize the darkness and mask it with joy.

In live performances, Mitchell often further varies the tone of these songs. For example, in the studio version of "The Last Time I Saw Richard," the repeated last words of each verse evoke a doubting pause, emphasized with suspended chords. These refrains are despairing, even cynical. In the live performance on *Miles of Aisles*, however, Mitchell shifted to a major tonality at those same points, her piano joined by a strongly rhythmic percussion and bass accompaniment. The combination creates a sudden forward, and oddly hopeful, motion. This tonal surprise, wrapped in enriched instrumentation, implies a reversal of the meaning of the studio version: perhaps it is possible that marriage and life—Richard's, specifically—can be fulfilling. Such changes render the meaning of the composition uncertain from performance to performance.

Traveling, traveling

Mitchell also evokes melancholy in her repeated use of barren terrains as narrative settings. In art and literature, melancholy evokes states of isolation; the contemplation of life in the face of death is the outsider's occupation (Bowring 2008, 161). Melancholy finds a pictorial representation in the desolate landscape (Wilson 2008, 34; Bowring 2008, 164; see also Radden 2009, 180–187). Many of Mitchell's songs open with descriptive lines that picture such landscapes, as in the moody and wintry skies of "Hejira," and the narrator's description of "Paprika Plains" (*Don Juan's Reckless Daughter*).[19] The longed-for invitation of "Come in from the Cold" (*Night Ride Home*) never arrives, remaining only imagined.[20] Instead, the song opposes the heat of sex, freedom, and longing with shivers of solitude and age.

Mitchell's music also depicts melancholy in its travels through (sometimes barren) landscapes, with motion occasionally rendered futile even as it continues. Often in her songs, the figure of the journey represents an undefined, liminal space of uncertainty; frequently, her travelers never arrive. For example, "All I Want" (*Blue*) describes a solitary traveler searching for something unknown. In other songs, midpoints don't mark progress, but instead emphasize the traveler's distance from both the beginning and end: the narrator of "Chinese Café" (*Wild Things Run Fast*) finds herself and Carol in the "middle," socially and chronologically. "That Song About the Midway" (*Clouds*) can be understood as a meditation on the paralysis of melancholy, its narrator remaining behind after its addressee has moved on, the midway itself a reference both to a fair's traditional center and also to a place of neither departure nor arrival. The youth of Mitchell's "Woodstock" (*Ladies of the Canyon*) are "caught" in a bargain with the devil. Andersen writes that "Woodstock's" oppositional images include the contrast of "the return and the journey forward," and that the song invites listeners to be part of a collective journey, "never quite arriving, perhaps, but always a little farther down the road" (Andersen 2013, 48).

The itinerancy of melancholy in Mitchell's work lies in more than lyrical portrayals of lone travelers in isolated landscapes. Her music gestures toward perpetual movement, whether by visiting the same point over and over, or, in her use of tonal polarities, moving between two points—in neither case permitting the resolution of an arrival. Contemporary scholars of melancholy source its instability in the mind's attempt to be in two places at once in an effort to accept or reconcile contradictory alternatives.[21] As a result, melancholy oscillates and vacillates (Wilson 2008, 32, 84, 90). Music is particularly suited to conveying this back-and-forth: the metrical repetition of chords or notes makes travel audible by rendering distance in rhythmic time, while its sounding in the same or nearby notes might limit a sense of progression.

Lloyd Whitesell hears such a vacillation in "Cold Blue Steel and Sweet Fire" (*For The Roses*). Noting that the song's tonal poles are C and G, he writes that "the C passages are infused with elements of G major, and vice versa. Arrival on one or the other tonal pole thus usually provides only a momentary stability, since an impetus toward the other pole is immediately set up [. . .] Neither pole is clearly differentiated from the other" (Whitesell 2008, 141). More than just vacillation, this two-point movement specifically performs the melancholic's restless rumination. The song's tonal polarity augments the contrast already noted here between its harmonics and lyrics, the combination of strategies further destabilizing this meditation on death as life's companion (Whitesell 2008, 142; see also 78, 104, 218).

In Mitchell's hands, the guitar strings also map this same terrain of oscillation. Her picking and strumming, particularly in her early studio recordings, create a regular undertone of persistent single- or two-point movement. Melancholy becomes both audible and visible: most pronounced in "Cactus Tree," "Nathan La Franeer," and "The Pirate of Penance" on *Song to a Seagull*. In "Roses Blue" on *Clouds*, a sense of urgency lingers, unresolved, through a relentless picking on the sixth string.[22] The sixth string becomes a drone—in music theory, the repetition of a single note throughout a composition.[23] Mitchell frequently uses "dropped D" tuning—tuning the guitar's sixth string as D, rather than E.[24] This tuning is also specifically melancholic in tone.[25] The same back-and-forth movement is visible, this time horizontally, in Mitchell's strumming of the dulcimer, in performances of "A Case of You" and "Carey" both from her compendium of melancholy, *Blue*.[26] Her dulcimer technique employs drone strings that play a constant, unchanging note, much like the repetitive plucking of the guitar's sixth string.[27]

"Dreams and False Alarms"

"Amelia" (*Hejira*), one of Mitchell's most enigmatic compositions, engages all of her approaches to melancholy. Some have found in the song a rejection of love or an embrace of solitude.[28] Yet its swings between the polarities of earth and sky, narrative and contemplation, movement and stasis, present and past, and suspended and major tonalities, are best understood as expressions of the melancholic's questioning sorrow. Here are the conflicts of lyric and tonality; the journey without arrival; two-point motion, lyrically, tonally, rhythmically, and thematically; and, ultimately, a work that lacks resolution, narratively or musically. Mitchell doubles and redoubles lyrical expressions of melancholy in their accompanying musical registers, layering questions in words and tones that work with and against each other, the effect of their oscillating movement unstable and restless. "Amelia" can be understood as a tale of rejection that opens onto a wider contemplation of rootlessness, but this analysis shows that it is just the reverse. At its center, "Amelia" conveys the inconstancy of the melancholic's life, one of chosen isolation. Rejection is merely its leitmotif.

In seven successive verses, Mitchell's narrator weaves her story with those of two others lost between sky and earth, sun and water, each longing to fly, physically or emotionally. These spaces are passageways, liminal and essentially melancholic. The song's narrator first counts jet vapor trails as she drives across the desert, referencing jets again in the second and final verses. In the third verse, she references arrival, but only as a rumor: its release is just out of sight, the narrator guessing that its experience might offer insight. In the fourth, she reveals a personal story: rejected by her lover, she is exiled to the road, melancholy's transient space. She is away, her location unspecified. The fifth contains the stories both of Amelia Earhart and of Icarus. The known narrative of Earhart's own journey lies somewhere between departure and arrival, the location of her ultimate descent and the circumstances of her death are unknown.[29] Man-made wax wings propel Icarus toward the sun. Each fails in their attempt to accomplish the physically impossible, doomed by a misplaced reliance on technology. In the sixth, the narrator describes herself as unable to love, perched in the cold upper air of the stratosphere, finally falling fatally into the arms of her lover. At the end of a single day of travel in the life of a late twentieth-century Ulysses, she sleeps in a motel with her wanderings beneath, and in, her head.

Ultimately, movement brings the narrator no closer to any destination: circular in structure, the composition arrives where it began, itinerant and without progress. In this way, the song invokes but then subverts the ring structure documented by anthropologist Mary Douglas in works that include the *Book of Numbers* (Douglas 2007). In Douglas's analysis, the ring is a fulfilling journey, its subjects venturing out, and, transformed or informed, returning along the same path. But "Amelia's" journey lacks a clearly defined beginning and/or end, serving also as metaphor for the melancholic's perpetual itinerancy. The first three verses convey, in turn, what the narrator saw; the disruptive effect of travel; and the uncertainty both of arrival and of any satisfaction it might bring. At the song's center—the fourth verse—is the narrator's story of her personal loss. From here, the lyrics circle back, each verse linked to its pair with narrative detail. In the fifth verse, Earhart and Icarus fail in their attempts, the counterpart to the uncertainties of arrival in the third; in the sixth, the narrator, too reserved, falls, and fails, in her relationship, the counterpart to the lure and disruptive effect of travel in the second; and in the final verse, asleep, she sees jets in her dreams as she did awake, in the first, no nearer and no farther from either place of departure or arrival. In Mitchell's construction, the ring simply spins. Like the melancholic, "Amelia" travels, but never arrives; it asks, but receives no answer.

Any convincing interpretation of "Amelia" requires more than a consideration of its narrative structure. In an apparent invocation of Freudian notions of loss and the Freudian melancholic's holding on to past objects, the song's lyrics reference tropes of melancholy from Mitchell's early albums, here reimagined as stops along Amelia's journey. The narrator has lived in "clouds," a look back to "Both Sides, Now" (*Clouds*) and comes to rest at the "Cactus Tree" motel, a reference to the ultimate track on *Song to a Seagull*.[30] But even as she employs referents that seem to suggest a longing for a lost past, Mitchell renders these markers themselves transitional and itinerant. Clouds move and shift, evanescent, incapable of supporting human life, sending visitors to their deaths; the "Cactus Tree" has become a motel, itself never a destination, but a temporary stop from which departure is always imminent.

Recurring, too, in "Amelia" is Mitchell's pairing of suspended chords with unstable lyrics, stressing their lived ambiguity. The last chord of the penultimate line of each verse, transcribed as Am7, emphasizes the chimera-like nature of the word it accompanies, each both enchanting and luring, and each a harbinger of as much potential evil as happiness. Here also are both unstable tonalities and rhythms.[31] Mitchell audibly isolates her musical line by employing a second: on the studio recording, Victor Feldman's vibraphone circles the melody but neither joins nor supports it. In the live performance (on *Shadows and Light*), Pat Metheny's guitar replaces the vibraphone, entering in the later verses and ultimately finding its own isolated course as his solo performance, itself leading into "Hejira."

Conclusion

In "Amelia," as in much of the work described here, Mitchell confronts and conveys the lived experience of melancholy. The methods she uses to do so are multilayered and sometimes in opposition. Her "chords of inquiry," ironic tonalities, and the trope of itinerant isolation mingle to create an overall effect of melancholy. Only by hearing the separate components of these layers does the intricacy of their structure become apparent; only by comparison with others' simpler, less melancholic performances of her music does the singularity of Mitchell's approach become evident. Ultimately, we can hear Mitchell's music as a travelogue of the terrain of melancholic thought, constantly in motion, but forever trapped.

Notes

1 On the early critical and popular positioning of Mitchell as "drowning in her own feelings," see Ruth Charnock, "Joni Mitchell: Music and Feminism," *United Academics: Journal of the Social Sciences*, 12.2 (2012): 91–92.

2 Mitchell told Malka Marom that at the time she went into analysis, she had "combed religions for certain answers, found them to be for the most part too idealistic for me to put into my everyday life except for some of the broader religions which include the yin-yang principle which give you a broader pendulum swing, you know?" "The Entertainers Interview," *CBC-AM* (February 3, 1974). http://jonimitchell.com/library/view.cfm?id=2542 (accessed: June 3, 2018).

3 "Well [. . .] look at my life—chronic illness, the bomb hanging over us. There were external iconic situations and personal chronic situations of tension. And stalker after stalker after stalker in my yard." In Malka Marom, *Joni Mitchell: In Her Own Words—Conversations with Malka Marom* (Toronto: ECW Press, 2014), 166.

4 Ibid., 80.

5 Whitesell calls it one of her "concept" albums, one "unified by melancholy and bittersweet tones," *The Music of Joni Mitchell* (Oxford: Oxford University Press, 2008), 199, 196; Eric G. Wilson calls it "an early product of Mitchell's acute sorrow." *Against Happiness* (New York: Farrar, Straus and Giroux, 2008), 98. On "Little Green," Kilauren Gibb, and her reunion with her mother, see Brian D. Johnson with Danylo Hawaleshka and Dale Eisler, "Joni's

Secret: Mother and Child Reunion," *MacLean's* (April 21, 1997), reprinted in *The Joni Mitchell Companion: Four Decades of Commentary*, ed. Stacey Luftig (New York: Schirmer Books, 2000), 191–197.

6 For example, James Bennighof uses the language of melancholy to describe uncertainty in Mitchell's music, writing that it "finds an analogy in the examination of society in general, as the singer's persona in various songs tends to despair of the possibilities for practices that will lead to desirable results, although occasionally (and often almost irrationally) expressions of hope emerge." Bennighof, *The Words and Music of Joni Mitchell* (Santa Barbara: Praeger, 2010), 178.

7 Mitchell has said that suspended chords are frequent in her work. Marom, *In Her Own Words*, 166.

8 On video spliced into a track of a live performance of *Chelsea Morning*, Mitchell says:

> "For years people said, Joni's weird chords, Joni's weird chords [. . .] Chords are depictions of emotions, these chords that I was getting by twisting the knobs on the guitar until I could get these chords that I heard inside that suited me. They feel like my feelings. I called them, not knowing, chords of inquiry. They have a question mark in them. There were so many unresolved things in me and that those chords suited me. I'd stay in unresolved emotionality for days and days."
>
> *Joni Mitchell: Woman of Heart and Mind (A Life Story)* (London: Eagle Rock Entertainment, 2003), DVD track 2, 15:16. Katherine Monk quotes Mitchell: "Most major chords are a depiction of well-being and happiness. My major chord will have a dissonant note leading to sorrow, then another note leading back to joy. There is always the possibility of the opposite emotion in my chords." *Joni: The Creative Odyssey of Joni Mitchell* (Vancouver: Greystone Books, 2012), 71. See also her explanation in "Interview Transcription: Times Talks Luminato Festival: Joni Mitchell and Brian Blade in conversation with Jon Pareles" (June 16, 2013), transcribed by Catherine McKay, *jonimitchell.com*, http://jonimitchell.com/library/view.cfm?id=3269.

9 Transcription at http://www.musicnotes.com/sheetmusic/mtd.asp?ppn=MN0074858 (standard tuning) (accessed: January 16, 2017).

10 Transcription in standard notation, *Hits* (Van Nuys, CA: Alfred Publishing Co., 2009), 70–73 ("Open E" tuning specified for guitar).

11 Transcription for guitar at https://www.azchords.com/c/crosbystillsnashandyoung-tabs-5029/woodstock-tabs-133807.html (accessed: September 28, 2017).

12 Transcription in standard notation for the piano and guitar, *Hits*, 20–26 (tuning down one-half step specified for guitar). The contrast is also noted by Whitesell, *Music*, 34.
13 Judy Collins, *Wildflowers* (New York: Elektra Records, 1967).
14 Crosby, Stills, Nash & Young, *Déjà Vu* (Los Angeles: Atlantic Records, 1970).
15 E.g., transcription by Sue McNamara, *jonimitchell.com*, http://jonimitchell.com/music/guitarfiles/144.pdf (accessed: January 16, 2017).
16 Shelley Fabares, "Johnny Angel," *Shelley!* (New York: Colpix, 1962).
17 Whitesell calls the disjunction an "affective dissociation" between words and music that conveys loss. *Music*, 115.
18 Whitesell has written in detail of this song:

> "The soldier's vortex of rage and despair hardly affects the musical environment – so polished, so transfixed. Joni's setting places a breathtaking emotional distance between her raw subject and her excessive artifice. There is also a defiance of gravity in the multiple musical suspensions, which are not hard to hear as gestures of buoyancy and release."
>
> Lloyd Whitesell, "A Joni Mitchell Aviary," *Women and Music*, Vol. 1, 1997, reprinted in Stacy Luftig, Ed., *The Joni Mitchell Companion: Four Decades of Commentary* (New York: Schirmer Books, 2000), 237–250, at 249. Bennighof has noted this same contrast, 136, and identified a similar effect in "For the Roses," noting that Mitchell sings it in a "rich, warm tone that, combined with the casual nature of the fingerpicked pattern, reflects ironically on the caustic nature of the text," *Words and Music*, 64, observing the same technique in "Trouble Child" and "Edith and the Kingpin" (*The Hissing of Summer Lawns*), 87, and "Cherokee Louise" (*Night Ride Home*), 141.

19 Nathan Wise writes that the landscape for Mitchell can be an active opposing force. "'Urge for Going' and the Luminosity of Genius," in *Gathered Light: The Poetry of Joni Mitchell's Songs*, ed. Lisa and John Sornberger (Toronto: Sumach Press, 2013), 3–4.
20 On the isolation of the house in snow, see Gaston Bachelard, *The Poetics of Space*. Trans. Maria Jolas. (Boston: Beacon Press, 1984), 38–42.
21 Wilson writes:

> "It is our own nervous fear, our melancholia, that leads to our awareness of the world's innate duplicity, its "both/and." Only by being unwilling to rest on one side of the world or the other do we come to sense the hidden marriage between both sides. Sadly inhabiting this rich limbo, we put ourselves in a position to grasp the profound meaning of life's deepest events. These

vexed events reveal to us what is already true of everything: all creatures are meldings of grandeur and gloom." *Against Happiness,* 81.

22 "How to Play Joni Mitchell 'Cactus Tree' (intro only)," Jerry's Guitar Bar, https://www.youtube.com/watch?v=ETiKTAdKSns, at 1:32. The instructor calls this "a drone on the sixth string." The repeated thumb-picking of the sixth string is also visible in Sue Tierney's rendering of Nathan La Franeer, https://www.youtube.com/watch?v=WQO9P-unloM.

23 The drone is "a sustained tone, usually rather low in pitch, providing a sonorous foundation for a melody or melodies sounding at a higher pitch level." *Encyclopaedia Britannica, s. v.* "Drone," https://www.britannica.com/art/drone-music (accessed: December 16, 2017).

24 On Mitchell's use of the "dropped D," see, e.g., Marc O'Hara, "Joni Mitchell's Guitars and Tunings," January 29, 2013. http://uniqueguitar.blogspot.com/2013/01/joni-mitchells-guitars-and-tunings.html (accessed: June 2, 2017).

25 On the melancholic effect of the "dropped D," see Jackie Bowring, *A Field Guide to Melancholy* (Harpenden, UK: Oldcastle Books, 2008), 183–184.

26 E.g., "A Case of You," performed in London in 1983, https://youtu.be/f_OtHVLAF4o, and "Carey," also performed in London in 1983, https://youtu.be/fFGrRSVW8jk (accessed: September 24, 2017).

27 Bennighof writes about "All I Want," also from *Blue,* that its first verse reveals that the singer, "like the dulcimer, is both uncertain and moving forward [. . .] Her vacillation between visions of a joyful companionship [. . .] and pain is framed in the journey metaphor and reflected in melodic and formal shifts." *Words and Music,* 50.

28 Ron Rosenbaum, "The Best Joni Mitchell Song Ever: An Ode to Obsessive Listening," *Slate.com* (December 14, 2007). http://www.slate.com/articles/life/the_spectator/2007/12/the_best_joni_mitchell_song_ever.html (accessed: June 2, 2017; emphasis in original):

> "It occurs to me that in some way that's what "Amelia's" enigma or paradox is about: True love is far more alarming than a false alarm. True love is truly alarming. Real danger. She's in some respects *grateful.* It was a false alarm. For an independent spirit like Joni Mitchell, it may be better to have loved and lost than to have loved and won, which can be *truly* terrifying."
>
> On "Amelia's" message of solitude, see Ariel Swartley, "Joni Mitchell: Hejira," *Rolling Stone* (February 10, 1977). http://www.rollingstone.com/music/albumreviews/hejira-19770210 (accessed: June 2, 2017).

29 E.g., Susan Butler, "Searching for Amelia Earhart," *New York Times* (July 11, 2017). https://www.nytimes.com/2017/07/11/opinion/amelia-earhart-photograph.html (accessed: September 24, 2017).
30 Whitesell notes, in addition, the mention of "paradise" in "Amelia" as a reference to "Big Yellow Taxi." *Music*, 209.
31 Mitchell, quoted in Whitesell, *Music*, 139, notes that the tonalities of "Amelia" modulate, and transcribers record the song as alternating between three-quarter and four-four time. E.g., Dave Blackburn, piano transcription of "Amelia," posted on *Joni Mitchell.com*, http://jonimitchell.com/music/guitarfiles/439.pdf (accessed: December 16, 2017).

Works Cited

Andersen, Jon. "Stardust in the Garden: On the Oppositional Poetry of 'Woodstock,'" in *Gathered Light: The Poetry of Joni Mitchell's Songs*, ed. Lisa and John Sornberger. Toronto: Sumach Press, 2013, 47–48.

Bachelard, Gaston. *The Poetics of Space*. Trans. Maria Jolas. Boston: Beacon Press, 1984.

Bennighof, James. *The Words and Music of Joni Mitchell*. Santa Barbara: Praeger, 2010.

Bowring, Jackie. *A Field Guide to Melancholy*. Harpenden, UK: Oldcastle Books, 2008.

Burton, Robert. *The Anatomy of Melancholy*. Ed. Holbrook Jackson, introduction by William H. Gass. New York: New York Review Books, 2001.

Butler, Susan. "Searching for Amelia Earhart," *New York Times*, July 11, 2017. https://www.nytimes.com/2017/07/11/opinion/amelia-earhart-photograph.html (accessed: September 24, 2017).

Charnock, Ruth. "Joni Mitchell: Music and Feminism," *United Academics: Journal of the Social Sciences*, 12.2 (2012): 91–106.

Douglas, Mary. *Thinking in Circles: An Essay on Ring Composition*. New Haven: Yale University Press, 2007.

Freud, Sigmund. "Mourning and Melancholia," in *Standard Edition of the Complete Psychological Works of Sigmund Freud, Volume XIV (1914–1916): On the History of the Psycho-Analytic Movement, Papers on Metapsychology and Other Works*, ed. James Strachey. London: Hogarth Press and the Institute of Psycho-Analysis, 1957.

Holly, Michael Ann. *The Melancholy Art*. Princeton: Princeton University Press, 2013.

Johnson, Brian D., with Danylo Hawaleshka and Dale Eisler. "Joni's Secret: Mother and Child Reunion," *MacLean's*, April 21, 1997. Reprinted in *The Joni Mitchell Companion: Four Decades of Commentary*, ed. Stacey Luftig. New York: Schirmer Books, 2000, 191–197.

Joni Mitchell: Woman of Heart and Mind (A Life Story). DVD. London: Eagle Rock Entertainment, 2003.

Luftig, Stacy, ed. *The Joni Mitchell Companion: Four Decades of Commentary*. New York: Schirmer Books, 2000.

Marom, Malka. *Joni Mitchell: In Her Own Words—Conversations with Malka Marom*. Toronto: ECW Press, 2014.

Mitchell, Joni. *Song to a Seagull*. Hollywood: Reprise Records, 1968.

Mitchell, Joni. *Clouds*. Hollywood: Reprise Records, 1969.

Mitchell, Joni. *Blue*. Hollywood: Reprise Records, 1971.

Mitchell, Joni. *Ladies of the Canyon*. Hollywood: Reprise Records, 1970.

Mitchell, Joni. *For The Roses*. Hollywood: Asylum Records, 1972.

Mitchell, Joni. *The Hissing of Summer Lawns*. Hollywood: Asylum Records, 1975.

Mitchell, Joni. *Hejira*. Hollywood: Asylum Records, 1976.

Mitchell, Joni. *Don Juan's Reckless Daughter*. Hollywood: Asylum Records, 1977.

Mitchell, Joni. *Mingus*. Hollywood: Asylum Records, 1979.

Mitchell, Joni. *Wild Things Run Fast*. Hollywood: Geffen Records, 1982.

Mitchell, Joni. *Dog Eat Dog*. Hollywood: Geffen Records, 1985.

Mitchell, Joni. *Night Ride Home*. Hollywood: Geffen Records, 1991.

Mitchell, Joni. *Turbulent Indigo*. Hollywood: Reprise Records, 1994.

Mitchell, Joni. *Taming the Tiger*. Hollywood: Reprise Records, 1998.

Mitchell, Joni. *Both Sides Now*. Hollywood: Reprise Records, 2000.

Mitchell, Joni. *Shine*. Santa Monica: Hear Music/Universal, 2007.

O'Hara, Marc. "Joni Mitchell's Guitars and Tunings," January 29, 2013. http://uniqueguitar.blogspot.com/2013/01/joni-mitchells-guitars-and-tunings.html (accessed: June 2, 2017).

Radden, Jennifer. *Moody Minds Distempered: Essays on Melancholy and Depression*. Oxford: Oxford University Press, 2009.

Radden, Jennifer. *Melancholic Habits: Burton's Anatomy and the Mind Sciences*. Oxford: Oxford University Press, 2017.

Radden, Jennifer, ed. *The Nature of Melancholy: From Aristotle to Kristeva*. Oxford: Oxford University Press, 2000.

Réunion des musées nationaux. *Mélancolie: Génie et Folie en Occident: en homage a Raymond Kilbansky, sous la direction de Jean Clair*. Paris: Gallimard, 2005.

Schwenger, Peter. *The Tears of Things: Melancholy and Physical Objects*. Minneapolis: University of Minneapolis Press, 2006.

Whitesell, Lloyd. *The Music of Joni Mitchell*. Oxford: Oxford University Press, 2008.

Wilson, Eric G. *Against Happiness*. New York: Farrar, Straus and Giroux, 2008.

Wise, Nathan. "'Urge for Going' and the Luminosity of Genius," in *Gathered Light: The Poetry of Joni Mitchell's Songs*, ed. Lisa and John Sornberger. Toronto: Sumach Press, 2013, 3–4.

Yaffe, David. *Reckless Daughter: A Portrait of Joni Mitchell*. New York: Farrar, Straus & Giroux, 2017.

Yeats, W. B. *The Collected Poems of W. B. Yeats*. 2nd edn. Ed. Richard J. Finneran. New York: Simon and Schuster, 2008.

Part Two

"The Only (Black) Man in the Room?" Mitchell's Milieu

5

In Search of Lost Chords: Joni Mitchell, *The Last Waltz*, and the Refuge of the Road

Gustavus Stadler

Murray Lerner's film *Message to Love: The Isle of Wight Festival 1970* documents Joni Mitchell's confrontation with an unruly crowd at an increasingly chaotic three-day concert, where an audience of 200,000 watched performances by acts like Jimi Hendrix, The Who, and The Doors. Her few minutes on screen will never fit as neatly with glib proclamations of the "end of the 60s" as the events at the free concert at Tracy, California's Altamont Speedway, organized by the Rolling Stones and documented in the far more canonical film *Gimme Shelter*. But *Message to Love's* depiction of Mitchell's confrontation with the festival audience carries some of the same force. In both films, dreams seeded at the Woodstock Music & Art Fair of 1969 turn into nightmares. Like *Gimme Shelter*, Lerner's film charts the breakdown of business-as-usual at a huge, outdoor, multi-artist concert. But in *Message to Love*, Woodstock's shadow looms more literally; just after Mitchell finishes playing her eponymous anthem of tribute to the already legendary affair, her microphone is commandeered by an apparently acid-baked hippie named Yogi Joe, who rather incoherently attempts to speak up for a group of people protesting outside the festival, demanding that it be made free.[1] Mitchell's manager finally pulls Joe offstage, prompting a chorus of boos and jeers from the audience. Mitchell tries to start her next song, "My Old Man," but breaks off after the opening chords. After some moments of awkward hesitancy, looking distraught and rather cowed ("Listen a minute—will ya listen a minute?"), she scolds the crowd at length in a breaking voice, reminding them of the vulnerability of performing ("you've got your life wrapped up in it") and accusing them of "acting like tourists," akin to onlookers she had recently witnessed at a "Hopi ceremonial dance."[2]

Soon, all appears to be well; the film cuts to the final seconds of a well-received performance of "Big Yellow Taxi," for which Mitchell even reproduces the song-punctuating giggle of the studio version. But a rift has emerged; she has suggested an insidious difference between performers and their audiences, one in which "indigeneity" stands in for the performers' authenticity and "tourism" for the audience's consumerism. The episode tries to paper over the fact that the boos by the Isle of Wight audience, however rude to Mitchell, were meant to protest the commodification of performance; instead, the representation of Yogi Joe's clumsy intervention becomes a lesson on etiquette. Eventually, however, crowds do break down the fences surrounding the concert grounds and stream into the festival, as Lerner's cameras record the festival organizers' descent into apoplexy. Indeed, more directly than *Gimme Shelter*, Lerner's film portends the growth of live rock as a well-oiled branch of big business in the 1970s, with performers and profits well-protected by police and professional security.

The Isle of Wight debacle represented in *Message to Love* contrasts starkly with Mitchell's best-known appearance in a concert documentary. This piece of film comes from the aftermath of the historical transformation that Lerner's film all but promises, in Martin Scorsese's movie about the final concert by The Band, *The Last Waltz* (1978), planned by guitarist/songwriter/honcho Robbie Robertson as their farewell to the trials of touring. Against the background of the incident depicted in the earlier movie, her appearance in the late-70s film feels as serene as twilight on a Laurel Canyon sundeck, her status as the only woman to perform at the concert safely blended into the proceedings by her "mesmerizing" appearance as, in Greil Marcus's words, "a goddess on the make" (2010, 82). But Mitchell's segment exposes some weaknesses in the tightly constructed film's efforts to assert the death and burial of the 1960s. In this chapter, I mean to unravel the way that Mitchell instigates a kind of structural breakdown in the cultural-historical narrative Scorsese and Robertson attempt to tell, in contrast to her quelling of chaos in *Message to Love*. As Scorsese's film, through the voice of Robertson, intones and inveighs against the chaos of the 1960s and early 1970s, as represented in the figure of "the road," Mitchell's appearance subtly draws out the counter-message she was articulating in her then-current album, *Hejira*, a record which depicts travel as a strange kind of refuge, a space in which ambivalence and uncertainty become forms of sustenance. Mitchell's presence—along with the *Hejira* song she performs onscreen, "Coyote"—achieves this effect, in particular, by quietly drawing attention to The Band's charismatic and gifted, yet troubled bass player/vocalist Rick Danko, whose interaction with Mitchell turns his appearance in the film into a challenge to the story told in the dominant key of Robertson's romanticized masculinity.

Message to Love and *Gimme Shelter*, as well as D. A. Pennebaker's *Monterey Pop* and Michael Hadleigh's Oscar-winning *Woodstock* (for which *The Last Waltz* director Martin Scorsese served as an assistant director), are verité documentaries, made with handheld cameras, and shunning both narration and talking-head sequences. They all also pay attention to the unpredictable responses of the concerts' audiences, and the generic spaces those audiences occupy. They are films whose aesthetics mirror how many prefer to imagine the sixties—as hard-scrabble, improvisatory, and organic. *The Last Waltz*, in contrast, presents a world that has moved beyond all that, depicting rock as a sumptuous and exclusive realm founded on the notion that the boundary between performers and audience is impassable. It is a tightly sealed, insular film, like the performance it depicts, which took place before a tidy crowd of 5,000, each of whom were served a traditional Thanksgiving dinner before the show. The film takes place in a relatively small, indoor performance space, and features no shots of the audience while the musicians are onstage. (Scenes of performances with Emmylou Harris and the Staples Singers were shot on a soundstage.) The concert was meticulously choreographed so that the film would avoid drawing any attention to its own process of construction. Moreover, songs are intercut with interviews with members of The Band, songwriter and guitarist Robbie Robertson in particular, which narrate (with some major gaps) the group's history, and the reasons for giving up on touring, which, in the movie's own terms, boil down to Robertson's dictum that "It's a goddamn impossible way of life."[3] No surprises can disrupt the film's structural hardware, it would seem—certainly not Joni Mitchell, whom we watch glide onto the stage in a flowery peasant skirt and thin burgundy sweater for a performance of her then-current single "Coyote" (from the LP *Hejira*, released that same month) in which nothing, least of all an onstage interloper, threatens her contented calm and focus; 40 years later, Robertson would refer to Mitchell's performance that evening as "like a cool breeze."[4]

Mitchell is one of a series of "friends" who perform their own songs in the film with The Band's backing: Bob Dylan, Neil Young, Van Morrison, Dr John, Neil Diamond, and Muddy Waters are among the artists on the star-studded bill, all of whom have some history of collaboration with the group, and none of whom, besides Mitchell, are women. There are a couple of ways of accounting for Mitchell's presence at the concert, among a star-studded series of performers, each of whom played a few of their own songs with The Band backing them. One of them, almost certainly, is her connection to Robertson, who had conceived of the concert, the film, and the abandonment of touring—a decision which in the following year led to the overall demise of the group. Mitchell had met fellow Canadian Robertson on various occasions, largely in southern California in the company of a mutual friend, the record company mogul David Geffen; Robertson played guitar on "Raised on Robbery" from Mitchell's 1974 *Court and Spark* LP and joined Mitchell and Geffen for the rollicking weekend depicted in the same album's "Free Man in Paris."

But Mitchell had another, less visible connection to The Band, one with less permanent musical documentation: her relationship with bassist Rick Danko, the other Band member who flanks her during the rendition of "Coyote," plucking his bass strings affably with his eyes glued on Mitchell's left hand as it fingers chords on her acoustic guitar. In late 1975 and early 1976, both Mitchell and Danko had joined up with Bob Dylan's Rolling Thunder cavalcade, playing multiple dates with the ensemble that included Dylan, Joan Baez, Roger McGuinn, Ramblin' Jack Elliott, Ronee Blakly, and others. Late in *Rolling Thunder Logbook*, his hysterical, Beat-aesthetic-tinged, panicked account of the tour he tagged along on, playwright Sam Shepard—often rumored to *be* the man the song calls "Coyote"—notices Mitchell watching Danko, describing the scene of spectatorship in a manner that could constitute a lyrical vignette for a slightly tweaked-up "Coyote": "Joni Mitchell is cross-legged on the floor, barefoot, writing something in a notebook. She bites her lip and looks over to Rick Danko, who's smashing the shit out of a pinball machine with both kneecaps, then pounding on the sides with both fists" (Shepard 1977, 82). In a recording of a Rolling Thunder performance in Montreal on December 4, 1975, Mitchell tells the audience that she is still adding verses to "Coyote"; Shepard's little tableau suggests the possibility that Danko, or some Danko-instigated suggestion of masculinity that tempted her curiosity, is present in the song they would play onstage together a little less than a year later.[5]

In *The Last Waltz*, Robertson and Scorsese try hard to make Danko and pianist Richard Manuel into tragic figures, the exhibits representing the toll of the years Robertson laments. Every member of The Band is clearly fucked-up in the interview segments, but Danko and Manuel appear especially full up on intoxicants. And indeed, the years that followed this concert bear out this depiction: both struggled with addiction, until Manuel committed suicide in 1985 and Danko died, at 56 in 1999, after long-term heroin addiction. Musically, Danko's biography became a narrative of lost promise. In the early days of the group, he had been a contributing songwriter; indeed, he and Dylan cowrote the powerful, oft-covered "This Wheel's on Fire" during the *Basement Tapes* sessions in pre-festival Woodstock. Part of what makes the story tragic is also on display in the film; in the performance scenes Danko, a marvelous and original player, bounces and beams through virtually every song, radiating gracious joy. His exuberance in the moment comes off as strong enough to cover what must have been a strong sense of ambivalence, at best, about giving up on live performances—at least regular ones, with this group of men who had played together steadily for a decade and a half.

Shepard's depiction of Mitchell watching Danko during a backstage moment in the Rolling Thunder festivities helps underscore the ocular dynamics between the two during her appearance in *The Last Waltz*, in which Danko watches Mitchell's guitar playing closely. It's an all but unnoticeable detail, but one whose easy disappearance belies its capacity to undo the film's neatness, its submission to the guiding authority that Scorsese and Robertson work hard to make unassailable. *Hejira*, the album Mitchell released the same month as the concert took place, is a key intertext here, a document of meditations on travel and gender formed during an itinerant year in her own life, which included several months on the Rolling Thunder tour.

In Scorsese's *The Last Waltz*, performance scenes alternate with interview segments, filmed almost a year after the concert, in which members of The Band respond to questions from the director. The film presents Robertson as the group's musical visionary and spokesperson, the one least ravaged by their history, actual details of which are fairly scant. The guitarist and chief songwriter lays out his case: The Band needs to stop touring, they are on the way toward an inevitably tragic fate to which their late contemporaries and colleagues Jimi Hendrix and Janis Joplin have already fallen victim. Ruggedly handsome, with a gravelly voice, bloodshot eyes, and a dense, brown helmet of blow-dried hair, Robertson reigns over the vast majority of the interview scenes. Both concert and film were his idea; accounts of the film's planning stress his degree of collaboration with Scorsese, including the production of a 200-page document of camera cues aligned with the structures of songs performed (Kelly 1980, 26). The film presents the rest of the group as either too uninterested or incapacitated to take on any real authority in telling the story of the band, concert, and film. Indeed, drummer Levon Helm, who in later years excoriated Robertson for minimizing the songwriting contributions—and thus royalty payments—of other members of the group, wrote in his 1993 memoir: "The film was more or less shoved down our throats [. . .] and we went along with it. Do it, puke, get out" (Helm with Davis 2000, 257). The film is as tightly controlled as Robertson's coiffure, a contrast not only to the older concert movies, but—perhaps intentionally—to *Renaldo and Clara*, the ragged and incomprehensible hybrid narrative-documentary film that Bob Dylan had constructed during Rolling Thunder.

Although Dylan's appearance is presented as the climax of the film, the interview sections included in *The Last Waltz* short shrift The Band's work with him, suggesting a bit of Oedipal anxiety. Oddly, the movie also contains no discussion of songs, songwriting, playing, or the recording process. Robertson is the film's discursive patriarch, and the narrative he relates in the interview segments focuses on their early days, playing with Ronnie Hawkins, visiting the southern United States for the first time in the company of native informant Helm. The focus becomes not so much music as a set of hackneyed talking points from a Frommer's guide to Americana. We have a young white band's trip to see elderly African American bluesman Sonny Boy Williamson in Arkansas. We have a long story about a hungry, broke-ass band shoplifting baloney from a grocery store. We have rubes arriving in New York and blithely checking into the "Times Square Hotel" because the name makes it sound centrally located, unaware that they are lodging at ground zero of the red-light district. In a scene that precedes the presentation of Mitchell performing, and which I'll return to, we have a brief and awkward discussion instigated by Scorsese's off-camera question, "So what about the women on the road?" Finally, we have Robertson intoning that "The road killed a lot of the great ones—Hank Williams [. . .] Janis, Jimi Hendrix, Elvis [. . .] It's a goddamned impossible way of life."[6] By the time of the concert and film, of course, the group was traveling to concert dates on jets in an industry whose upper echelons, since calamities like Altamont and Isle of Wight, had become increasingly corporatized.

Across Mitchell's *Hejira* LP, however, the view we get of travel and life on the road is variegated, multi-patterned, ambivalent; in a song like "Coyote," Mitchell's narrator seems simultaneously enchanted and undone in her life as a "hitcher, a prisoner of the white lines on the freeway." The album seems determined to explode the singularity of the notion of "the" road, to prevent travel from symbolizing any one thing, from standing in as a figure for any singular myth. "Hejira" is the Arabic word for journey, often used to refer to Mohammad's escape to Medina from persecution in Mecca. Multiple modes of travel populate the songs, from skateboards to 747s, as "Black Crow" suggests, in a knowingly hyperbolic manner:

> I took a ferry to the highway
> Then I drove to a pontoon place
> I took a plane to a taxi
> And a taxi to a train.

For Mitchell, if anything, the road is a "refuge" (as the title of one song has it), because it offers experiences and encounters so diverse and multiple that they can't be mythologized through a single frame. It brings new forms of contact with others and oneself, and persistently proffers more of the same; it makes available and palpable new terms and concepts, new senses and forms of perception. It continually self-undermines and regenerates. In a way, it *is*, as Robertson has it, "goddamned impossible"—but, from this orientation, largely because it is impossible to confine within a narrative. It's not even necessarily discursive, at least in the modality of explanation—and this, for Mitchell, is a good thing, a sentiment ripened in the opening verse, in which the singer is sheltered in a non-place where "There's comfort in melancholy/When there's no need to explain."[7] A decade ago, writer Ron Rosenbaum described the song "Amelia" in terms that resonate beautifully with the entire album: "[Mitchell] seems in some ruefully voluptuous way to be reveling in her hejira, getting deliriously deep into her disillusion and disenchantment, exploring the unmapped territory of her newfound solitude like the eponymous aviator in the dreamy solace of long motel-punctuated drives."[8] This is not to say that the road is not threatening and, potentially, deathly. In many ways, the ur-figure of the LP is Amelia Earhart, the addressee of "Amelia," history's most famous female pilot, "swallowed by the sky." But of course, the mystery of Earhart's disappearance, embodied in this image of a gulping sky—in contrast with the literal warning in the deaths of musicians like Hendrix and Joplin—is what attracts Mitchell, as well as the recurrent phrase "false alarm"—a figure of dissipated warning, of emotions in flight from their initial, or representable, catalysts.

The sexiest of these songs is "Coyote," which may be either the most flirtatious song about fucking or the most graphic song about flirting ever written, an ambiguity underwritten and accelerated by the fact that the title character is alternately a male human and an actual, wild coyote. A few specific details provide ballast for seeing Sam Shepard as the model for the song's protagonist, such as the reference to Nova Scotia's "Bay of Fundy," where the playwright kept a waterside home. But I prefer to hear Mitchell's ode to life as a "prisoner of the white lines on the freeway" as a more general luxuriation in the frame-shifting of movement, a sentiment underwritten by the light touch of her syncopated guitar strumming as it gently leads the song's loping rhythm and melody. The road is a place of serial impressions, in which a "farmhouse burning down" quickly changes into "some road house lights/Where a local band was playing," and in which the narrator, recognizing that Coyote has "a woman at home" and "another woman down the hall" seems titillated by the precariousness surrounding his advances.⁹ The road, in this portrayal, is a space of flirtation; in this verse, that flirtation is explicitly sexual, but the LP as a whole finds an erotic charge more broadly in the road as a space that cultivates the constant raising of questions, the continual renewal of possibility.

* * *

A moment in Robbie Robertson's recent autobiography is richly suggestive:

> After dinner, Joni told me she had a new song almost finished. There were a couple of acoustic guitars in the living room, and she picked one up, changed the tuning, and motioned for me to pick up the other. Then she soared into the cosmos with her angelic voice. I tried to follow her on guitar, but between her unusual tunings and obscure fingering, I was a man in search of lost chords. (2016, 408)

The contrast between Mitchell's and Robertson's aesthetic-psychic imagination of the road might seem overdetermined, in advance, by the simplest understanding of the cultural politics of gender. Robertson's depiction of the road is authoritative, agonized, romantic, masculine; Mitchell's, in her contemporaneous work, is speculative, questioning, fluid, feminine—as non-solid as her brief pre-appearance in *The Last Waltz* through a scrim, singing backup from backstage on Neil Young's "Helpless." The way this buried conflict registers structurally in *The Last Waltz*, however, is messier, and draws out Rick Danko as an unassuming counter-authority to Robertson.

Mitchell's appearance in *The Last Waltz* takes place just past the midpoint of the film. It is brief and, ostensibly, reprises the mise-en-scene of all the performances presented in the film: she walks out on stage, and sings "Coyote" standing, playing acoustic guitar, in the space where most of the "special guests" appeared, in between guitarist Robertson (to her left, our right) and bassist Danko (to her right, our left). To this point in the film, Danko hasn't had much screen time during the interview scenes, and if he does not come off as quite as wasted as Richard Manuel, he is still, clearly, substantially wrecked. But it's Danko who de facto introduces Mitchell's scene, at the end of an interview segment in which Band members respond to the question from Scorsese about "women on the road." In this sequence, Robertson stays uncharacteristically quiet. The question brings Manuel to the fore with the exclamation, "I love 'em! That's probably why we've *been* on the road!" Levon Helm demonstrates both his visual acuity and his negative feelings about the project by attempting to lean out of the frame as he softly asserts, "I thought you weren't supposed to talk about that stuff." The segment turns into a full-blown introduction to Mitchell, though, when Danko says, "As we've grown, the women have grown." The film seems to endorse this patronizing comment by turning to a shot of Mitchell's back as Robertson intones to the crowd, "Who? Joni Mitchell, right." Offered up to the film's audience as representative, if "grown," woman, Mitchell walks onstage, bows to the crowd, and kisses Robertson on the cheek. She strums the opening chords and rhythm of "Coyote"; after a measure or two, the group fall in behind her.

With the film's serial presentation of The Band-backed guest performances, it's easy to miss a couple of formal peculiarities that have just appeared on the screen. One is that Mitchell is the only performer we have seen—or, over the course of the movie, do see—emerge from backstage; she is shown from the back walking out to greet the musicians. Another is that the film and sound editing are markedly choppier here than in the other segments; there is an awkward cut after she kisses Robertson to the first chord of the song, an edit which excises any embrace of recent Rolling Thunder fellow traveler Danko. It is as though the film doesn't quite know how to integrate what happens when a woman walks into its frame, and this difficulty has a kind of musical analogue in the gentle gallop of the song, which contrasts greatly with the swampy blues foundation—The Band's favored musical idiom—that underlies the songs they perform with the other "friends."

Through most of the scene, we are positioned on Robertson's side, looking over at Mitchell, with Danko in the background. We are looking, then, at Mitchell, but also at where Danko is looking, and his eyes are riveted on one part of Mitchell's body: her left hand, fingering out the song's chords. In preparing for the concert, The Band had only a few weeks to learn songs by nearly a dozen guest artists, so it's not surprising that he would be watching Mitchell's hand for the chords and changes; musicians playing in blues-based idioms in ensembles often rely on vision, in this manner, to suture them into the music. The positions of a guitarist's fingers on the fret board provide a kind of map, or code, for musicians who play without printed notation. But in this instance, because of the unconventional way(s) Mitchell plays guitar, tuning her strings in ways generated by her own ear, the fingered frets are not producing the notes they usually do. The object of Danko's gaze is providing him with no information, no semiosis. Like Mitchell's framing of the hejira, it resists the confinement of sign and symbol.

Joni Mitchell's nonstandard guitar tunings comprise one of the most distinctive aspects of her music. Early in her career, like many folk and blues guitarists, she began to move away from standard tuning (from low to high strings, E-A-D-G-B-E) toward open tunings—tuning the open strings of the guitar to a particular chord (usually G- or D-major), creating a dronier sound as multiple open strings ring out with the root note of the song's key, basically throughout the composition. At some point after the release of her first album, as her compositions became more formally complicated, she became fascinated with developing her own, highly idiosyncratic tunings, often to "sus" or suspended chords—although, in general, she developed tunings only from how they sounded to her and had no idea what chords and notes she was playing. On "Coyote," her guitar is tuned to a D-minor 11 chord, a very rare one indeed in the blues-based rock idiom. As a result, the positions in which she places her fingers on the fretboard are completely opaque to other musicians. Mitchell has said, "I'm handicapped in communicating with other musicians," and that she often has no idea how to identify the chords she plays in any communicable musical sign system (Marom 2014, 75). Consequently, her collaborations in the 1970s, as she did more ensemble playing while her songs became more complex, were marked by lengthy transcription sessions; a participating musician who, unlike most working in popular idioms, had an operative knowledge of music theory, would identify Mitchell's chords for the other players. In the case of The Band, classically trained keyboardist Garth Hudson played this role during the rushed rehearsals for the *The Last Waltz* concert.

Unconventional tunings produce unconventional finger positions; virtually unheard-of tunings produce never-before-seen fingerings. Sight underwrites the sounds musicians make when everyone knows where the fingers go for a specific chord, but in Mitchell's *The Last Waltz* scene, watching Danko watch Mitchell's fingers, the spectacle is one of sight *not* working, at least not in a way that produces knowledge for the bassist in any conventional manner. Mitchell has detuned not just her guitar, but that lynchpin of cinematic spectatorship itself, the male gaze. Mitchell was not unfamiliar with this dynamic of vision, one that, in Robertson's words in his recent memoir, put her collaborating musicians "in search of lost chords."

In her book of interviews with Malka Marom, the Canadian writer shows Mitchell a photograph of her sitting on a lawn, playing guitar, alongside Eric Clapton, David Crosby, Mickey Dolenz, and an unidentified baby. Her response to the photo:

> Eric Clapton is watching my hands, his mouth is gaping open because he couldn't figure out what I was doing: "What is she doing? How is she getting those sounds?"
>
> People would comment on my hands from the start, like when Chuck Mitchell and his partner then, Lauren James, came to see me. Lauren James went, "Look at her right hand," and Chuck went, "Hell, look at her legs." [laughs] (Marom 2014, 72)

Poignantly, in this vignette in Marom's book, she looks back at an image of a man looking at her, and that man, virtually a knighted figure in the annals of rock guitar, is left in a feminine position, with his mouth "gaping open." Moreover, Mitchell here presents herself as a dilemma for straight male musicians: Do they look at her hands or at a more traditionally erotic (and highly legible) object of vision like her legs? In her scene in *The Last Waltz*, Rick Danko has made his choice, sending his gaze toward Mitchell's hand in a manner that veers off the routes traveled by conventional, heterosexually structured markers of gendered difference. That Danko, Clapton, and the rest can't identify the chords also means they can't *hear* them—they need vision to identify what, for Mitchell, is a self-generated aural formation. Their ocular failure repeats an auditory failure. For Mitchell, this acoustic failure—the evasiveness of her chords' *sound*—is also gendered. In the same interview with Marom, Mitchell discusses the confusion her frequent use of suspended chords—whose harmonic structure creates, for many listeners, a sense of tension—has posed for male collaborators: "I used to call them, not knowing what a sus chord was myself, I called them chords of inquiry. They have a question mark in them. They're sustained. Men don't like them because they like resolution, just like they do in life" (Marom 2014, 74). In fact, plenty of rock songs use suspended chords, but Mitchell makes them more frequent and more central—less like brief variations of a song's staple chords—than tends to happen in rock songwriting. In spatial terms, the idiom of travel, this tenor of irresolution gives her music a sense of detachment from origin and destination. It underwrites an ethos, charted in *Hejira*, of wandering and flirtation as ways of being.

"Coyote" is five-and-a-half minutes long in *The Last Waltz*; it gently unravels at the end, perhaps because putting together a tight ending was a low priority on The Band's rushed schedule.[10] The film moves along. Mitchell reappears for the all-hands version of Dylan's "I Shall Be Released" that closed the concert, in advance of several jam sessions and an encore. Her accrued screen time hardly makes her a presence of any exceptional weight in the film.

Yet her performance does reverberate, in another sequence, focusing on Rick Danko. It was Danko who, in effect, introduced Mitchell into the film by awkwardly assimilating her into its chapter on the topic of "women on the road." It was Danko who drew attention to the spectacle of her sound, irreducible to naming, manifest in her fingers' arrangement on the guitar frets. Slightly later, the film devotes an interview sequence to Danko alone; it is the longest sequence in which a member of The Band appears without Robbie Robertson present. It is also the most extended sequence in this two-hour lamentation of "the road" in which someone is *moving*, is actually engaged in a physical journey, however miniature. This part of the film begins with Danko, in an echo of Mitchell's stage entrance, shot from the back as he walks through the halls of Shangri-La, The Band's studio and recreation complex in Los Angeles, giving Scorsese a tour. As docent to this tourist and his accompanying camera operator, Danko describes the individual rooms, and at first, we appear to be on our way into another Robertson-style tale of romance. "This used to be a bordello," he begins, apparently launching into another narrative akin to the ones told earlier in the film by Robertson, stories designed to cement The Band's fit with American myth. But in Danko's demeanor and disposition, that sort of narrative can't take hold. As we emerge into the facility's recording studio, his story about the building's past trails off, "You can't believe most of what you hear, but [inaudible]."

A struggle drives this scene. On the one hand, it seems designed, again, to affirm Robertson's argument by showing Danko as road-ravaged, a shell of the man who cowrote "This Wheel's on Fire" with Bob Dylan in a basement in pre-festival Woodstock. Danko isn't as articulate as Robertson, the segment seems meant to suggest. But there is a subversive eloquence to his inarticulateness in uttering, haltingly, with his back to us, "You can't believe most of what you hear, [mumble]," a statement whose form and content so deeply contrasts with Robertson's stories and discursive domination of the film. The bassist troubles that flow of chatter and continues to do so when Scorsese asks what he's going to do now that The Band has ceased to exist. Danko doesn't respond in words. Instead, sitting behind the mixing board, he cues up a recording of "Sip the Wine," a song from his forthcoming, eponymous, first foray into solo LPs, a song which, in its simple lyrics and bare-bones, repeated 1–4 chord pattern contrasts starkly with the formal complexity of a song like Mitchell's "Coyote." It's hard not to imagine that Scorsese and Robertson included Danko's song precisely because it sounds, in a manner sad and steeped in pathos, like a trashed, anemic version of a Band song. The camera focuses on Danko as he looks down at his lap, listening and, the implication seems to be, confronting the specter of having to learn how to live sitting still.

The salve to this scene may lie in the title track from *Hejira*, in which Mitchell counsels, "there's comfort in melancholy/when there's no need to explain," an observation made from a characteristically directionless, non-instrumental depiction of travel "in some vehicle." That is, what Danko needs at this moment is less talk, less badgering from the film's discursive authority, more succor drawn from the ways movement undermines explanation. He might also take some solace from "Refuge of the Road," with its imagery of "spring along the ditches," and "good times in the cities" circumventing the threat of a "thunderhead of judgment" she associates with "analyzing" and "her old ways."[11] In this fantasy, Mitchell proffers Danko something that he might not have been able to hear, but may have caught a glimpse of in Mitchell's hands—something that may well have served him better than Robertson's "thunderhead of judgment" that dictated the story of The Band, who broke up at some point right around the taping of the film's interview segments, a year after the final concert performance. She offers access to a road outside of judgment, to a search for lost chords that is, as we've seen, a search for something one can't identify in advance.

Robertson wants to sign off on The Band—he wants to leave his sole signature on The Band's songs and on its story. In the story his film *wants* to tell, Danko's song "Sip the Wine" sounds so sad and desiccated because it's the detritus left after Robertson's sundering of the group. But Mitchell's disruption won't let this happen, won't succumb. "You just picked up a hitcher/A prisoner of the white lines on the freeway": the song and the album from which it comes are deeply drawn to the road as an inescapable place, an inescapable way of being—rather than a simple form of escape. Despite their eminent talents, Robertson and Scorsese seem unable to free themselves of another prison: the entitled Americanness (in Robertson's case, adopted) of believing one always has access to freedom, that one can always get away, escape, de-attach. Danko, staring a hole in his lap or watching Mitchell's fingers, embodies the spirit of Mitchell, though their relationship seems a sadly missed encounter. And yet, what at first seemed a merely halting inarticulacy becomes a deep will to attachment, a far more inviting engagement than just another story of roadkill.

Notes

1 Mitchell wrote the song in a New York hotel room during the festival, having stayed in the city to avoid missing a scheduled appearance on *The Dick Cavett Show*.
2 *Message of Love: The Isle of Wight Festival*, DVD, directed by Murray Lerner. 1996. Sony Music Video, 1997. As if infected by the problems of the festival, Lerner's film did not find adequate financial backing for release until a quarter of a century after it was shot.
3 *The Last Waltz*, dir. Martin Scorsese (1978), MGM DVD 2006. As for the gaps, the story the group tells makes remarkably little mention of their relationship with Bob Dylan, such as their work on his legendary 1966 "going electric" tour or the bare-bones Woodstock collaborations that later became known as *The Basement Tapes*.

4 At the live concert, Mitchell sang three additional songs, all from *Hejira*. The Robertson quote is from his memoir *Testimony* (New York: Crown Archetype, 2016), 482.
5 Joni Mitchell, "The Rolling Thunder Revue—Montreal Forum December 4, 1975," https://www.youtube.com/watch?v=PgS-txfQbqQ (accessed: May 15, 2017).
6 Elvis Presley died ten months after the concert, so this interview marks the distance from which (at least some of) these segments were filmed, even though the film implies that they were filmed backstage or around the time of the performance.
7 Mitchell, "Hejira," *Hejira*.
8 Ron Rosenbaum, "The Best Joni Mitchell Song Ever," *Slate.com*. http://www.slate.com/articles/life/the_spectator/2007/12/the_best_joni_mitchell_song_ever.2.html (accessed: May 14, 2017).
9 Mitchell, "Coyote," *Hejira*.
10 Mitchell also sang backup on Neil Young's performance of "Helpless" from offstage; in the film, she is presented in silhouette, behind a scrim. At the concert, she performed two other songs of her own, "Furry Sings the Blues" and "Shadows and Light," and, alongside Young, sang backup on The Band's "Acadian Driftwood."
11 Mitchell, "Refuge of the Road," *Hejira*.

Works Cited

Danko, Rick. *Rick Danko*, 1977. Albany: One Way Records, 1997.

Gimme Shelter. Dir. Albert and David Maysles and Charlotte Zwerin, 20th Century Fox, 1970.

Helm, Levon with Stephen Davis. *This Wheel's on Fire: Levon Helm and the Story of The Band*. Chicago: A Cappella Books, 2000.

Kelly, Mary Pat. *Martin Scorsese: The First Decade*. Pleasantville, NY: Redgrave Publishing, 1980.

The Last Waltz. Dir. Martin Scorsese, 1978. MGM, 2006.

Marcus, Greil. *Bob Dylan by Greil Marcus, 1968–2010*. New York: PublicAffairs, 2010.

Marom, Malka. *Joni Mitchell: In Her Own Words—Conversations with Malka Marom*. Toronto: ECW Press, 2014.

Message to Love: The Isle of Wight Festival. Dir. Murray Lerner, 1996. Sony Music Video, 1997.

Mitchell, Joni. "The Rolling Thunder Revue—Montreal Forum December 4, 1975." https://www.youtube.com/watch?v=PgS-txfQbqQ (accessed: May 15, 2017).

Mitchell, Joni. Mitchell, Joni. *Hejira*. Hollywood: Asylum Records, 1976.

Robertson, Robbie. *Testimony*. New York: Crown Archetype, 2016.

Rosenbaum, Ron. "The Best Joni Mitchell Song Ever." *Slate.com*. http://www.slate.com/articles/life/the_spectator/2007/12/the_best_joni_mitchell_song_ever.2.html (accessed: May 14, 2017).

Shepard, Sam. *Rolling Thunder Logbook*. New York: Viking, 1977.

6

"Tar Baby and the Great White Wonder": Joni Mitchell's Pimp Game

Eric Lott

Tar baby and the Great White Wonder
Talking over a glass of rum
Burning on the inside
With the knowledge of things to come
There's gambling out on the terrace
And midnight ramblin' on the lawn
As they lead toward temptation
With dreamland coming on

—Joni Mitchell, "Dreamland," 1977

J. D. Souther tells the story of a day, in late 1977, at record producer Peter Asher's house. Souther was introduced by Asher and his wife Betsy to a thin black man with huge sunglasses and a big mustache. His name was Claude, and Souther concluded that he was a pimp. He was decked out in dark pants, white vest, and white jacket, his Afro tamed down by a fancy chapeau. Claude didn't say much as the group, which also included guitarist Danny Kortchmar, made small talk.

After a short while, as Sheila Weller recounts the episode in *Girls Like Us: Carole King, Joni Mitchell, Carly Simon—and the Journey of a Generation*, "Claude took off his hat. And then he took off his *wig*. Claude was *Joni*, in blackface. Souther and Joni had been lovers, but he hadn't recognized her under the costume. This was her new alter ego, a character she would imminently name 'Art Nouveau,' her 'inner black person.'" Mitchell has often repeated what she says will be the first line of her autobiography: "I was the only black man in the room" (Weller 2008, 424–425; Marom 2014).[1]

Mitchell pulled this stunt more than once. A candid snapshot by famed rock photographer Henry Diltz surfaced not long ago, showing Mitchell at bassist Leland Sklar's 1976 Halloween party in full Art Nouveau regalia. Sklar's annual party was a mainstay of the closely knit southern California musical star system, and it was curious, says Diltz, to see this unfamiliar face at the affair.

> Everyone thought it was someone whom someone else knew: "Is that guy your friend?" "I thought he came with you." I was taking a picture of my wife—we went as pirates—and this guy happened to be in the background.
>
> I can't remember how this person's true identity came to be known, but it wasn't until an hour or two into the party that we figured out he was Joni Mitchell—she dressed herself up that way to see if she could fool all her friends, and she did. She was a dear friend of everyone in that room, and no one got it. Joni was very into observing street life—pimps and hookers, and characters like that—so she could write about it. She was fascinated by that side of life. [. . .]
>
> Joni was proud she was able to pull this off. (Diltz 2010, 88)

Such cagey acts of everyday performance art are of interest not least for the way in which they produce an offense against intimacy, registered in Diltz's vaguely miffed tone: Mitchell was proud to pull this off, in the midst of friends and ex-lovers who should have known better. It's more important to ask what she was trying to prove. The pose is hardly unprecedented, and its appeal hasn't yet departed, as Daphne Brooks observes in her rousing critique of Amy Winehouse as a "retro-soul Jolson in a dress." Brooks proposes that Winehouse's "real innovation" is that she "created a record about a white woman wanting to be a black man—and an imaginary one at that" (2008, 36; see also Brooks 2010, 37–60). If Joni, as she did on so many other counts, got there long before, she also did it in a more corrosively sociological vein, evincing her inner pimp in her music and her everyday life to make sense of the scene in which she found herself, which as she knew meant the "star-maker machinery" of the 1970s southern California culture industry. Something of a (Saskatchewan) spy in the house of its pimps and pirates, she "observed" its rather different "street life" in a guise at once undercover and all too racially revealing—of it as much as of her. She was, after all, the only black man in the room.

As the 1970s began, Joni Mitchell was at the center of the Laurel Canyon singer-songwriter aristocracy, penning such countercultural anthems as "Both Sides, Now," "Big Yellow Taxi," "Woodstock," and "The Circle Game." She was the blond damsel with a dulcimer, crowded by other laureates of female autonomy such as Laura Nyro, Carole King, and Carly Simon, not to mention industry stalwarts such as David Crosby, Neil Young, Jackson Browne, and Graham Nash, but her early songs were quickly covered by other artists and her albums *Ladies of the Canyon* (1970) and *Blue* (1971) established her unusually liberated musical, lyrical, and political intelligence. Mitchell's following albums *For The Roses* (1972), *Court and Spark* (1974), *The Hissing of Summer Lawns* (1975), and *Hejira* (1976), if not indeed several subsequent records, constituted a period of sustained brilliance that, while certainly appreciated today, still has not gotten its full critical due. Always restless in her search for new sounds, even at the cost of her pop audience, Mitchell by the end of the decade had produced a concept album about jazz great Charles Mingus—the culmination of a gathering fascination across these years with African American culture and her relationship to it. The nadir (or maybe just the pivot) of this fascination came with Mitchell's appearance in blackface drag—as Art Nouveau, or Claude the pimp—on the cover of her 1977 album *Don Juan's Reckless Daughter*. Mitchell here doubles, even triples herself (she appears as a little girl in First Nations costume on the cover's back), an insistent mirroring she deployed again in the 1980 concert film *Shadows and Light*, where during a song about bluesman Furry Lewis the face of her Art Nouveau is superimposed over her own. The mirror becomes literal in a short film she did around this moment titled *The Black Cat in the Black Mouse Socks*, one of nine female-authored contributions commissioned by producer Barry Levinson for a cinematic compendium called *Love* (1980).[2] Dressing up as Art before the mirror, surrounded by manifold accoutrements of "blackness" (a hustler's manual, bling, a boombox playing Miles Davis), Mitchell attends a Halloween party and meets up with a former lover.

With a couple of notable exceptions, Mitchell's decade-long plunge into black culture has more or less mystified most commentators, despite the professed admiration for her work by artists including Prince, who recorded a fabulous cover of "A Case of You"; Q-Tip ("Joni Mitchell never lies," he intones on Janet Jackson's 1997 song "Got Til It's Gone," which samples Mitchell's "Big Yellow Taxi"); and Herbie Hancock, whose fine 2007 album *River: The Joni Letters*, featuring Mitchell compositions sung and played by a variety of performers, won two Grammy awards. Greg Tate long ago remarked upon Mitchell's "black" and even "hip-hop" sensibility and attitude, "not a parrot, a pirate, or a parody." Kevin Fellezs counts Mitchell a defining figure in a field of male musical influences on the formation of jazz-rock fusion. Miles Park Grier has undertaken the most sustained study of Mitchell's blackface drag and the way it afforded the artist a way out of the singer-songwriter pigeonhole and into the ranks of the male rock canon (Tate 1998; Fellezs 2011, 148–182; Grier 2012; see also Nelson 2007; Whitesell 2008; Yaffe 2017).

I am interested in the way Art Nouveau's black mirror gave Mitchell the unlikely but provocative critical leverage she needed on the presumptively white and male 1970s LA social and musical scene. Mitchell's employment of backing jazz musicians; race-driven songs like "The Jungle Line," "The Boho Dance," "Furry Sings the Blues," and "Dreamland"; Beat garb like the beret she sports on the cover of *Hejira*; romantic relationships with black men like percussionist Don Alias; and, ultimately, her collaboration with Mingus form a revealing chapter in 1970s pop life, not to mention the cultural history of Los Angeles. Operating in a notoriously racist and segregated LA cultural scene, at the height of the post-Watts-riot "urban crisis," and amid a climate of race-war fantasy and fact (most obviously in the mind of Charles Manson and in the Hell's Angels' murder of a black man at Altamont), Mitchell left the folkie retreat of Laurel Canyon and, as it were, came down into the streets in imaginary cross-racial identification (the streets were those of Bel Air, but hey). Working with Mingus, himself from Watts, and formerly a pimp to boot, Mitchell walked some way out of whiteness; but given that *Mingus* (1979) was her least satisfying album of the decade—Robert Christgau rightly called it a "brave" but failed experiment—here I mean to ask what cognitive gain comes with her mix of interest in, identification with, and appropriation of black sounds and styles (1981, 263). In a cultural domain known for its hideous racial entailments, Mitchell's valiant move certainly shows the limits of any merely individual attempt to undermine whiteness, but it curiously afforded a telling perspective on one ambitious woman artist's ascendancy, at a high pitch of second-wave feminism, in that weird new service industry to the American youth imaginary, commercial song.

Between 1963 and 1965, as Charlie Gillett long ago observed, the epicenter of US pop music shifted from New York to Los Angeles: where records made in New York stayed at No. 1 on the charts for twenty-six weeks (to LA's three) in 1963, by 1965 LA-made records had jumped to twenty weeks at No. 1 (to New York's one), and things stayed that way (Gillett 1983, 324–325). The political economy and social formation of Los Angeles are therefore key to understanding the consequences, and perhaps sources, of this westward drift. Eric Avila's *Popular Culture in the Age of White Flight* offers one notable account of the way in which the postwar LA dialectic of chocolate city and vanilla suburb (or canyon) came about. Hollywood, Disneyland (opened in 1955), Dodger Stadium (built in time for the 1962 season), and the Eisenhower-initiated state-sponsored freeway system helped push-pull suburban/inner-city racial and class formations into being; mid-century Los Angeles was self-consciously made into a white or white-dominated city. As in other US conurbations, housing in Los Angeles was concertedly racially redlined by a host of agencies and activities, not least among them the New Deal's Home Owners' Loan Corporation and Federal Housing Authority. Disney's choice of Orange County's Anaheim for the location of Disneyland certified the sanitized suburban ethos he meant to foster there. Dodger Stadium was set down atop a working-class Chicano neighborhood (Chavez Ravine) in an attempt by city fathers to "renew" the historic downtown area. Key to this entire cultural geography was the freeway, whose supplanting of an extensive, demographically diverse, public streetcar system cemented the new urban regime of privatized racially segmented living. (As California historian and activist Carey McWilliams put it in 1965, the "freeways have been carefully designed to skim over and skirt around such eyesores as Watts and East Lost Angeles; even the downtown section, a portion of which has become a shopping area for minorities, has been partially bypassed.") The figurehead for these developments, Avila observes, was Ronald Reagan, who aided the House Un-American Activities Committee in its quest for "subversive" influences in Hollywood, emceed the televised opening ceremonies at Disneyland, and appeared on live television to promote the building of Dodger Stadium. Reagan was, of course, governor of California from 1967 to 1975, precisely the years of Laurel Canyon musical hegemony (Avila 2006, 213).

The Watts uprising in 1965 made spectacular protest specifically against the racial dimensions of this urban regime. Southern in-migration, particularly during the Second World War, had radically recomposed the city's demographics and geography; while whites settled in such locales as the San Fernando Valley, African Americans swelled the ranks of South-Central Los Angeles, the LA black population actually doubling in the munitions boom-time of the war years. This gave rise, for one thing, to the sounds of LA's Central Avenue, with its crowds congregating in clubs like the Plantation, the Downbeat, and the Savoy. In his history of LA pop, *Waiting for the Sun*, Barney Hoskyns goes so far as to suggest we think of LA, not Memphis or Chicago or Detroit or New Orleans, as the defining American R&B town (Hoskyns 1996, 21). (Even Motown was to migrate there in 1971.) This scene was martially policed by an Los Angeles Police Department significantly shaped by white southern sensibilities; for this and other reasons, the LA black music scene had by 1965 been attenuated and supplanted by white pop reveling in one or another strain of endless-summer romanticism—this at a time when unemployment in Watts ran to a whopping 30 percent. In August, these tinderbox conditions ignited when a motorcycle cop's traffic stop escalated into insurrection, resulting in thirty-four deaths, thousands injured, more than that arrested, and $40 million in damage over six days of pitched battle. LA songwriter Randy Newman later remarked, "I always felt that the race situation was worse here than anywhere" (Hoskyns 1996, 107), while Thomas Pynchon wrote in a now-famous 1966 piece that Watts was a "country which lies, psychologically, uncounted miles further than most whites seem at present willing to travel," the so-called LA scene "a little unreal, a little less than substantial," "a white Scene" with illusion everywhere in it, the Sunset Strip itself a puny enclave of unfulfillment (Pynchon 1966, 4–5).

All of which is to say that mid-1960s Los Angeles became a racially segmented scene structured violently in dominance at the moment it emerged as *the* port of entry into the US pop mainstream. The signature event of the British Invasion, for example, may have been the Beatles' 1965 show at Shea Stadium, but their label (before they formed Apple) was Hollywood's Capitol Records. The British Invasion, I would argue, is best understood as the invasion of Los Angeles. From the defining conceptual contributions to Los Angeles of Reyner Banham, Christopher Isherwood and David Hockney, to the LA presence of the Beatles and the Stones—1965's "Satisfaction" was recorded in Los Angeles, not Swinging London—to the import of British pop sensibilities through teen shows like *Shindig* and *Where the Action Is*, UK minds and mentalities had very much to do with the West Coast's opening of "the doors of perception," as LA emigrant Aldous Huxley had it (Jim Morrison heard the call). The aforementioned Peter Asher, producer in the 1970s of such artists as James Taylor and Linda Ronstadt, had been the Peter of the British duo Peter and Gordon, known best for their 1964 hit "A World Without Love" (Asher's sister Jane had been Paul McCartney's girlfriend). The organizing of youth as a pop collective in the late 1960s, that is to say, was very much a matter of a certain style of California dreamin'. The Sunset Strip was itself undergoing a perhaps Watts-emulating series of upheavals. The fall 1966 disturbances later depicted in the B-movie *Riot on Sunset Strip* (1967) were the Strip's answer to police repression in Los Angeles. The scene was politicized not around race, however, but rather around youth leisure rights; in response to a business consortium's plan to replace Strip pop clubs with high-rises, youth revolted, with at least one massive march (featuring fixtures such as Peter Fonda, Dennis Hopper, and Sonny and Cher) and massive arrests. It is utterly symptomatic of this Strip scene that Stephen Stills' signature protest song of this moment, "For What It's Worth" ("Stop, hey, what's that sound / Everybody look what's goin' down"), is not about the Vietnam War, still less about injustices across town in Watts, but instead refers to the hassles on the Strip. The pop juggernaut fueled by revolting youth bore the decisive impress of LA white dominance.

In the wake of Watts, in other words, Laurel Canyon scarcely batted an eye. Buffalo Springfield; the Byrds; the Flying Burrito Brothers; Crosby, Stills, & Nash; Jackson Browne; Linda Ronstadt; The Eagles: amid the ashes, find me any real engagement with race in the United States of the 1970s. Even for Neil Young, racism took place in "Alabama," not, say, Malibu. (I mean no disrespect to Young's brilliant songs broaching US genocide and Native American extermination, among them "Cortez the Killer" and "Pocahontas.") A budding Laurel Canyon cultural historiography, including the books *Hotel California* by Barney Hoskyns and *Laurel Canyon* by Michael Walker, mimics and perpetuates this racial complacency (Hoskyns 2006, 233; Walker 2007).[3] When Joe Smith took over Elektra-Asylum Records from David Geffen in 1975, he worried that his blackest artist was Joni Mitchell—which is to say that alone of all the white LA crew, Mitchell was paying attention to race. Beginning with *For The Roses* (1972) and *Court and Spark* (1974), Mitchell used jazz musicians (albeit the fusiony bunch of Tom Scott's LA Express) for her backing band, and the inclusion of a cover of Lambert, Hendricks, and Ross's "Twisted" on *Court and Spark* marked the start of her own foray into jazz singing. By this time, she had partnered with jazz-identified drummer John Guerin, whose playing was key to the sound and shape of this music. But it is really with 1975's *The Hissing of Summer Lawns* that Mitchell ventured self-conscious explorations of racial difference, blackness, and her own privileged whiteness (this was apparently Prince's favorite Joni album). From the celebration of rock 'n' roll in "In France They Kiss on Main Street" to the dissing of suburban whiteness in the title track, "Shades of Scarlett [as in O'Hara] Conquering," and "Harry's House," there's a new turn in Mitchell's work toward both social dissection and musical genre jumping. "The Jungle Line," with its Burundi warrior drummers in the background, is a witty satire of white primitivism and exoticism—"safaris to the heart of all that jazz" by "those cannibals of shuck and jive"—including, I think, her own; not for nothing does the song depict a slumming Henri Rousseau, like Mitchell a painter, and another in a line of powerful men perfect for the singer's inveterate transvestism, as in the previous year's channeling of David Geffen in "Free Man in Paris."

The *ars poetica* of this strategy is "The Boho Dance," Mitchell's nod to Tom Wolfe. "Down in the cellar in the Boho zone / I went looking for some sweet inspiration, oh well / Just another hard-time band with Negro affectations," she sings. But she's way too smart to leave it at that: "I was a hopeful in rooms like this / When I was working cheap / It's an old romance—the Boho dance / It hasn't gone to sleep." Rich boho Joni with Negro affectations: she sure knows who she is. And yet there's self-congratulation here too in Mitchell's defiance toward bohemia, a certain self-satisfaction: Jesus may have been a "beggar, rich in grace," she sings, but Solomon—whom I take as Mitchell's figure for herself—"kept his head in all his glory." "It's just that some steps outside the Boho dance / Have a fascination for me." Conclusion? "Nothing is capsulized in me / On either side of town / The streets were never really mine / Not mine these glamour gowns." Joni is large, she contains multitudes, and she is forthright about the resulting contradictions.

Thus, on one hand, the ever-so-slightly self-parodic "Blue Motel Room" from the following year's *Hejira*, an amusing romantic moue sung like a road-weary blues mama crossed with Billie Holiday. On the other, the same record's "Furry Sings the Blues," as striking for Mitchell's sudden mimicry of bluesman Furry Lewis—during a visit, Lewis looks Mitchell in the eye and says "I don't like you"—as it is for its rather withering self-portrait of Joni in Memphis longing to channel the souls of Lewis and W. C. Handy: "W. C. Handy I'm rich and I'm fey / And I'm not familiar with what you played / But I get such strong impressions of your hey day / Looking up and down old Beale Street." And then this, as self-scathing as a Steely Dan tune: "Why should I expect that guy to give it to me true / Fallen to hard luck / And time and other thieves / While our limo is shining on his shanty street / Old Furry sings the blues." You've got to credit her honesty here, even if the cross-gender, cross-racial yearning is a trifle embarrassing. No question that Mitchell counts herself as one of the above "thieves." In other words, here blackface or at least blackvoice has become a not altogether negligible mode of racial self-awareness.

These moves are especially arresting given that *Hejira* was the record of an extended, meditational solo road trip Mitchell made in the wake of her short stint with Bob Dylan's Rolling Thunder Revue in 1975, the latter documented in Dylan's film *Renaldo and Clara* (1978). Rolling Thunder was a sort of vagabond carnival extravaganza with a constantly varying cast of performers including Joan Baez, Ronnie Hawkins, Ramblin' Jack Elliot, Sam Shepard, Allen Ginsberg, and many others; "Coyote," Mitchell's beautiful signature song of this period (the one she plays, for example, in Martin Scorsese's *The Last Waltz*), addresses with a sort of wistful buoyancy her affair with Shepard.[4] Mitchell had any number of such liaisons and kept right at her business, which often involved conjuring art out of them; that was part of the point, that was very much the persona and one of the reasons she was so compelling, that she sang (as the song "Help Me" summarized it) about loving her loving but loving her freedom even more, even if it often meant pain and isolation. This persona also occasioned a certain queenly rancor toward Joan Baez on the Rolling Thunder tour, alas, only one of the undermining forces besetting the tour's attempt to circumvent the star system by picking up artists in whatever locales it visited (including off the street). In any case, much of Rolling Thunder's importance to this period of Mitchell's work comes in the benefit concerts the Revue did for Rubin "Hurricane" Carter, the promising boxer convicted of murder who occasioned one of Dylan's most famous mid-70s songs, "Hurricane." Michael Denning has written of the benefit concert format as an artifact specifically of what he calls the post-1973 Great Recession, and the agitation and performing on Carter's behalf, including a show at Carter's Clinton State Prison itself, incubated a weird mix of activism, celebrity, and racial affect (Denning 2009, 28–41). Carter himself recounted one nasty episode in which Mitchell, after a poor reception at the prison, called him a "jive-ass nigger."[5] This post-countercultural address to the state's carceral apparatus thus both reveled in and foundered upon the white-Negro fantasies Mitchell had for some time been skewering in her music. It thickens the context for her subsequent exploration of such fantasies, as does the larger political-economic context of the Great Recession, a context to which I will return. Sexual freedom, female mobility, vested cross-racial interests, the lures and snares of male power: all would be condensed in the next turns of Mitchell's life and career.

It was at about this moment that Mitchell fell in love with Don Alias. Stanley Crouch could have been describing Mitchell's relationship with Alias in his novel *Don't the Moon Look Lonesome* (2000), in which a young, blond South Dakota (Mitchell hailed from Saskatoon, just to the north) jazz singer's relationship with a black jazz musician mixes crossover urgency with crossover's obvious limits. Mitchell and Alias, an Afro-Cuban music specialist who worked with everyone from Nina Simone to Miles Davis, had a deep but conflicted three-and-a-half-year relationship, and Alias thereafter remained close to her heart. His presence on *Don Juan's Reckless Daughter* helps give that record its distinctive, bristling sound, and he commanded the drum kit on the Shadows and Light tour. But Mitchell surely tested his mettle; the one-time premed student was alarmed, for example, to find Mitchell's nude portrait of him, complete with hard-on, suddenly hanging in the living room of their New York loft. She called it a "testament to his sexuality"; he called it "an embarrassment" (Weller 2008, 430). Alias insisted she repaint it, and she ultimately did, but Mitchell fought him every step of the way. This painterly investment in the black penis is of a piece with Mitchell's other racial and gender peregrinations, and it is the cover of *Reckless Daughter*, the music of this particular moment in her life, that sports Mitchell's Claude-the-pimp getup. The painting and the scuffle it occasioned are of interest for the race and gender reversals impacted there. The painting reverses the relations of looking by which hundreds of years of painted nudes have been structured; in assuming the male prerogative to look and to represent there is something of the self-portrait in it; its figuration celebrates but also appropriates, exoticizes as well as owns, recapitulating her fantasy of her own black maleness. Having a black man, for Mitchell, came satisfyingly close to being one.

The turn to the pimp guise, then, however bizarre it might seem, does bring all of Mitchell's 1970s concerns together, and more besides: the question of sexual dominance and its emotional fallout, the attractions of male power, particularly black male power, and the matter of money—who has it, who is in a position to dispense it, and what it will get you in a recessionary economy nonetheless governed in part by the pop power machine. When you contemplate Joni as pimp, you realize that in her work the dialectic or conflict between women's romantic susceptibility over against the desire for liberty and ambition, the pull of racial otherness and the street characters, including Rubin Carter, who seem to embody it, was all across the decade underwritten by a clear-eyed emphasis on cold hard cash. "He was playin' real good / For free," goes the self-deflating "For Free," way back in 1970, on the same record, *Ladies of the Canyon*, that features the myth-making "Woodstock" and the environmentalist whimsy of "Big Yellow Taxi." Mitchell was, from the start, able to offer withering critiques of her own willing place in the pop cash nexus. In so doing she offered up demystifying tales of what has been termed "countercultural capital." Michael Szalay and Sean McCann, in their introduction and conclusion to a 2005 volume of the *Yale Journal of Criticism* entitled *Countercultural Capital: Essays on the Sixties from Some Who Weren't*

There, assailed the magical thinking and "merely cultural" thrust of much of the post-Woodstock generation's artistic and critical production, its disregard of, for example, what McCann calls "presidential government" (and they take me to task for the same tendency, incorrectly I might add) (Szalay and McCann 2005; Lott 2005, 471–472; McCann 2008). Mitchell, I am arguing, always knew the "back to the garden" fantasy was precisely that. The song "Court and Spark," again, to take one of many examples, is structured in this fashion; though she falls in love with a deep soul who plays for "passing change" on the streets and in People's Park, she can't "let go of L.A. / City of the fallen angels." The very cover of *The Hissing of Summer Lawns* features Mitchell's painting of a long snake in the suburban garden, Mitchell as Tom Wolfe again, while inside the gatefold comes a double-album-sized photograph of Joni luxuriating in her backyard pool! And *Hissing*'s "Edith and the Kingpin" is a tale of pimp and stable outright, making clear not only that the political economy of sex (as Gayle Rubin called it the year the song was released) is an economy structured in gender and financial dominance but also, and crucially, that pimp and whore are locked in an ineluctable codependency. As in—or better, as a version of— Hegel's master/slave dialectic, both parties realize themselves each through the other, need each other to exist "for themselves," might at any moment upend the balance of power that holds them together: "Edith and the Kingpin / Each with charm to sway / Are staring eye to eye / They dare not look away / You know they dare not look away." Mitchell's perhaps characteristic response: Why not be both? (Rubin 1975; Hegel 1977, 111–119).[6]

A little backstory here. As David Yaffe has shown, a jazz-lore lineage of the pimp/whore dialectic extends back through such texts as Ralph Ellison's *Invisible Man* (1952), Billie Holiday and William Dufty's *Lady Sings the Blues* (1956), and most importantly for Mitchell, Charles Mingus's *Beneath the Underdog* (1971) (Yaffe 2005). An LA-centric pulp pimp heir to such representations suddenly erupted in the late 1960s. Justin Gifford documents how the Los Angeles pulp publisher Holloway House almost single-handedly made available vivid, visceral stories of the pimp game in dozens of books by such writers as Iceberg Slim, Donald Goines, and many others (Gifford 2013; see also Coleman 2003, 68–80). By the early 1970s, Blaxploitation film had emerged to throw such stories up on the big screen. Joni Mitchell seems to have keyed into the persona's usefulness in commenting on what Jean-Paul Sartre might have called her "situation" in the culture industry of her moment (Sartre 1965). Transmogrifying the pimp figure's South-to-North migration and defiant self-making into her own passage from Saskatoon to Los Angeles via Toronto and then Detroit—Joan Anderson became Joni Mitchell through her Detroit marriage to Chuck Mitchell, and Joni, perhaps tellingly, experienced firsthand Detroit's late-1960s "urban crisis" (though not the summer of '67's Great Rebellion, by which time she had made her way to Greenwich Village)—Mitchell absorbed the pimp's stance and saw the logic of what Gifford calls a "pimp poetics." To wit, the pimp of Iceberg Slim's 1967 autobiography, Gifford argues, is a figure who adapts structures of white power and economic exploitation in order to achieve a radically individualized form of liberty: "Slim," an associate tells him, "a pimp is really a whore who's reversed the game on whores [. . .] a good pimp is like a slick white boss" (2013, 67). Which leads to the conclusion that pimping is not a sex game but rather a "skull game," all about ice-cold attitude and pile after pile of cash money (Gifford 2013, 68). Floated by second-wave feminism but never feminist-identified, Mitchell bought into the radically individualized perspective of all this—a perspective purchased through the "star-maker machinery" she was tough-minded enough to analyze so clearly because of her self-understanding as whore become pimp. If, as various critics have perceived, pimps and pimp writers both are service workers bound up in culture-industry protocols, Mitchell, I would argue, alludes in precisely this way to her own artistic practice. In this light, the great song "Free Man in Paris" comes to seem an act of pimp David Geffen being turned out by his friend, mack daddy Joni. Limning the pressures of the "star-maker machinery" on one of its own biggest operators, *she* hustles *him*, punks him into a character in a tune that *reads* him and that, not incidentally, made them both a lot of money. It's as though the best you could do in this crazy new exploding industry as a female artistic sole proprietor was aspire to hustle yourself, be your own pimp—that was Mitchell's implicit, and then explicit, claim.

Charles Mingus certainly understood himself this way in the political economy of jazz, as he makes elaborately, outrageously evident in his 1971 autobiography *Beneath the Underdog*, a bulging, sprawling, brilliant mixture of self-psychoanalysis, sex manual, pimp narrative, and modernist character study that depicts Mingus, in whatever domain he chooses, always struggling to get a leg up, and over (Mingus 1971). One of the great minds in jazz history, at once composer, arranger, bandleader, and bassist, Mingus called Mitchell out of the blue in the fall of 1978 with six new tunes he wanted Mitchell to write lyrics for. If Mitchell had dreamed that someday her pimp would come, this was it: Mitchell immediately devoured Mingus's autobiography and agreed to meet with him. The result was *Mingus* (1979), released shortly after Mingus's death at 56 from Lou Gehrig's disease.[7] In the album's liner notes Mitchell writes about the experience: "It was as if I had been standing by a river—one toe in the water—feeling it out—and Charlie came by and pushed me in—"sink or swim"—him laughing at me dog paddling around in the currents of black classical music." The river is no longer frozen like the one Mitchell wished to skate away on in her famous 1971 song "River"; and pimped out or herself doing the pimping, little dog Joni swims in jazz, appropriating Mingus's voice and persona in songs such as "A Chair in the Sky," which riffs on Mingus's confinement to a wheelchair in the last months of his life. Mitchell here becomes one of what the song nicely terms "mutts of the planet"—an achievement that does not, however, preclude, and may even precipitate, some of the worst writing of her career to that point (it was to get much worse). The biggest payoff of black drag king Joni may be the discordant, angry guitar work on *Mingus*. But songs like "Sweet Sucker Dance" have an embarrassing tendency to claim ownership over Mingus's heart: "We're dancing fools / You and me / Tonight it's a dance of insecurity / It's my solo / While you're away / And shadows have the saddest things to say." And while Mitchell becomes white once more in her lyrics to Mingus's "Goodbye Pork Pie Hat," the slack, "Strange Fruit"-style lyrics meld Mingus and Alias into a single, iconic figure, and produce precisely the exoticism she lampooned just a few years earlier: "So the sidewalk leads us with music / To two little dancers / Dancing outside a black bar / There's a sign up on the awning / It says "Pork Pie Hat Bar" / And there's black babies dancing . . . / Tonight!" This cul-de-sac of cross-racial identification played out equivocally in the Shadows and Light Tour that followed it, buttressed as it was by an almost entirely white host of backing jazz musicians, among them Mitchell veterans Alias and Jaco Pastorius as well as newbies Michael Brecker, Pat Metheny, and Lyle Mays.

If *Mingus* plays somewhat like a struggle for pimp supremacy, it also, like the whole pimp fantasy for Mitchell, gives new meaning to her idea of "Both Sides, Now," as Alexander Corey has suggested—Mitchell's oft-covered late-1960s song about love's and life's illusions. Traversing gender, racial, and class binaries, looking at them from both sides of the street, cruising between them as it were, Mitchell hits on the difference, or is it the sameness, of "being" and "having" the phallus, as Jacques Lacan's writings elaborate it (Lacan 1977; see also Grosz 1990). White woman and black man are twinned in the US racial imaginary as threats to white masculinity—it's why their coupling is taboo, and possibly why Mitchell wants to inhabit them both. The phallic investments of Mingus's autobiography might also have titillated her into this stance. As Corey puts it,

> when Joni Mitchell dresses up as the embodied possessor of the black penis, she is also drawing on her feminine ability to "be the phallus," which is her ability to turn the bodily allusion to the phallic symbol into the illusion of the phallus itself. It is a moment at which she triangulates a danger to white masculinity through simultaneous invocation of dangerous white feminine sexuality and a threatening black masculinity—a moment which may not have been fully realized, but maybe [sic] a kind of opening or unanimated potentiality that resists the racial and sexual power structures that continued to govern American culture, albeit in a constantly shifting way. Castrating the white male comes from both sides; the white woman like Mitchell and the black man like, say, Eldridge Cleaver and Amiri Baraka. (Personal correspondence)

Blackface drag is perfect for taking down or just surmounting white masculinist domination from "both sides now," a fraught way of negotiating the 1970s sex/gender system at the intersection of second-wave feminism and Black Power—a way, as Miles Grier writes, to criticize sexism as if it were racism against black men.[8]

California pimpin' in the Great Recession: in the words of Walter Sobchak (the John Goodman character in *The Big Lebowski*, another recessionary LA story), "at least it's an ethos." Walter's comic preference for Nazis over nihilists might seem uncomfortably analogous to Joni Mitchell's late 1970s moves. However outré and racially problematic, they at least offered a figural meditation on an artistic political predicament that she understood as such. Consider the alternative, which I'm sure she did. Succeeding Ronald Reagan in the California governor's seat was Jerry Brown, who famously cozied up to the Laurel Canyon firmament—figuratively in the case of artists like Jackson Browne and The Eagles, who did a benefit show in 1979 to raise funds for Brown's 1980 presidential run, and quite literally in the case of Linda Ronstadt, who for a time became his girlfriend. Compromised politics met compromised music in a small-s state imaginary that The Eagles' *Hotel California* all-too-easefully assailed: they did indeed check out anytime they liked, and sure enough they never did leave. Brown addressed recessionary times with a fiscal austerity that was widely seen as to the right of anything Reagan had overseen, and the musicians mostly did a lot of blow, shilling for it all and soundtracking a late-1970s malaise. It was, in a way, a local version of what Michael Szalay examines in his study of the post-Second World War American novel, *Hip Figures*, which argues that the figure of the hipster, imagined above all in Norman Mailer's "The White Negro," was key to the postwar formation of the Democratic Party, clinched in the figure of "hipster president" John F. Kennedy but compelling in various guises beyond his life and example (Szalay 2012). To be "in," as Mailer had it, was to be in tune with the forces of history, out of office or in. It was no doubt difficult to dissent from this vibe in the late-1970s California pop-political landscape, so it was not nothing in this context for Joni Mitchell to ask, essentially, and with respect to race and the cash nexus, who's zoomin' who? Especially at a moment when the Bakke decision threatened to reverse significant aspects of affirmative action, and when the anti-tax revolt of Proposition 13 began to lay the groundwork for a national version of such revanchism. As Mike Davis argued in *Prisoners of the American Dream*, the groundwork for the Reagan 1980s was pioneered in California (Davis 1986, 157–180). Black drag-kinging the pimp gave Joni Mitchell purchase on several contexts and conundrums at once, and in a state whose politics would come to define the federal apparatus across the decades to come. It wasn't pretty, and it's hardly defensible, but as she put it in the song "Shadows and Light": "Every picture has its shadows / And it has some source of light / Blindness, blindness and sight."

Coda: for the roses

Edwardsville, Illinois, summer 1979, the Shadows and Light Tour: my friend Tom Byrne and I snuck backstage after seeing the show, filing in behind VIPs strolling into a little hut behind the outdoor festival stage. I was twenty and utterly starstruck. We were suddenly in the intimate presence of the band, several musicians including Jaco Pastorius and Michael Brecker gathered around an upright piano, Joni sitting regally in a wicker chair. She had gotten that late-1970s perm, blond kink, black and blond as Greg Tate has it. She greeted us warmly and casually and in doing so left us tongue-tied. Courteous and almost courtly, she asked us about ourselves, and when she found out that I play drums she called Don Alias over and introduced us: tongue-tied again. She recounted her enjoyment of her recent musical moves, particularly playing with Pastorius, and way too soon people started to split. Joni spontaneously offered us the good-luck flowers that had been sent over by the record company—I still have the note that came with them. It reminded me of her acid irony about the business in "For the Roses"—"And now you're seen / On giant screens / And at parties for the press / And for people who have slices of you / From the company." And then I was struck by the way, as she did with her music, Joni had turned a company man's obligation into a gift.

Notes

1 The origins of this getup are told in, among other sources, O'Brien (2002); another set of Mitchell tellings occurs in Swanson (2015), 88–94.
2 Joni Mitchell's official website. http://jonimitchell.com/library/video.cfm?id=412 (accessed: June 3, 2018).
3 Joe Smith remark in Hoskyns at 233.
4 Shepard's take can be found in *The Rolling Thunder Logbook* (2004, 117); more generally, see Kutulas (2010).
5 Rubin Carter documentary; the quote appears as well, in Mitchell's own telling, in Bego (2005, 145).
6 Tina Turner's version of "Edith" on Herbie Hancock's *River: The Joni Letters* strikes me as perhaps the definitive one, sung by one who was forced to know, and then left, the life.

7 Joni Mitchell, *Mingus* (Hollywood: Asylum Records, 1979); Santoro (2000, 374–376, 381–384); Bego (2005, 167–179); Monk (2012, 27–34).
8 I am indebted for these formulations to Alex Corey's illuminating, extended written responses to an earlier version of this work, personal communication on July 29, 2011; Grier (2012); Halberstam (1998, 231–66). Subject for further study: Joni Mitchell exploring ideas contemporaneous with and closely adjacent to Irigaray (1985).

Works Cited

Avila, Eric. *Popular Culture in the Age of White Flight: Fear and Fantasy in Suburban Los Angeles*. Berkeley and Los Angeles: University of California Press, 2006; McWilliams quoted at 213.

Bego, Mark. *Joni Mitchell*. Lanham, MD: Taylor, 2005, 145.

Brooks, Daphne A. "Tainted Love," *Nation*, September 29, 2008.

Brooks, Daphne A. "'This Voice Which Is Not One': Amy Winehouse Sings the Ballad of Sonic Blue(s)Face Culture," *Women and Performance*, 20.1 (2010): 37–60.

Christgau, Robert. *Rock Albums of the 70s: A Critical Guide*. Boston: Da Capo, 1981.

Coleman, Beth. "Pimp Notes on Autonomy," in *Everything but the Burden: What White People Are Taking from Black Culture*, ed. Greg Tate. New York: Broadway, 2003, 68–80.

Crouch, Stanley. *Don't the Moon Look Lonesome: A Novel in Blues and Swing*. New York: Vintage, 2000.

Davis, Mike. *Prisoners of the American Dream: Politics and Economy in the History of the U.S. Working Class*. London: Verso, 1986.

Denning, Michael. "Bob Dylan and Rolling Thunder," in *The Cambridge Companion to Bob Dylan*, ed. Kevin J. H. Dettmar. Cambridge: Cambridge University Press, 2009, 28–41.

Diltz, Henry. "Black Like . . . Joni Mitchell," *Spin* (October 2010): 88.

Fellezs, Kevin. *Birds of Fire: Jazz, Rock, Funk, and the Creation of Fusion*. Durham, NC: Duke University Press, 2011.

Gifford, Justin *Pimping Fictions: African American Crime Literature and the Untold Story of Black Pulp Publishing*. Philadelphia: Temple University Press, 2013.

Gillett, Charlie. *The Sound of the City: The Rise of Rock and Roll*, New York: Pantheon, 1983, 324–325.

Grier, Miles Park. "The Only Black Man at the Party: Joni Mitchell Enters the Rock Canon," *Genders*, Online 56 (2012). http://jonimitchell.com/library/view.cfm?id=2532 (accessed: August 1, 2018).

Grosz, Elizabeth. *Jacques Lacan: A Feminist Introduction*. New York: Routledge, 1990.

Halberstam, Judith. *Female Masculinity*. Durham, NC: Duke University Press, 1998.

Hegel, G. W. F. *Phenomenology of Spirit*. Trans. A. V. Miller (1807). Oxford: Oxford University Press, 1977.

Hoskyns, Barney. *Hotel California*. Hoboken, NJ: John Wiley, 2006.

Hoskyns, Barney. *Waiting for the Sun: Strange Days, Weird Scenes, and the Sound of Los Angeles*. New York: St. Martin's Press, 1996.

Irigaray, Luce. *This Sex Which Is Not One*. Ithaca, NY: Cornell University Press, 1985.

Kutulas, Judy. " 'That's the Way I've Always Heard It Should Be': Baby Boomers, 1970s Singer-Songwriters, and Romantic Relationships," *Journal of American History*, 97.3 (2010): 682–702.

Lacan, Jacques. *Ecrits: A Selection*. Trans. Alan Sheridan. New York: Norton, 1977.

Lott, Eric. "Chants Demagogic," *Yale Journal of Criticism*, 18.2 (2005): 471–472.

McCann, Sean. *A Pinnacle of Feeling: American Literature and Presidential Government*. Princeton, NJ: Princeton University Press, 2008.

Marom, Malka. *Joni Mitchell: In Her Own Words—Conversations with Malka Marom*. Toronto: ECW, 2014.

Mingus, Charles. *Beneath the Underdog: His World as Composed by Mingus*. Ed. Nel King. New York: Vintage, 1971.

Mitchell, Joni. *The Hissing of Summer Lawns*. Hollywood: Asylum Records, 1975.

Mitchell, Joni. *Don Juan's Reckless Daughter*. Hollywood: Asylum Records, 1977.

Mitchell, Joni. *Mingus*. Hollywood: Asylum Records, 1979.

Monk, Katherine. *Joni: The Creative Odyssey of Joni Mitchell*. Vancouver, BC: Greystone, 2012.

Nelson, Sean. *Court and Spark (33 1/3)*. New York: Continuum, 2007.

O'Brien, Karen. *Shadows and Light: Joni Mitchell, the Definitive Biography*. London: Virgin, 2002.

Pynchon, Thomas. "A Journey into the Mind of Watts," *New York Times Magazine* (June 12, 1966): 4–5.

Renaldo and Clara. Dir. Bob Dylan. Circuit Films, 1968.

Riot on Sunset Strip. Dir. Arthur Dreifuss. American International Pictures, 1967.

Rubin, Gayle. "The Traffic in Women: Notes on the 'Political Economy' of Sex," in *Toward an Anthropology of Women*, ed. Rayna R. Reiter. New York: Monthly Review Press, 1975, 157–210.

Santoro, Gene. *Myself When I Am Real: The Life and Music of Charles Mingus*. New York: Oxford University Press, 2000.

Sartre, Jean-Paul. *Situations*. Trans. Benita Eisler. New York: George Braziller, 1965.

Swanson, Carl. "Joni Mitchell, Unyielding," *New York Magazine* (February 9–22, 2015): 88–94.

Szalay, Michael. *Hip Figures: A Literary History of the Democratic Party*. Stanford, CA: Stanford University Press, 2012.

Szalay, Michael, and Sean McCann, eds., *Countercultural Capital: Essays on the Sixties from Some Who Weren't There*, Yale Journal of Criticism, 18.2 (2005).

Tate, Greg. "Black and Blond," *Vibe* (December 1998).

The Rolling Thunder Logbook. New York: Da Capo, 2004, 117.

Walker, Michael. *Laurel Canyon: The Inside Story of Rock-and-Roll's Legendary Neighborhood*. New York: Farrar, Straus and Giroux, 2007.

Weller, Sheila. *Girls Like Us: Carole King, Joni Mitchell, Carly Simon—and the Journey of a Generation*. New York: Atria, 2008.

Whitesell, Lloyd. *The Music of Joni Mitchell*. New York: Oxford University Press, 2008.

Yaffe, David. *Fascinating Rhythm: Reading Jazz in American Writing*. Princeton, NJ: Princeton University Press, 2005.

Yaffe, David. *Reckless Daughter: A Portrait of Joni Mitchell*. New York: Farrar, Straus and Giroux, 2017.

7

Tangled up in *Blue*: The Shadow of Dylan and Stylistic Swerves in Early-Seventies Joni Mitchell

Howard Wilde

It has become a cliché of rock journalism to label Joni Mitchell a "female Dylan," something she has quite understandably resisted. In an interview with Morrissey in 1996, she noted that "They tend to lump me always with groups of women. I always thought: "they don't put Dylan with the Men of Rock; why do they do that to me with women?"[1] Not only does Mitchell echo Morrissey's complaint about the phrase "female singer-songwriter" as a marked form, but she instinctively uses Dylan as her go-to example.[2] In a lively polemic from 2012, Katherine Monk labels Dylan "the male Joni Mitchell," a counterblast against the patriarchy that underpins the construction of the rock canon (2012, 149).[3] However, Mitchell's relationship with Dylan's work has always been double-edged: though the pair toured together and occasionally covered each other's songs, Mitchell later described herself as "almost anti-Dylan," and in a famous 2010 interview, suggested that Dylan's songs were "not authentic" and "not written honestly."[4]

This chapter seeks to explore Dylan and Mitchell's influences on each other, as well as Mitchell's stylistic influences on the next generation of songwriters, in a field characterized by male hegemony. I will try to avoid the traditional pitfalls of assessing Mitchell's work *against* Dylan's, as though his songwriting language were a definitive template by which hers should be judged. Likewise, I will not be aiming to produce a list of "echoes" between Dylan's work and Mitchell's, although of course there are many intertextual connections for those willing to search for them. Nor do I want to erase Dylan from a critical evaluation of Mitchell's songwriting influences. Instead, I want to propose the idea of Mitchell as "anti-Dylan": an equal and opposite aesthetic pole of influence.

The canonization of Dylan is an inescapable fact of history. He has been scrutinized by rock critics, thrust into the critical limelight whether he liked it or not, politicized as a "spokesman of his generation," compared favorably with Shakespeare, analyzed hagiographically by scholars like Wilfred Mellers, and projected as a successor to the English Romantics (Mellers 1984; Ricks 2003).[5] Rightly or wrongly, he has come to stand metonymically for the very idea of songwriter as auteur, while Mitchell's work has been consigned to his penumbra. Even the most careful scholarly considerations of the Mitchell–Dylan relationship have tended to be slightly apologetic. Mitchell's work is more harmonically complex, arguably broader in its literary references, every bit as novel in its musical forms, and more wide-ranging in its range of musical influences. Yet so many commentators, including a sample I will critique later in this chapter, insist on "validating" Mitchell's work in the context of Dylan's, as though the mere comparison were the greatest compliment they could bestow. This critical imbalance can legitimately be critiqued along gendered lines, not least because the corpus of rock journalism is so overwhelmingly male-dominated.

In this chapter, I will aim to redress this balance by identifying some of the defining aesthetic criteria by which critics have traditionally validated Dylan's work, and suggesting an alternative, largely antithetical, set of criteria which apply to Mitchell. I will not be attempting a sociological critique of rock journalism and its attendant biases: there are already plenty of excellent critiques in the musicological literature (e.g., Leonard 2007; Hopper 2015). Instead, I will propose a binary division between Dylan and Mitchell's songwriting styles based on close readings of selected songs. I will propose that Dylan's work is essentially *sermonic*: his songs can be apocalyptic, vatic, oblique, accusatory or confessional, and their narrative complexity (his main claim to auteur status) is offset by harmonic simplicity. Mitchell's work, by contrast, is often conversational, intimate, questioning, uncertain; her complex narratives are often enriched by some equally complex and ambiguous harmonies, influenced by jazz, classic-romantic music, painting, and high modernism. Instead of "validating" Mitchell's work by occasional "nods to Bob," I will suggest that she achieved a decisive stylistic swerve on the album *Blue*, which in turn exerted a recursive influence on Dylan's output, as well as providing a blueprint for a new generation of songwriters.

Canonization and influence as anxiety

In considering the ambivalent relationship, both personal and aesthetic, between Mitchell and Dylan, it is worth considering two theoretical topics that are broadly intertwined, and generally more developed in literary criticism than in pop-rock musicology: first, theories of the canon; and second, theories of influence. Both are ideologically problematic and politically polarized, and although much of the debate will be outside the scope of this chapter, a number of key concepts might be useful. Central to these ideas are the writings of Harold Bloom, a figure who has divided critics with his unfashionable defense of the "high art" canon, his use of the terms "strong" and "weak" poets, and his bold use of the word "authenticity" without the layers of anxious irony that accompany that word in twenty-first-century literary and musicological circles.[6] More controversial still is his contempt for what he has termed the "school of resentment" (postcolonial theory, feminism, black literature) (Bloom 1995, 4). In particular, Bloom is notoriously dismissive of the idea that popular songwriting might be poetry, let alone "great" or canonical poetry. In an appendix, Bloom updated his canonical list of twentieth and twenty-first-century poets to include John Ashbery, Geoffrey Hill, Elizabeth Bishop, Marianne Moore, and others (1995, Appendices A–D). Although it is not an especially sexist list, it is notable for its exclusion of musicians, or indeed anything "populist": Dylan, Cohen, Mitchell, and others are notably absent. This position echoes the "high art" purism of the Marxist critic Theodor Adorno, who regarded the "serious" protest songs of the sixties (by Joan Baez and others) as fatally tainted by commodification and banality.[7] Slam poetry, said Bloom, was "the death of art" (in Somers-Willett 2009, 21).

Other poetry scholars, however, have been passionate advocates for the canonization of Dylan in particular. Christopher Ricks's ambitious *Dylan's*

Visions of Sin aims to locate Dylan's body of work within the tradition of nineteenth-century Romanticism, offering cross-readings between Dylan songs and poems by John Keats and Alfred Tennyson.[8] This has the effect of reinforcing Dylan's canonical status by removing him from his immediate milieu, and giving him the aura of the misunderstood outsider: "the poet and the painter, far *behind* his rattled time" (as Dylan himself put it).[9] In this text-centered critical approach to Dylan, we are invited to "read" his "work" (both words are loaded) outside the traditions of rock and roll, beat poetry, the Never Ending Tour, the blues, and all the messy, rhizomatic, multicultural cross-threads that make Dylan's songwriting what it is.[10] If this approach elevates one aspect of Dylan's writing at the expense of others (the textual over the performative), it seems even more problematic when dealing with the melodic and harmonic complexities of an artist like Mitchell.

Dylan himself has always been ambivalent about his canonization by the critics. In fact, critic-mockery has been a common theme of his writings, interviews, and songs. It is probably fair to say that he has written as many songs about his critical reception as about war and politics (the two topics often ascribed to him by lazy critics): "Ballad of a Thin Man" (1965) satirizes an earnest Bob-worshipping journalist; "It Ain't Me, Babe" (1964) is often delivered in a finger-pointing philippic against his adoring audiences; "Maggie's Farm" (1965) captures the anger of a folksinger dragged unwillingly on to a canonical pedestal: "They say 'Sing while you slave' and I just get bored." Later, however, in the *Chronicles*, Dylan is at pains to rebrand himself a folksinger once more, casting a snide barb in the direction of the melancholic poet Archibald MacLeish (Dylan 2004, 141). He also suggested that he had deliberately released light country songs on *Nashville Skyline* (1969) to put critics off the scent. So, Dylan's entire career has been infused with a kind of meta-critical jouissance, flirting with canonical immortality but never quite letting the critics have the upper hand.

While the idea of a canon is still common currency in journalistic circles (now more than ever, in the age of top-hundred lists and clickbait), it has been largely discredited in the musicological literature.[11] Marcia Citron's deconstruction of patriarchal narratives in the (classical) musical canon was followed by Cerys Wyn Jones's feminist critique of the rock canon, and a study by Ralf von Appen and André Doehring, which hinted that the idea of a rock canon was a preserve of middle-aged white men, subconsciously asserting their own hegemony (Citron 2000; von Appen and Doehring 2006; Jones 2008). Indeed, von Appen and Doehring's meta-canonic list (compiled from dozens of journalistic top-hundred lists), is striking for its exclusion of female, LGBTQ, and nonwhite artists. This bias has been reflected every year in my undergraduate classes; when students have been asked to list the ten "most influential albums" released since 1960, fewer than 5 percent of their nominations feature a female artist, let alone a female songwriter.[12] The annual (and now painfully predictable) omission of Joni Mitchell seems significant, given her vast critical acclaim and the diverse ambit of her influence. Why is Joni Mitchell's work so little-known, and so under-appreciated, among popular music students? (Dylan's name features in their lists, although they often admit to unfamiliarity with his work.)

Of course, my questionnaire uses loaded questions: Why, for instance, do we tend to privilege albums over singles? Why, almost 30 years after Christopher Small's radical book *Musicking: The Meanings of Performing and Listening*, do we still try to reify the rock album as an artefact?[13] And what is it to be "influential"? To this end, I want to invoke Bloom's most celebrated idea: the idea of influence as *anxiety*. Poets, argues Bloom, invoke other poets, and cannot become poets without first having been inspired by other poets. In an ironic echo of the leftist intertextual criticism largely despised by Bloom, poems (for him) achieve their meaning only in relation to other poems. As we have already seen, Bloom has shown no interest in extending his theory to popular music, but the idea of influence as anxiety might be helpful in explaining changes of style, especially in key albums like Joni Mitchell's *Blue*: a radical departure from the Dylanesque norm of folk rock at a critical historical juncture. In particular, Bloom's theory of influence invokes the idea of the "swerve": a break with tradition that comes from the anxiety of sounding too much like one's precursor.[14]

In fact, it might be fair to say that, of the interesting singer-songwriters to emerge around the revolutionary year 1968, no one really sounds *less* like Dylan than Joni Mitchell. Unlike him, she did not extensively borrow the twelve-bar blues form; she did not learn traditional guitar tunings by default but reinvented tunings according to her own caprice; she was largely an autodidact when it came to piano and guitar technique (like her fellow Canadian, Leonard Cohen); she was a poet and painter before she was a folk singer; she might have adopted the folk-rock idioms of the time for *Clouds* but certainly did not style herself as a folk troubadour in the mold of Baez; she distanced herself from certain political movements and causes, preferring environmentalism to radical feminism, and so on. Her status as a Canadian woman might also have lent her the aura of an outsider, perhaps making it easier, rather than more difficult, to escape the oppressive shadow of Dylan and the inevitable comparisons. In Bloom's model, the act of "swerving" often takes the form of invoking an earlier, or "other" style in order to escape the burden of the immediate past: thus Stravinsky would invoke Machaut, Gesualdo and jazz as a way of wriggling free from Russian Romanticism; the Second Viennese School would evoke Bach not as a kind of sentimental archaism but as a means of renewing the musical lexis after two generations of Austro-German Romantic tradition.[15] So it is tempting to read Mitchell's excursions into jazz (on *Hejira*) and progressive tonality (on *Blue*) as "swerves," conscious or otherwise, from a hegemonic tradition: in this case, that of the three-chord folk song as exemplified by, say, Joan Baez's covers of Dylan.

Inevitably, critical reviews of Mitchell's work in the seventies would invoke Dylan. When they did, however, it was not as a stick with which to beat Mitchell, but more often a way of sneering at His Bobness, knocking him off the pedestal they had constructed. After all, by the seventies he was all but buried by the critics: they were already searching for a new Bob Dylan, and the lackluster *Self Portrait*, released the year before *Blue*, was widely regarded as the end of Dylan's influential phase, and the beginning of a period of mediocrity. David Bowie's "Song for Dylan" (1971) and Wainwright's later "Talking New Bob Dylan" (1991) both hint at the anxiety of the songwriter in a post-Dylan era. The tone of this review of *The Hissing of Summer Lawns*, by Stephen Holden for *Rolling Stone* in 1976, is not untypical:

> [Mitchell] has amassed the most impressive body of work of any post-Dylan singer-songwriter, elaborating the free-form narrative ballad form that Dylan thrust into popular song, and polishing a melismatic melodic line more flexible than Dylan's and many times more sophisticated.[16]

Better Than Dylan, then, but only to be read and appreciated through the prism of Dylan, and only better in respect of her vocal embellishments, not necessarily her imagery or narratives. It is also debatable whether Mitchell's songs are really reducible to "narrative ballads," at least in the folk sense of that term, with all the moralizing and storytelling that we find in Dylan.

More recently, in his encyclopedic study of Mitchell's work, Lloyd Whitesell devotes a section to the influence of Dylan (his excellent musical analyses propose a typography of her song forms, again tellingly using Dylan songs as a template). However, Mitchell herself refers very sparingly to Dylan songs when discussing her influences. One exception occurs in the following interview, cited more elaborately by Whitesell: "When I heard "Positively Fourth Street," I realized that this was a whole new ballgame: now you could make your songs literature" (2008, 77). In a later remark about the same song, she praised the "direct, confronting speech, commingled with imagery." This remark, for Whitesell, constitutes a "galvanic spark" originating from her "first encounter with the seminal Dylan song." He calls this moment "an early conversion experience":

> We know from Mitchell's subsequent career that this early conversion experience did not cancel out her love of rock 'n' roll. The Dylanesque model of serious poetic ambition merely took its place alongside the Little Richard model, in an expanded understanding of what words in pop songs can accomplish. (Whitesell 2008, 77)

This account is not without its problems, though. For one thing, it assumes a dichotomy between the "high art" ambitions of Dylan as auteur and the populist aesthetic of Little Richard; yet Little Richard was an enormous early influence on Dylan, too.[17] Many of Dylan's songs, not just the simple Elvis pastiches on *Nashville Skyline* or *The Basement Tapes*, draw on rock 'n' roll to a much greater extent than any Mitchell song; the country blues is a staple of Dylan's songwriting, from "Highway 51" to "Thunder on the Mountain" and all points in between. Equally, the choice of "Positively Fourth Street" is interesting: it was never released on an album, and so stands somewhat outside the canonical "body of work"; it is hardly "literary" in its language; it contains no obvious poetic imagery, metaphor or poetic conceits. It is certainly direct and vituperative, more so than any typical pop song of the time; it is also uncompromisingly strophic, without any hook, chorus, bridge, or other conventions of current chart pop. But *literature*? We might be skeptical about taking her remarks at face value here, given the breadth of literary allusions that pervade her own work. In any case, she was already immersed in Western art songs, referencing German lieder and jazz. She needed no Damascene conversion to song-as-literature by a (reluctantly) canonized Dylan.

That said, it is impossible to escape the fact that Mitchell's career began in an era of unbridled Dylanolatry. Singer-songwriters needed to take a position vis-à-vis Dylan, whether imitating him passively, covering his songs, responding to his words in what would nowadays be called a "backatcha," paying homage, or self-consciously swerving from his influence. Several singers began their careers by covering Dylan songs in a respectful fashion, often smoothing down their rough edges: Judy Collins, Joan Baez and Nico among others. Others executed more obvious swerves and symbolic rejections of Dylan's influence: John Lennon's symbolic rejection of Dylanolatry came in his famous post-Beatles song "God" ("I don't *believe* in Zimmerman"—emphasis mine) (1970), while Paul Simon's "A Simple Desultory Philippic" (1966) was a perfect satirical impression of Dylan that captured the absurdity of the Bob-worshipping zeitgeist. The anxiety of influence was quite palpable. If Joni Mitchell had stopped recording after *Ladies of the Canyon*, her career might legitimately have been characterized as "post-Dylan," along with his other imitators. But the harmonic and prosodic adventures on *Blue* evoke not a post-Dylan landscape but a vigorously anti-Dylan language, whether conscious or otherwise.

Song as sermon; song as conversation

In the following discussion, then, I would like to argue the case for Joni Mitchell as an opposite pole of influence, at least equal to Dylan but diametrically opposed in several ways: linguistic register, harmonic vocabulary, phrasing, diction, rhyme-schemes, and musical structure. To summarize this dichotomy, we might think of two broad tropes of folk-rock songwriting: song as sermon and song as conversation (see Table 7.1).

Of course, not all Dylan songs are literal sermons, and not all Mitchell songs are conversations (although "Hard Rain" and "A Case of You" might be useful exemplars of each). I have also hesitated to map this loose schema on to a gender binary, because plenty of female songwriters use a sermonic style (Ani DiFranco comes to mind), while some male writers aim for a prose register (such as Maynard James Keenan, who has often acknowledged Mitchell's influence). It would also be too simplistic to regard the division as "political versus apolitical": Mitchell's songs are often politically charged without lecturing, as when she sings about the Magdalene Laundries. Equally, the caricature of Dylan as a political songwriter fails to do justice to his hundreds of love songs.[18]

The musicologist Dai Griffiths hints at a similar kind of dichotomy between the self-consciously poetic and the conversational. In his interesting concept of the "anti-lyric," the term "lyric" is double-edged: in its literal sense it denotes the words of a popular song, but it also carries historical connotations of lyric poetry (as distinct from epic poetry): poetry which foregrounds the writer's emotions and situates the self at the center of the narrative (Griffiths 2009). Griffiths defines the "lyric" tendency as "words that tend to be like poetry" and "anti-lyric" as "words that tend to be like prose" (2009, 42). A famous example occurs in "A Case of You":

Table 7.1 Song as sermon and song as conversation

Song as Sermon ("Bob" Trope)	Song as Conversation ("Joni" Trope)
Teleology	Discursiveness
Monologue	Dialogue
Moral certainty	Ambivalence
Clear key centre	Tonal ambiguity
Echoes of Romanticism	Echoes of early Modernism
End-rhyme	Internal or absent rhyme
Virtuosic rhyme	Concealed rhyme
Metrical regularity	Metrical irregularity
"Folk ballad" trope	"Jazz solo" trope
Poetic register	Prose register
Peroration	Bathos / anticlimax

Source: From author's data.

> Just before our love got lost you said
> "I am as constant as the northern star" and I said,
> "Constantly in the darkness
> Where's that at?
> If you want me I'll be in the bar"

The structural rhyme (star/bar) is partially erased by the "and I said," shifting the rhyming word into the middle of the line, and moving the banal, conversational signifiers (you said, I said) to the end of the musical phrase. In the narrative, Mitchell's male interlocutor comes out with a vatic *Julius Caesar* quotation and is gently cut down to size by the narrator, switching effortlessly to world-weary vernacular. This is just one example of the kind of ironic bathos that characterizes her writing on *Blue*.

This mode of delivery is in marked contrast with Dylan's typical style of declamation. Dylan's rhymes can be astonishingly playful and creative, but they almost always have the effect of reinforcing the sense of teleology and closed structure.[19] Indeed, some of Dylan's most impressive comedic rhymes appear in songs with the most pointedly moralistic message. A famous example is "Hurricane" (1976), where internal rhymes jostle with structural end-rhymes in a way that prefigures hip-hop, not least in anger and visceral energy:

> And ride a horse along a *trail*
> But then they took him to the *jail / house*
> Where they tried to turn a man into a *mouse.*

This is no random, improvised piece of rhyming virtuosity, though: it is part of the song's design, entirely consistent across the song's eleven verses. The effect of the short penultimate line is teleological, and essentially sermonic: to drive toward the angry, righteous peroration (in this example, the word "mouse" is prolonged passionately for a whole bar, in a way that simply would not be possible on the page, or in a poetry reading). A similar effect is achieved in "Tangled up in Blue" (1975), in which the tagline is prepared by a shorter line, in order to drive to the final cadence on "blue": this word is progressively stretched from verse to verse, in both the album version and several live recordings. This drive toward the peroration is starkly at odds with Mitchell's style of delivery in many of the songs on *Blue*. This example, from "California" is typical: "They won't give peace a chance / That was just a dream some of us had." The syllable "had" (rhyming with "bad") falls on a weak beat, giving a sense of bathos and understated resignation. If Dylan's rhymes take us by surprise us when we hear them, Mitchell's rhymes are easy to miss, even on the page.

Another distinctive feature of Dylan's declamation is the very deliberate variation in syllabic density—to use a term of Leonard Cohen's (Zollo 1997, 341). This is a parameter of song which does not normally exist in written poetry: the relationship between the syllable-count of the line and the musical meter. Some Dylan songs have varied syllabic densities which make them appear unconvincing on the page, but extremely powerful in their sung delivery, as here, in "Not Dark Yet" (1997), where eighteen syllables are crammed into a two-bar phrase:

> Every nerve in my body is so vacant and *numb*
> I can't even remember what I was I came here to get away *from*.[20]

Again, the effect is teleological: the tone may be conversational, but the narrative is still essentially a sermon, prophesying the end of the world. Indeed, Dylan's embrace of the "song as sermon" aesthetic is a defining feature of his style, from the early "A Hard Rain's A-Gonna Fall" (1964) (one of his very rare unrhymed songs), through his Christian period ("Gotta Serve Somebody" from 1979) to the various apocalypse songs, some of which (from 1963's "Talkin' World War III Blues" to "Tempest," 2012) are faintly comedic. The binary opposite of the "preaching" song is the confessional song, something occasionally embraced by Dylan, when he moves from the pulpit to the confession box ("Every Grain of Sand" from 1981, for example).

Mitchell is famously averse to the idea of the "confessional" songwriter. In a recent article for the *Guardian*, Alexandra Pollard has argued that the label is almost always applied to women poets (Sylvia Plath, Ann Sexton, and others), and quotes this particularly offensive (but not untypical) comment on Plath's work by a male reviewer: "The personal character of the confessional detail is embarrassing, and the tone of hysterical melodrama which pervades most of the writing is finally irritating."[21] Mitchell recently expanded on this idea, suggesting that there are two types of confession: the involuntary confession of sins under torture, or the "voluntary" self-abasement of the confession box (Mitchell, cited in Pollard 2015). Unlike so many of Dylan's songs, Mitchell's are never sermons, lectures, or confessions.

"The Last Time I Saw Richard": songwriting and cubism

"The Last Time I Saw Richard," the last track on *Blue,* is neither moralistic nor confessional. Instead, it is an early example of the conversational trope, in which a female narrator, world-weary and slightly cynical, looks back on a conversation in a bar with a male interlocutor.[22] Such a simple narrative device is rare in the pop songs of the late sixties and early seventies, but it occurs in later examples by Alanis Morissette, like the epistolary song "Unsent" (1998) and "Joining You" (1998) in which the narrator writes supportively to a friend who was contemplating suicide. In its narrativity, "Richard" frames the conversation in the past tense, shot through with nostalgia: to that extent, it harks back to the nostalgic song cycles of Schubert and Schumann (both *Winterreise* and *Dichterliebe* begin with memories, and the narrative arc of both cycles is clearly framed in a happier past). The device has already been prefigured in the preceding song "A Case of You," in that poignant line "Just before our love got lost, you said," but here it becomes a structural framing device: the conversation is interspersed with factual banalities of suburban life (the dishwasher and coffee percolator being the early-seventies equivalents of the "gramophone" famously evoked in Eliot's *The Waste Land*).[23] I mention Eliot here, not as a way of "legitimizing" Mitchell's work through comparisons with dead male poets (as Ricks does in his Dylan–Keats cross-readings), but to show just how vastly Mitchell's idiolect differs from that of Dylan. If Dylan has one foot in the nineteenth century, far behind his rattled time, Mitchell's literary reference points are firmly rooted in the twentieth. If Dylan's images resonate with Romantic poetry and antebellum Americana, Mitchell's are alive with modernism.[24] The gently prosaic references to dishwashers and coffee percolators in "Richard" would seem very out of place in a Dylan song.

The musical structure of "Richard" is similarly conversational. It feels largely improvised, although a careful comparison of the three verses reveals a very deliberate strophic structure. Likewise, there are variations in syllabic density, perhaps even more dramatic than those in Dylan: the "gorgeous wings" line is set to an almost madrigal-like melisma, but its sentimentality is undercut by the prosodic diction of the verses, sung to a speech-like oscillation of fifth and third scale degrees:

> The last time I saw Richard was Detroit in 68 and he told me
> All romantics meet the same *fate*, someday. (Emphasis mine)

This is the diametrical opposite of Dylan's style of declamation: instead of the teleological drive toward the rhymed word at the end of each line, the delivery effaces the rhyme, and shunts it into the middle of the line. It is not quite the same as the internal rhyme mentioned by Whitesell in his reading of "I Had a King": in that earlier song, each line contains an end-rhyme and a concealed rhyme as a deliberate structural device, but here there seems to be an equally deliberate dovetailing between the closures implied by the rhymes and those articulated at musical phrase endings (2008, 17).

However, it is in her musical structures that Mitchell takes the most decisive stylistic swerves from the folk-rock tradition and forges a genuinely new technique that was to prove influential for songwriters of the next generation. Several commentators have found echoes of jazz in this early phase of her career (e.g., Whitesell 2008, 22–23 on *Court and Spark*),[25] and it is possible to hear "Richard" as a bridge between the folk idioms of her earlier writing and the rich additive harmony and quasi-improvisatory storytelling of her seminal jazz album, *Hejira*. Though Dylan's harmonic language is rooted in the blues, he almost never uses the additive harmonies of jazz, and his tonal centers are nearly always unambiguous. Conversely, "Richard" is full of tonal ambiguity, reflecting the emotional ambivalence of the lyric.

The identification of a tonic is problematic: many online transcriptions, including some endorsed by Mitchell herself, notate the song in two sharps, perhaps influenced by the prolonged D chords of the intro, and perhaps by the cryptic final chord of Bm11 (a "jazz" chord or Stravinskian "bitonal" chord, depending on how we want to interpret it). However, the body of the song is clearly in G major, even though this is undermined by the ambiguity of the surrounding piano episodes. Whitesell, in his taxonomy of tonality and modality in Mitchell's songs, assigns "Richard" to the "polytonal" category, as distinct from the commoner "polymodal" category, which implies chromatic variations in melody lines over an undisputed tonic (Whitesell 2008, 122). However, "polytonal" does not imply two simultaneous tonics, as in sections of Stravinsky's *Petrouchka* or the bitonal folk-melody arrangements in Bartók's *Mikrokosmos*. Instead, it implies tonal ambiguity: there are no perfect (or, indeed plagal) cadences to provide closure in the key of G major (the only V- I progressions being at the start of each strophe), and the outer sections undermine the tonal center.

Tonal ambiguity can be explained in two very different ways: first, as a modernistic tendency paralleling the "extended tonality" found in the art music of the late nineteenth century and codified by theorists such as Deborah Stein in her study of the songs of Hugo Wolf (Stein 1985). In this model, the songwriter uses tonal ambiguity to "swerve" from an established framework of tonal closure: it is essentially an avant-gardist gesture. The second explanation is that tonal ambiguity arises in rock songs because our Western-centered paradigm of tonality is biased towards a single, controlling tonic, and in trying to interpret a particular blues or rock sequence in terms of a single key center, we are misreading one musical language through the prism of another.

A famous example of this idea is in Lynyrd Skynyrd's "Sweet Home Alabama" (1974): the familiar D-C9-G loop can be parsed as I-bVII-IV in D mixolydian or as V-IV-I in the key of G. Philip Tagg, in his excellent taxonomy of loops and shuttles in pop songs, effectively cuts the Gordian knot by suggesting that such loops are merely motions from one point to another, without any need to decide which is the hegemonic tonal center (Tagg 2014, 371–400). In other words, by asking whether G or D is the "real" tonic, we may be asking an unnecessarily loaded question.

In "Richard," however, the tonal ambiguity seems both deliberate and poetic: the three sung verses can be explained quite unproblematically in terms of a G major tonic (admittedly, not with a "common practice" type of voice-leading or harmonic progression), while the piano sections flirt with D major, F sharp minor and B minor.[26] If we disregard the piano introduction and outro, the three strophes all outline a "flat side" chordal loop of [G – Am (x2)] – C – F – G, corresponding to I – ii – IV – bVII – I in G mixolydian.

Behind the additive dissonances of the surface, then, the schema is not unlike that of Cohen's "One of Us Cannot Be Wrong" (1967), which also uses a I – ii oscillation, and moves to the chord of bVII at the end of each strophe. While the internal structure of the strophes emphasizes the flat side of the circle of fifths, each strophe is linked by a more traditional circle-of-fifths progression from the sharp side: A – D – G (or V/V – V – I). These underlying progressions have plenty of precedents in the folk rock of the late sixties and early seventies, but here the vocal line takes a startling swerve into a jazz aesthetic that prefigures *Hejira*: in the line "look at your eyes, they're full of moon," Mitchell sings an unprepared ninth above the bass. Likewise, in the sigh-like codettas of each strophe ("pretty lies," "love so sweet" and "dark café days"), the vocal melody presents unresolved elevenths over the A in the bass. The last two notes of the melody line in the song ("café days"), and indeed the entire album, *would* be consonant with the tonic, but the tonic has yet to arrive. When it does, it is a brief closure, eclipsed by the cryptic Bm11 that closes the track: a dissonant collision of two chords (Bm and A) heard simultaneously.

This kind of ambitious harmonic language is the antithesis of the Dylan folk-rock aesthetic. Although Dylan talked about the flattening out of time in his lyrics (specifically "Tangled up in Blue"), there is nothing in his work that comes close to this kind of structural stasis in the music, where tonal centers occur synchronically.[27] To find an origin of this startling style-shift, we might look instead to high-art modernism. In a famous book on Stravinsky, Roman Vlad introduces the intriguing concept of musical cubism. Cubism in painting involves the simultaneous representation of objects from different perspectives, yet the inherently non-representational nature of music means that "cubist music" is perhaps, at best, a metaphor.[28] Vlad, however, points to a number of interesting chords and heterophonic details in Stravinsky's music which disrupt the tonal syntax by presenting tonics and dominants simultaneously: an example is the dissonant chord that closes the *Symphony in C* (1940). Edward T. Cone, in an early analysis of the *Symphonies of Wind Instruments*, offered a similar reading in which familiar chord progressions were made strange and unsettling by being interspliced in a kaleidoscopic fashion (Cone 1968, 18–26). It is tempting, then, to suggest that Mitchell's songwriting language draws as much on her experience as a painter as on her exposure to the folk-rock tradition. *Blue* is, after all, a "painterly" album, suffused with references to colors: "I miss my clean white linen"; "Let's have a round for the bright red devil," "I am a lonely painter / I live in a box of paints," as well as "Little Green" and of course "Blue" itself, with its references to ink and tattoos.

As a poet and a painter before she became known as a songwriter, Mitchell was already equipped with a songwriting paint box that allowed her to eschew the Dylan paradigm with greater ease and assurance than many of her contemporaries. In fact, her influence is keenly felt on Dylan's *Blood on the Tracks*, released four years after *Blue*. It was a time when Mitchell's star was in the ascendant, at least in terms of critical reception, rather more than his own. "Tangled up in Blue" may not be a direct reference to the Mitchell album, although one critic recently claimed that Dylan told him precisely this.[29] However, it was written in a renewed creative phase in 1974–1975, after a brief hiatus filled with the study of painting and modernist poetry. He himself suggested that the song was concerned with the flattening of time, and the use of discontinuous, fragmented narrative. It is certainly the first, and perhaps the only, Dylan song to use the quasi-cubist, nonlinear narrative more familiar from Hollywood flashbacks or the modernist novel. Though its melodic and harmonic structure is infinitely simpler than "Richard" or indeed anything on *Blue*, its startling, almost filmic imagery ("rain falling on my shoes") and its seamy adult themes of drug dealers in basements seem to suggest a stylistic affinity with the Mitchell of "acid, booze and ass / needles, guns and grass."[30]

Influence and legacy

The idea of influence as anxiety, then, seems useful to the extent that it can help us identify decisive stylistic swerves, not just in comparing one songwriter's style with another, but in tracing the stylistic evolution of each. The anxiety of influence might apply just as well to the burden of living up to one's own stylistic reputation: so Dylan's career is littered with anti-Dylan swerves, in which he ritually disavows earlier styles, and challenges the caricatures erected by the critics. The most dramatic of these swerves came in his Christian period, beginning with *Slow Train Coming* in 1979, but his touring career has been marked by dramatic changes in the interpretations of his own songs. Likewise, Mitchell's long recording career is marked by significant style-shifts, the tonal ambiguities and complexities on *Court and Spark* (1973) and *Hejira* (1976) being prefigured by the assured, relaxed harmonic complexity of "The Last Time I Saw Richard."

In turn, Mitchell herself casts a long shadow, and provides a source of inspiration (and perhaps anxiety) for a later generation. Inevitably, Mitchell comparisons have been foisted on female songwriters: Laura Marling, for instance, was being dubbed the successor to Joni Mitchell at a very early stage in her career, and her excellent "Reversal of the Muse" series explores the role of women in the creative arts (presenting women as inspired creators rather than as muses).[31] Alanis Morissette, for example, spent some time in India between her first and second albums, wrestling not so much with the "anxiety of influence" as the anxiety of her own fame. If the songs on *Jagged Little Pill* (1995) were Dylanesque and sermonic (even down to the harmonica solos and the political anger on the closing track, directed at the misogyny of the Catholic Church), the more striking tracks on *Supposed Former Infatuation Junkie* (1998) seem unthinkable without Mitchell: in particular, the radical tonal scheme of "Joining You," which alternates conversational verses (in a static C minor) with sermonic choruses (modulating sharpwise through C, G, D and A).

But is there a danger, in reassessing Mitchell's legacy, of casting her as a role model purely for *women* songwriters? As David Bennun remarks: "When Mitchell's influence is mentioned, it is almost exclusively in terms of how she inspired those female singer-songwriters, as if a female artist may be the creative begetter only of other women."[32] Perhaps, although both Marling and Morissette have embraced the "Bob" trope in their work every bit as much as the "Joni" trope, while a growing number of male singers and songwriters cite Mitchell as an influence. The sixties phenomenon of women covering Dylan songs has given way, encouragingly, to a growing trend of men covering Mitchell songs: Ian Shaw, James Blake, and Rufus Wainwright among the more creative examples.

I have not tried to claim that Mitchell is superior to Dylan (although her musical language is undeniably more complex), but that her body of work has shown a generation of songwriters that a creative auteur does not need to tread in Dylan's footsteps. Just as the tradition of "progressive" songwriting from *Sgt Pepper* to Pink Floyd would be unthinkable without Dylan, so a growing body of music would be unthinkable without the radical stylistic excursions of *Blue*. Rather than interpreting Mitchell's work as an antithetical "reaction" to Dylan (as per Bloom's lines of thought, and the critical positions that regard her as "post-Dylan") it might be more fruitful, and fairer to both, to regard them as equal and opposite poles of influence: two artistic traditions which bifurcated significantly in the early seventies. Whether Dylan's influence was a source of creative anxiety in any literal or psychological sense is a moot point: as I hope to have shown, the internal evidence of her songs seems not to suggest some sort of Freudian wrestling with a precursor, but rather a startlingly fresh idiolect that showed a generation of songwriters that there is another, at least equally interesting, way of approaching the craft.

Notes

1 Reprinted in David Wild: "Morrissey Interviews Joni Mitchell: Melancholy Meets the Infinite Sadness," *Rolling Stone* (March 6, 1997).
2 Morrissey's comment was "to use the term 'female songwriter' implies that the term 'songwriter' belongs to men" (cited in Wild, "Morrissey," 1997).
3 It reflects the playfulness of Ricks's comment about "that Dylanesque writer William Shakespeare" (Ricks 2003, 60).
4 Matt Diehl: "It's a Joni Mitchell Concert, Sans Joni," *Los Angeles Times* (April 22, 2010).
5 For a sarcastic debunking of the "spokesman of a generation" label, see Bob Dylan (2004, 115).
6 The concept of strong and weak poets is introduced in Bloom (1997). The defense of the canon and the attacks on leftist postmodernism appear in Bloom (1995, 4–7). For a nuanced defense of the concept of "authenticity" in popular music, see, for example, Moore (2002, 209–23).
7 Lola Calamidades, *Theodor Adorno—Music and Protest* (2010). www.youtube.com/watch?v=-njxKF8CkoU (accessed: January, 2 2017).
8 For the Tennyson allusions, see Ricks (2003, 192–193).
9 Bob Dylan: "Chimes of Freedom," *Another Side of Bob Dylan* (New York: Columbia, 1964).

10 "Rhizomatics" is a term coined by philosopher Gilles Deleuze and psychiatrist and activist Félix Guattari to denote recursive, non-linear influence, cited in Tate (2005, 177–197).
11 The unfashionable concept of genius is discussed in Pickering and Negus (2004, 198–203).
12 Informal surveys carried out as part of my "canon" topic in the second-year undergraduate module "Rock and Popular Musicology," University of Hull, 2010–16.
13 For some interesting critiques of the problematic idea of music as artefact, see Small (1998) and Goehr (2007). In the medium of song, Regina Spektor's "All the Rowboats" (*What We Saw from the Cheap Seats*, 2012) is a wonderful lament on the idea of music as ossified museum-piece.
14 The terms "swerve" and "clinamen" are used almost interchangeably, the latter being the first of the Six Revisionary Ratios, defined as "a swerve of the atoms"; see Harold Bloom: *The Anxiety of Influence: A Theory of Poetry* (Oxford: Oxford University Press, 1997), 14–16.
15 The musical examples are mine. Bloom did not apply his theory to music, and it does not have significant traction amongst musicologists. An interesting example is Korsyn (1991), who reads a Brahms piece in terms of its "misprision" of Chopin.
16 Stephen Holden, "Review of *The Hissing of Summer Lawns*," *Rolling Stone*, January 15, 1976.
17 For footage of a young Dylan, circa 1958, enthusing about Little Richard, see *Tales of Rock and Roll: Highway 61 Revisited*, dire. James Marsh, 1993.
18 But I would contend that his love songs are Romantic in the nineteenth-century sense: they are fundamentally expressions of the self, whether tender (as in "Love Minus Zero: No Limit") or vituperative ("Idiot Wind"; "It Ain't Me, Babe").
19 Some feminist scholars have argued that teleology in musical structure is a manifestation of male hegemony: see, for example, McClary (2002, 112–131).
20 Bob Dylan: "Not Dark Yet," *Time Out Of Mind* (New York: Columbia Records, 1997).
21 Charles Gullans, cited in Alexandra Pollard: "Why Are Only Women Described as 'Confessional' Singer-Songwriters?" *Guardian* (April 9, 2015).
22 Named men in the titles of pop and rock songs are extremely rare, with the exception of heroes and outlaws: John Wesley Hardin(g), Joey (Gallo), and the like. Women's names in song titles are too numerous to mention.
23 T. S. Eliot: *The Waste Land* (1922). "When lovely woman stoops to folly and / Paces about the room again, alone / She smooths her hair with automatic hand / And puts a record on the gramophone." The first six words are an ironic

quotation from Oliver Goldsmith, and the music technology evokes the banality of modern life. The shunting of Goldsmith's end-rhymed "folly," as well as the new rhyme of the banal word "and" seems playfully Mitchellesque.

24 To give just one example of each: Dylan's 2006 song "When the Deal Does Down" borrows lines from the obscure nineteenth-century poet Henry Timrod (a subject of lively journalistic debate about his authenticity at the time), while the title track of Mitchell's *Hejira* paraphrases Albert Camus no less closely. For the Dylan-Timrod debate, see Robert Polito: "Bob Dylan: Henry Timrod Revisited," Poetry Foundation, October 2006 [Online] available at: https://www.poetryfoundation.org/articles/68697/bob-dylan-henry-timrod-revisited (accessed: June 3, 2018). Camus wrote "This is the most obvious benefit of travel. At that moment we are feverish but also porous, so that the slightest touch makes us quiver to the depths of our being" (*Notebooks 1935–1942*, vol. 1), paraphrased by Mitchell in "Hejira," v.2.

25 For example, Whitesell, *The Music of Joni Mitchell* (New York: Oxford University Press, 2008), 22–23, on *Court and Spark* (1973).

26 This duality of voice and piano is another echo of the German lied tradition: Schubert's late song "Am Meer," for example, frames a fairly unproblematic C minor tonality in the verses with a rippling diminished seventh chord in the piano sections, which never resolves (at the time, an astonishingly radical gesture). Schumann's "Im Wunderschönen Monat Mai" uses a similar device, with the song ending on a dominant seventh. Like the Mitchell song, this song uses a narrative framing device in which the optimism of new love is seen through the prism of memory. In "Richard," the voice and piano are in an uneasy dialogue with one another, in which a sense of pained nostalgia is undercutting the prosaic anti-romantic message of the text.

27 Jonathan Cott, "Bob Dylan: The Rolling Stone Interview, Part 2," *Rolling Stone* (November 16, 1978).

28 Roman Vlad: *Stravinsky*. Trans. Frederick Fuller and Ann Fuller (London: Oxford University Press, 1967), 58–60.

29 Ron Rosenbaum: "The Best Joni Mitchell Song Ever," *Slate* (December, 14 2007). http://www.slate.com/articles/life/the_spectator/2007/12/the_best_joni_mitchell_song_ever.html (accessed: December 17, 2016).

30 Joni Mitchell, "Blue," *Blue* (Hollywood: Reprise Records, 1971).

31 Laura Marling: "Reversal of the Muse: An Exploration of Femininity in Creativity," http://www.reversalofthemuse.com/ (accessed: April 30, 2018).

32 David Bennun: "How Joni Mitchell Changed Music," *1843* Magazine *[The Economist]* (April 10, 2015). http://www.1843magazine.com/blog/joni-mitchell (accessed: June 3, 2018).

Works Cited

Bennun, David. "How Joni Mitchell Changed Music," *1843* Magazine *[The Economist]*. April 10, 2015 [Online] Available from: http://www.1843magazine.com/blog/joni-mitchell (accessed: August 1, 2018).

Bloom, Harold. *The Western Canon: The Books and School of the Ages.* New York: Riverhead Books, 1995.

Bloom, Harold. *The Anxiety of Influence: A Theory of Poetry.* Oxford: Oxford University Press, 1997.

Calamidades, Lola. *Theodor Adorno—Music and Protest.* www.youtube.com/watch?v=-njxKF8CkoU (accessed: January 2, 2017).

Camus, Albert. *Notebooks 1935–1942*, vol. 1. Trans. Philip Thody. Chicago: Ivan R Dee, 2010.

Citron, Marcia. *Gender and the Musical Canon.* Chicago: University of Illinois Press, 2000.

Cohen, Leonard. *Songs of Leonard Cohen.* New York: Columbia, 1967.

Cone, Edward. "Stravinsky: The Progress of a Method," *Perspectives of New Music*, 1.1 (1968): 18–26.

Cott, Jonathan. "Bob Dylan: The Rolling Stone Interview, Part 2," *Rolling Stone*, November 16, 1978. https://www.rollingstone.com/music/music-news/bob-dylan-the-rolling-stone-interview-part-2-173545/ (accessed: August 1, 2018).

Diehl, Matt. "It's a Joni Mitchell Concert, Sans Joni," *Los Angeles Times*, April 22, 2010.

Dylan, Bob. *The Freewheelin' Bob Dylan.* New York: Columbia, 1963.

Dylan, Bob. *Another Side of Bob Dylan.* New York: Columbia, 1964.

Dylan, Bob. *Bringing It All Back Home.* New York: Columbia, 1965.

Dylan, Bob. *Highway 61 Revisited.* New York: Columbia, 1965.

Dylan, Bob. *Blood on the Tracks.* New York: Columbia, 1975.

Dylan, Bob. *Desire.* New York: Columbia, 1975.

Dylan, Bob. *Slow Train Coming.* New York: Columbia, 1979.

Dylan, Bob. *Shot of Love.* New York: Columbia, 1981.

Dylan, Bob. *Time Out of Mind.* New York: Columbia, 1997.

Dylan, Bob. *Chronicles, Volume One.* London: Simon and Schuster, 2004.

Dylan, Bob. *Tempest.* New York: Columbia, 2012.

Goehr, Lydia. *The Imaginary Museum of Musical Works: An Essay in the Philosophy of Music.* New York: Oxford University Press, 2007.

Griffiths, Dai. "From Lyric to Anti-Lyric: Analyzing the Words in Pop Song," in *Analyzing Popular Music*, ed. Allan F Moore. Cambridge: Cambridge University Press, 2009, 39–60.

Holden, Stephen. "Review of *The Hissing of Summer Lawns*," *Rolling Stone*, January 15, 1976.

Hopper, Jessica. *The First Collection of Criticism by a Living Female Rock Critic*. Berkeley: Featherproof, 2015.

Jones, Carys Wyn. *The Rock Canon: Canonical Values in the Reception of Rock Albums*. London: Ashgate, 2008.

Korsyn, Kevin. "Towards a New Poetics of Musical Influence," *Music Analysis*, 10.1 (1991): 3–72.

Leonard, Marion. *Gender in the Music Industry*. London: Routledge, 2007.

Lynyrd Skynyrd. *Second Helping*. USA: Sounds of the South/MCA, 1974.

Marling, Laura. "Reversal of the Muse: An Exploration of Femininity in Creativity," http://www.reversalofthemuse.com/ (accessed: April 30, 2018).

Marsh, James. *Tales of Rock and Roll: Highway 61 Revisited*. [documentary], 1993.

McClary, Susan. *Feminine Endings: Music, Gender and Sexuality*. Minneapolis: University of Minnesota Press, 2002.

Mellers, Wilfred. *A Darker Shade of Pale: A Backdrop to Bob Dylan*. London: Faber and Faber, 1984.

Mitchell, Joni. *Blue*. Hollywood: Reprise Records, 1971.

Monk, Katherine. *Joni: The Creative Odyssey of Joni Mitchell*. Vancouver: Greystone Books, 2012.

Moore, Allan. "Authenticity as Authentication," *Popular Music*, 21.2 (2002): 209–223.

Morissette, Alanis. *Supposed Former Infatuation Junkie*. Hollywood: Maverick, 1998.

Pickering, Michael, and Negus, Keith. "Rethinking Creative Genius," *Popular Music*, 23.2 (2004): 198–203.

Polito, Robert. "Bob Dylan: Henry Timrod Revisited," Poetry Foundation, October 2006. https://www.poetryfoundation.org/articles/68697/bob-dylan-henry-timrod-revisited (accessed: June 3, 2018).

Pollard, Alexandra. "Why Are Only Women Described as "Confessional" Singer-Songwriters?" *Guardian*, April 9, 2015.

Ricks, Christopher. *Dylan's Visions of Sin*. New York: Viking Press, 2003.

Rosenbaum, Ron. "The Best Joni Mitchell Song Ever," *Slate*, December 14, 2007. http://www.slate.com/articles/life/the_spectator/2007/12/the_best_joni_mitchell_song_ever.html (accessed: December 17, 2016).

Small, Christopher. *Musicking: The Meanings of Performing and Listening*. Middletown, CT: Wesleyan University Press, 1998.

Somers-Willett, Susan. *The Cultural Politics of Slam Poetry: Race, Identity, and the Performance of Popular Verse in America*. Ann Arbor: University of Michigan Press, 2009.

Stein, Deborah. *Hugo Wolf's Lieder and Extensions of Tonality.* Ann Arbor: UMI Research Press, 1985.

Tagg, Philip. *Everyday Tonality II.* New York and Huddersfield: The Mass Media Music Scholars' Press, 2014.

Tate, Joseph. *The Music and Art of Radiohead.* London: Ashgate, 2005.

Vlad, Roman. *Stravinsky.* Trans. Frederick Fuller and Ann Fuller. London, Oxford University Press, 1967.

von Appen, Ralf and Doehring, André. "Nevermind the Beatles, Here's Exile 61 and Nico: "The Top 100 Records of All Time"—a Canon of Pop and Rock Albums from a Sociological and an Aesthetic Perspective," *Popular Music*, 25.1 (2006): 25–39.

Whitesell, Lloyd. *The Music of Joni Mitchell.* New York: Oxford University Press, 2008.

Wild, David. "Morrissey Interviews Joni Mitchell: Melancholy Meets the Infinite Sadness," *Rolling Stone*, March 6, 1997.

Zollo, Paul: *Songwriters on Songwriting.* Boston, MA: Da Capo Press, 1997.

Part Three

"Busy Being Free": Love, Time, Feminism

8

"Here's a Man and a Woman Sitting on a Rock": Joni Mitchell, Margaret Atwood, and Irritable Feminism

Pamela Thurschwell

In this chapter I chart multiple connections between Joni Mitchell and Margaret Atwood, as brilliant, angry, self-conscious, Canadian women artists of the same generation.[1] I explore the crossovers between Mitchell's songs (focusing on "Come in from the Cold," "Song for Sharon," and "Refuge of the Roads") and Atwood's writings (focusing on the quasi-autobiographical novel, *Cat's Eye*) to uncover a shared sensibility as well as a shared history and sense of place. Mitchell's and Atwood's works speak to each other through a similar affective landscape—simultaneously tough, vulnerable, and imbued with a desire for freedom that merges with a deep sense of loneliness. A critique of patriarchy, via a feminism that I want to call irritable, is a central plank of both authors' techniques and sensibilities.

Mitchell and Atwood's work in relationship to feminism can be seen to provoke irritation in two different directions. First, feminist fans, such as myself, might find ourselves occasionally irritated at both of these hugely admired artists for their periodic refusals to inhabit the word "feminist," which we want to assign to them. Second, Mitchell and Atwood sometimes seem annoyed, in return, by fans' desire to annex them and their work. They regularly express their desire not to be pinned down by any one term such as "feminist." There is a relationship then of mutual, but I'd like to think productive, irritation between Mitchell and Atwood and their feminist fans. At the end of the chapter, I will connect this dynamic of shared irritation to Mitchell's sense of humor, which is frequently overlooked because it often appears in relation to her dissatisfaction with a heterosexuality she is also constantly drawn back toward, as both a good and bad object. Joni's optimism (what there is of it) is, in Lauren Berlant's terms, cruel but also wry; she and Atwood both cast sidelong, skeptical glances at their own nexus of desires and its structural impossibility (Berlant 2011).[2]

Making the case for irritable feminism, or indeed, any sort of feminism, as central to understanding Mitchell and Atwood's artistic output, is complicated by the fact that both artists have had an ambivalent relationship to feminism throughout their careers. Mitchell, more vehemently than Atwood, has disavowed the label "feminist" in relation to her work. To take just one example, in an interview with Malka Marom in 1973, Mitchell claims "I was never a feminist. I was in argument with them. They were so down on the domestic female, the family, and it was breaking down. And even though my problems were somewhat female, they were of no help to mine. I was already past that. I don't want to get a posse against guys" (Marom 2014, 62). Similarly, echoing a familiar disavowal of an anti-male feminism in favor of an apparently more encompassing "humanism," Atwood too has expressed some dissatisfaction with the term. Most recently, in relation to the TV series of *The Handmaid's Tale*, she found herself again being asked about the feminist credentials of the novel, and again demurring (McNamara 2017). In Rebecca Mead's profile of her in a 2017 *New Yorker* piece, Mead explains the paradoxes of this in relation to Atwood's work:

> Given that her works are a mainstay of women's-studies curricula, and that she is clearly committed to women's rights, Atwood's resistance to a straightforward association with feminism can come as a surprise. But this wariness reflects her bent toward precision, and a scientific sensibility that was ingrained from childhood: Atwood wants the terms defined before she will state her position. Her feminism assumes women's rights to be human rights and is born of having been raised with a presumption of absolute equality between the sexes. "My problem was not that people wanted me to wear frilly pink dresses—it was that *I* wanted to wear frilly pink dresses, and my mother, being as she was, didn't see any reason for that," she said. Atwood's early years in the forest endowed her with a sense of self-determination, and with a critical distance on codes of femininity—an ability to see those codes

as cultural practices worthy of investigation, not as necessary conditions to be accepted unthinkingly. (Mead 2017)

Atwood's occasionally grumpy relationship to feminism is here posited as a product of the unusual freedom in her upbringing; her father was an entomologist and, like the character Elaine in *Cat's Eye*, Atwood spent her early years traveling with her parents in the woods of northern Quebec while he did research, her family finally settling in Toronto when she was eight.[3] Atwood's refusal to identify herself with a single identity category can be connected, via this analysis of her early years, to an anthropological distance that her narrators maintain in many of her works. It can be found, for instance, in the metafictional academic-conference epilogue to *The Handmaid's Tale*, which interrupts the trauma and immediacy of Offred's story and replaces it with academic infighting and historical distance. *Cat's Eye* also sets up its protagonist, Elaine as a kind of anthropologist. The reader witnesses the young Elaine's struggles to understand the codes of adolescent and adult femininity that surround her in her new environment. Elaine's estrangement from these codes also estranges us as readers; why, the book asks, would anyone find it desirable to wear a "twinset" or even know what one was? (Atwood 1990, 50). But then again, why be denied a twinset, or a frilly pink bow, if you want one? When does freedom from the trappings of femininity actually turn into another demand that the young woman perform her feminism, and her gender, a certain way (without makeup or frilly pink bows)? As the previous quote from Mead indicates, Atwood sees femininity as a performative structure, viewing it from a critical distance; in *Cat's Eye* she both questions the efficacy of, and exposes the cruelty of, gender policing. However, in other sections of the novel, when the grown-up Elaine is a painter claimed by 1980s Toronto feminists, she also bristles at a different kind of policing—that which would make her a spokesperson for 1970s second-wave feminism. When Elaine is interviewed by a young woman reporter, she is asked about her debts to feminism, "A lot of people call you a feminist painter." Elaine responds: "I hate party lines, I hate ghettoes" (Atwood 1990, 90).

Neither Mitchell nor Atwood are comfortable being pinned down, then, in relation to their gender and sexual politics. Although they are both often tough and hard-headed in their dissections of patriarchy, romantic love, and the ruses of heterosexuality, they are also often unforgiving in their representation of dynamics between women.[4] I'd like to place this shared attitude in relation to their shared generational history. Both writers chart the toll a certain version of middle-class heteronormativity has taken historically on women, from the 1950s through the 1980s. ("Come in from the Cold" came out on *Night Ride Home* in 1991; Atwood's *Cat's Eye* came out in 1988); Mitchell and Atwood both portray the ways in which femininity was instilled and policed by their 1950s Canadian upbringing. Think of the first line of "Come in from the Cold": "Back in 1957 we had to dance a foot apart." The oppressive chaperoning of the 1950s high school dance ignites a lifetime of erotic yearning that suffuses the rest of the song as we listen to the narrator grow older, although not necessarily wiser—still longing for the sexual frisson of youth. Both Mitchell and Atwood are skeptical about the idea that growing older means gaining wisdom. The analysis that underpins these self-critical lines, and takes apart the romantic spark, are uncompromisingly honest: "Are you just checking out your mojo? Am I just fighting off growing old?" But as the singer ages, she emphasizes a continued shared vulnerability and neediness in relation to romance, hurting and panicking, "we strike out/out of fear."[5]

Atwood covers similar terrain in *Cat's Eye*. There's an uncompromising, scratchy, clear-sightedness in the way they both portray women's desire for men, for art, and for freedom—showing women breaking away from heteronormative narratives of desire and getting sucked back in again, knowing the stakes and dangers but unable to fully extricate themselves. This problem—the contradictions of heterosexuality, of being caught in a certain version of romance, and of the myths surrounding the female artist—can be tragic, but also funny, a point to which I will return at the end. A line such as this from *Cat's Eye*, "Old lovers go the way of old photographs, bleaching out gradually as in a slow bath of acid," would not be out of place in a Mitchell song such as "Down to You": "Everything comes and goes/marked by lovers and styles of clothes" (Mitchell 1974; Atwood 1990, 266).

Atwood and Mitchell have some obvious biographical similarities. They are of the same generation, only a few years apart in age: Atwood was born in November 1939 and Mitchell was born in November 1943. They shared a childhood in the 1940s shadowed by the Second World War, and the sometimes harsh conditions of small town Canadian life. Mitchell talks about the kinds of texts which influenced her as a child in an interview with Malka Marom:

> There were only two stores in town. My dad ran the grocery store and Marilyn McGee's dad ran the general store. She and I called the Simpsons-Sears catalog "The Book of Dreams." It was so glamorous when I was a child, four or five. We'd be down on our bellies looking at every page, and she and I would pick out our favorite object from the front page to the back page. We would cut out our favorite matron's girdle and our favorite saw and our favorite hammer. "I like that one best." Every page, "That's my favorite." So in that way you learned to shop before you have money, you learn the addiction of the process of selection. (Marom 2014, 2–3)

The Sears catalog signifies a kind of constricted feminine consumerist fantasy, but also a sense of play and enjoyment: the young girl's right to have desires. However, contained in the material reality of the fantasy is also a harsh reminder of economic reality: "The Book of Dreams, when everybody had read it, because we were on rations, it became toilet paper. Even the mayor, if you could imagine, wiped his ass with the Simpsons-Sears catalog, glossy coloured paper" (Marom 2014, 13–14). In *Cat's Eye*, Atwood shows her character Elaine, as a young girl, cutting up the Eaton catalog in a kind of bewildered conformity with the games her friends Grace and Carol want to play:

> Or we sit on the floor in Grace's room with piles of old Eaton's Catalogs. I've seen lots of Eaton Catalogs before: up north they're hung in outhouses for use as toilet paper. Eaton's catalogs always remind me of the stench of such outhouses, the buzzing of the flies down the hole underneath [. . .] But here we treat these catalogs with reverence. We cut the small coloured figures out of them and paste them into scrapbooks. Then we cut out other things—cookware, furniture—and paste them around the figures. The figures themselves are always women. We call them "My lady." "My lady's going to have this refrigerator," we say. "My lady's getting this rug." "This is my lady's umbrella." (Atwood 1990, 53)

These games, in which store catalogs become "books of dreams" for young girls aspiring toward domestic bliss in 1940s Canada, and then are used to wipe up shit, indicate that 1940s and 1950s fantasies of the "good life" never go unquestioned in Mitchell's and Atwood's works.[6] *Cat's Eye*, in its brutal depiction of cruel and bullying friendships between girls, proceeds to dismantle this domestic idyll for girls, exposing the anxieties and fears of otherness that grounds the dream of romance, marriage, and buying refrigerators. Mitchell's "Song for Sharon" from *Hejira* (1976) mines some similar territory, comparing the singer's grappling with fame and love to the different path of a childhood friend. As a child, the singer wanted romance and the wedding dress most of all, "the ceremony of bells and lace/still veils this reckless fool here." Sharon ends the song with a husband and a farm, while the singer has "the apple of temptation/and a diamond snake around [her]arm." The desire to connect to the childhood girlfriend, who understands the woman artist and what made her who she is, is intense and palpable in both "Song for Sharon" and *Cat's Eye*. The crushing effects of female competitiveness and cruelty are foregrounded in Atwood's novel, yet the protagonist Elaine ends the book with a sense of longing for the lost frenemy who had nearly destroyed her life as an adolescent: "This is what I miss, Cordelia: not something that's gone, but something that will never happen. Two old women giggling over their tea" (Atwood 1990, 421). Addressing an old friend provides more comfort in "Song for Sharon" amid the comparisons between the singer's life and Sharon's. Many of Mitchell's songs chart the contortions of the woman artist unsuccessfully attempting to have both romance and a creative identity; however, the end of "Song for Sharon" gives both Sharon and the singer music and the landscape of their childhood ("I've still got my eyes on the land and the sky").[7] The friendship between the women seems alive and potentially nourishing, at least in this telling.

Time and location also connect Mitchell's work to Atwood's. Both were teenagers in the 1950s, and both negotiated the complex and fractious business of being a woman artist in the 1960s and beyond. Further, their Canadian roots are central to their work. They both write about the geography of Canada, taking its skies, rivers, mountains, and clouds as metaphors and backdrops. As Atwood puts it: "One of the primary interests for a Canadian writer has to be geology followed by geography" (Mercer 2009, 51–52). Rocks and maps, vast spaces, and bodies of water populate their art. As Mitchell claims of her relationship to the Canadian landscape: "I've always thought

Neil [Young] and I [...] carried a loping prairie walk in our music" (Mercer 2009, 53). There is, I think, a specifically Canadian sense of loneliness here, that combines with the possibility of completion in the landscape; wandering through it, facing the cold, and not just coming in from it, will get you somewhere.[8]

Many of Mitchell's reminiscences of her childhood in Michelle Mercer's *Will You Take Me as I Am: Joni Mitchell's Blue Period* and Malka Marom's book of interviews, *Both Sides Now—Conversations with Malka Marom*, chime deeply with Atwood's portrayal of the harsh winters the adolescent girls experience in *Cat's Eye*. Mercer writes:

> Every year in early spring, Joni remembers, she and her best friend Sharolyn would wait for the day the ice broke on the Saskatchewan River. They'd head to the river bluffs after school, looking for signs the big event was coming. Snow and ice slowly melted into the water, which then rose under the surface ice and began to degrade it [...] They watched closely for cracks because once the break started it was over quickly and they didn't want to miss it. When this rite of spring finally came, its violence was mesmerizing, the great plates of splitting ice sounding like rifle shots, or sometimes cannon booms. The broken ice chunks thudded and crashed downstream, pulling along trees torn from the riverbank and whatever else didn't get out of the way. With a couple of days, the ice would be gone. (Mercer 2009, 64)

The ice and thaw are central for Atwood too. In a traumatic central scene in *Cat's Eye*, Elaine, abandoned by her bullying, torturing school friends, falls through the ice. Something about this chilling, menacingly violent, but also potentially freeing version of mother nature resonates for both artists, who often seem to be skating on thin emotional ice. In an interview with Malka Marom, Mitchell talks about her reasons for leaving the sometimes-idyllic Laurel Canyon, as a longing for a remembered Canadian harshness:

> It's like when I left my house in Laurel Canyon, which seemed too soft and too comfortable, too dimly lit, too much red upholstery [...] And the place that I built up on my land in British Columbia was almost like a monastery [...] Stone and hardwood floors and hardwood benches. Everything that would be corrective. No mirrors [...] I made this place very uncomfortable, like a corrective shoe. (Marom 2014, 87)

Mitchell and Atwood both chafe at a version of softness that is so often ascribed to women artists; what I am calling their irritable Canadian feminism is itself a kind of corrective, an ethics and aesthetics of the uncomfortable place. In her book on Canadian literature, Atwood suggests that, if the United States claims the frontier as a central organizing symbol, and England, the island, the central symbol for Canada is "survival" (*Survival*, Atwood 1972, 31). Survival as an idea is multifaceted, Atwood suggests:

> For early settlers or explorers it meant bare survival in the face of "hostile" elements and/or natives: carving out a place and way of keeping alive. But the word can also suggest survival of a crisis or disaster, like a hurricane or wreck, and many Canadian poems have this kind of survival as a theme; what you might call "grim" survival as opposed to "bare" survival. (*Survival*, Atwood 1972, 32)

Atwood and Mitchell both face, and work with grim survival. It limns their ways of being women artists.[9]

There are other more mundane biographical connections between Mitchell and Atwood as well; they both lived in the same neighborhood in Toronto, and perhaps most obviously, they know each other. Atwood paid tribute to Mitchell in a speech inducting her into the Canadian Songwriters Hall of Fame in 2007, and they received stars on Toronto's Walk of Fame at the same time. Atwood reflects on this in a 2012 interview: thinking about the perks of being Margaret Atwood, she says: "Winning the Booker after three previous nominations—that was certainly a lot of fun[. . .] Getting the Toronto Walk of Fame with Joni Mitchell—that was fun because it was Joni Mitchell."[10] I have not found any evidence of Mitchell talking about Atwood's work, but there is a lovely photograph of the two hugging after attending the unveiling of their stars on the Canadian Walk of Fame in October, 2001.[11] Mitchell is on record as being a fan of another great Canadian fiction writer, Alice Munro, and the thematic connections between Munro and Mitchell are strong as well.[12] These three fierce modern Canadian women writers all write about female desire, and the way it is punished and disciplined, with wry humor as well as, more than occasionally, despair. One of my favorite Mitchell lines, from "The Same Situation" off *Court and Spark*, "Send me somebody who's strong and somewhat sincere," does not dismiss the possibility of love entirely, but it weighs in with diminished expectations. It's a line that might well appear in a story by Munro or Atwood. Is there a specifically ambivalent shared Canadian feminist sensibility that these women writer share? To speculate via potentially dubious stereotypes, I wonder if the imperative on the Canadian woman isn't doubled; women are required by our heteronormative, patriarchal culture to be nice, to placate, to show an idealized maternal unselfishness, always thinking of others before themselves. Canadians are often stereotyped as nice as well. Is it possible that writers like Mitchell, Atwood, maybe Munro, claim an artist's version of self and ego in response to these imperatives? A connection to desire and freedom that is refracted through a cold and sometimes harsh landscape, a refusal to placate men, that codes as doubly ornery for Canadian women?

The two artists' shared thematics do not end there. Atwood's first book of poetry was called *The Circle Game*, and came out in 1964, shortly before Mitchell wrote her song "The Circle Game" which was covered by Tom Rush and Buffy Sainte-Marie before Mitchell herself recorded a version of it for *Ladies of the Canyon* (1970).[13] If you Google "circle games" (rather than "*the* circle game") you get a list of kids' party games such as Duck, Duck, Goose. The idea of "circle games" was available as a metaphor in the early 1960s, but it is Mitchell's song that lingers in people's memories when you mention the phrase. Atwood's poem of that title does not simply mirror Mitchell's use of the phrase. Mitchell's image of the carousel as childhood, the seasons of life going around in a movement of hopeless and hopeful aging and return, contrasts with Atwood's less reassuringly cyclical image of "circle games," although Atwood's poem also refers to childhood games. In Atwood's poem, the circles are enclosing and entrapping for the woman speaker: "So now you trace me/like a country's boundary/or a strange new wrinkle in/your wellknown skin" (Atwood 1964). The imagery of the circling children's game, and some of the language is similar: "The children on the lawn/joined hand to hand/go round and round . . ." (Atwood 1964). In Atwood's poem, the childhood game turns sinister and a circle must be broken; whereas, for Mitchell, the carousel of time is inevitable for everyone, and comforting at least in the beauty of the song, and the promise of renewal.[14] Is there a clear connection between the two circle games? According to the Joni Mitchell website, Joni introduced "The Circle

Game" at a concert in 1966 while Atwood's "Circle Game" poem sequence was first published in a magazine, and then in book form in 1964.[15] Mitchell's song was written in response to Neil Young's "Sugar Mountain," which was composed when Young was 19 and unhappy at the thought of growing older ("You can't be twenty on Sugar Mountain"). "The Circle Game" as a response to Young, is less despairing and more reflective. It also shifts the imagery of the childhood competitive version of the circle game. In Duck, Duck, Goose, someone is always "It," the goose, the loser, while the carousel symbolizes a race that never ends and which the child can never win, partly because we all grow old and die, but also because winning is not the point. In Mitchell's "Circle Game" living is the point.

Margaret Atwood said in response to a tweeted question, that she has "never known" whether Joni knew of her poem sequence, but the shared sensibility, emerging from the shared Canadian literary and artistic scene is strong.[16] From this 1940s–1960s backdrop of emerging progressive politics, played out in cold places, comes their shared wry humor and their "irritable feminism" in relation to heterosexual relations. I want to suggest that, among other things, Mitchell's songs twist romance in unexpected ways. Her songs allow us to see relations between men and women as romantic: seductive, attractive, and exhilarating but also, as well as being dangerous, they are often, also perhaps doomed from the start, being rooted in lies. The best you can hope for in a man is "somewhat sincere." Mitchell's perspective also meshes with her interest in original sin, as in "Woodstock's" wish to "get ourselves back to the Garden." However, if from one point of view, the sexual relation is originally constituted by a tragic curse, then, from another less grandiose perspective, it is just kind of annoying. Kind of inevitable. Something to be laughed at, as well as cried along with. Hence my title, "Here's a man and woman sitting on a rock" from "Hejira." The visual, deictic gesture—"Here's"—makes it seem as if the listener chances upon this couple, as the last or only people on earth, mythical, stranded only each other. "They're either going to thaw out or freeze" suggests this is an Adam and Eve myth playing out on a desert island. This is a back-to-basics gesture that suggests not so much an ideal original pairing, but a continually evolving lovers' quarrel, a *Huis Clos* of relationships.[17]

In Mitchell's love songs which are often also irritated-with-love songs, there is often an assumed-to-be-confessional portrait of a woman artist finding ways to be taken seriously, to take herself seriously. But within this structure she encounters a moment when she also turns a harsh eye back on herself, allowing for the sense that perhaps she also has been taking herself too seriously. This back-and-forth between melodramatic desires for freedom, and realizations of the potential comforts of self-deflation, of ordinariness, or a lack of transcendent meaning, is characteristic of Mitchell's work. In "Come in from the Cold" she looks back on a time when she thought life had meaning, and she had choices to make, "And I made some value judgements/In a self-important voice." Mitchell recognizes the absurdity of the grand claim, especially in relation to the vicissitudes of love and desire; however, she still longs "to lose control." Clear-sightedness resides in the moment that you excuse no one, even or especially yourself, from your own canny judgmental eye.

In a song she has referred to as one of her own favorites, "Refuge of the Roads" off *Hejira*, Mitchell turns her amused and deflationary gaze outward and then inward (Weller 2008, 415). I will conclude by talking a little about the first and last verses of this song. It begins by recalling a meeting with a charismatic man, "a friend of spirit" who drinks and womanizes, but who also becomes a part of an intense relationship—almost a folie à deux—with the singer, who sees herself in him, and him in herself. "He saw my complications and he mirrored me back simplified/And we laughed at how our perfection would always be denied." Up to this point in the song there is a characteristic wry doubled recognition; the two of them are mirrors of each other, awesome and perfect. It's just such a shame that so few others realize it. But then the man takes a wrong turn, dispensing words of wisdom to the singer. He starts telling her what to do to make herself more content, that she needs "heart and humor and humility" to lighten her burden. Is it any wonder she abandons him for the roads?

Putting aside, for a moment, Mitchell's on-record statement that the song is about the Buddhist spiritual leader, Trungpa, who was making the celebrity rounds in the early 1970s, this first verse is interesting to me because it seems to portray a relationship of equals.[18] (I say "relationship" because I think it does not matter much whether it's a relationship between friends or lovers.)

Although the man "drinks and womanizes" and the woman, initially, seems charged with holding him together, grounding the man's sanity in her tears, this dynamic quickly shifts. On the one hand, he seems to really see her—there's a mutual recognition between them, and she is complicated. Being "simplified" for her is not a bad thing. And they are funny together—in their shared egotism, laughing at how their perfection will always be denied. This is unusual—what other portrayals of heterosexual relationships can you think of, especially in pop music, in which both participants joke about their own shared narcissism?[19] But then, as the verse finishes, he ruins it all by mansplaining enlightenment, and she leaves. Heart and humility might be nice in the abstract, but not coming from him, not to her. She's got other fish to fry. I find here that wry, amused, refreshingly unforgiving, reaction to heterosexual role-playing that I am calling Canadian irritable feminism.

The rest of the song charts her wandering away from the one-on-one connection toward something freer—she falls in with drifters and cooks them dinner, finds fun in cities, listens to the crickets while losing herself in nature. There is a movement here away from individual enlightenment, or the fulfilment a woman might hope to find in a romantic entanglement, toward an itinerant sense of community and the intense freedom, the aloneness and possible connection, of travel. In the final verse of the song she is in the most mundane of places, a highway service station, looking at a famous photograph of the earth taken from the moon. The first of these photographs dates from August 23, 1966, and several famous ones followed in the late 1960s and early 1970s.[20] When used on the cover of the countercultural consumer bible, *The Whole Earth Catalog* in 1968, and in many other contexts, these photographs become inseparable from a sense of infinite possibility for humanity; yet they also suggest a humbling sense of scale. The photo in the gas station sets the scene for what follows in "Refuge of the Roads," what you can and can't see when you see the earth whole,

> You couldn't see a city
> On that marbled bowling ball
> Or a forest or a highway
> Or me here least of all.

The final objects that can't be seen in this grand photograph, after the artist herself, are the mundane and unpleasant details of traveling—restrooms without hot water, luggage that is bursting at the seams. The ending of the song is all about perspective—moving out and moving in again. The roads, in the final verse, lead to the stars—to the point where the self-seeking, free, woman artist, is no longer visible, even to herself. "Refuge of the Roads" charts a characteristic version of perspective in Mitchell's work; how could one hope to find a single individual on the earth as seen from the sky? But perhaps this disappearance of the female self—the me who is invisible—is also a kind of glorious reassertion, a shot in the dark from the woman artist, staking a claim for freedom against the mansplaining egocentrism of the first verse. Like Atwood, her sister in irritable Canadian feminism, I see Mitchell as finally very happy, as the song says, to keep "mak[ing] most people nervous," with her unforgiving and unforgettable analyses of the truths and lies people tell themselves about their own significance, and their feelings for others, in relationships and in solitude. Whether Mitchell and Atwood would grudgingly acknowledge my "irritable feminism" label or, dismiss it with a characteristic desire for freedom, an insistence on not being pinned down, for me, their exasperated, wry, funny, sometimes grim, Canadian feminism is, and will continue to be, an extraordinary refuge, charting an ethics and aesthetics of some of the late twentieth century's most uncomfortable places.

Notes

1 I'd like to thank Ian Balfour and Ruth Charnock for their editorial contributions to this chapter. Wild speculations and wrong stuff is, of course, all my own fault.
2 In *Cruel Optimism* (Durham: Duke University Press, 2011), Lauren Berlant defines the affective state of "cruel optimism" as an attachment to an object that is not conducive to our thriving structures. I am suggesting that Mitchell and Atwood both have a strongly self-reflexive attitude toward this state.
3 "Margaret Atwood," http://www.luminarium.org/contemporary/atwood/atwood.htm (accessed: June 3, 2018).
4 Think of Mitchell in a song such as "Conversation" in which the lover has no sympathy whatsoever for the mistreated partner of the man she is in love

with: "She only takes him out to show her friends/I want to free him." *Ladies of the Canyon* (Hollywood: Reprise Records, 1970).
5 Mitchell, "Come in from the Cold," *Night Ride Home* (Hollywood: Geffen Records, 1991).
6 Leopold Bloom similarly wipes his ass with a newspaper in James Joyce's *Ulysses* in a commentary on the tabloids.
7 "Song for Sharon" is dedicated to Joni's best friend when she was growing up in Maidstone, Saskatchewan in the 1950s. It refers to the fact that Sharon wanted to be a professional singer, while Joni wanted to get married and live on a farm. As adults the two changed places. See Joseph Dobrian, "'Song for Sharon' brings back memories," *Iowa City Press-Citizen*, February 7, 2017. https://eu.press-citizen.com/story/opinion/contributors/writers-group/2017/02/07/joni-mitchell-song-sharon-brings-back-memories/97296996/ (accessed: June 11, 2018).
8 Think, for instance, of Mitchell's "River" from *Blue*, where a river is both something frozen, but also a means of escape after a ruined love affair, something "to skate away on" (Hollywood: Reprise Records, 1971).
9 Drowning in cold water is also a threat and a promise for both artists. See for instance, Mitchell, "Song for Sharon," *Hejira* (Hollywood: Asylum Records, 1976); Margaret Atwood, *Surfacing* (Toronto: McClelland and Stewart Ltd, 1972) and the poem "This is a photograph of me" from *The Circle Game* (Contact Press, 1964).
10 Carolyn Lawrence, "Canadian Literary Icon Margaret Atwood Reflects on Her Career Longevity, Her Confidence in Her Art, and Names Her Greatest Accomplishment," *Women of Influence*, September 10, 2012. http://www.womenofinfluence.ca/2012/09/10/margaret-atwood-success-story/ (accessed: June 11, 2018).
11 http://www.baltimoresun.com/la-et-ms-joni-mitchell-pictures-20150331-005-photo.html.
12 Quoted in Mercer (2009, 208–209). Taken from Sean O'Hagan, "Idol Talk," *New Musical Express*, June 4, 1988 (n.p.) Joni pictures herself as a frustrated short story writer:

> You heard of Alice Munro? Boy! I connect with her. She's a fellow Canadian and she writes about things I lived through. But I kinda slept through them. I didn't absorb them like her—detailed memories of childhood, family gatherings, events. I used to look to Dylan or Neil [Young] for songwriting inspiration but now, there's no one really cutting it, so you gotta turn to the short story tellers—Munro, Raymond Carver, the dirty realists. Since *The Hissing of Summer Lawns*, I've been a frustrated short story writer but whereas Carver makes me think I can write short stories, Munro makes me think I can't.

13. Buffy Sainte-Marie was the first to release it on her 1967 album *Fire and Fleet and Candlelight*. Tom Rush also recorded the song, making it the title track of his 1968 album. This was a breakthrough for Mitchell, who spent much of 1967 performing in Philadelphia and Toronto as she built up her career. Rush saw her perform in Detroit that year and recorded "The Circle Game" along with two other Mitchell compositions for the album: "Urge For Going" and "Tin Angel." Mitchell's own version came out in 1970 on *Ladies of the Canyon*. See "'The Circle Game' by Joni Mitchell," *Songfacts*. http://www.songfacts.com/detail.php?id=5649 (accessed: June 11, 2018).
14. This might have to do with the way the two texts are gendered. Mitchell's "Circle Game" is about a boy ("words like, when you're older, must appease him") whereas Atwood's "Circle Game" is about a woman trapped in a relationship.
15. "'The Circle Game' by Joni Mitchell," *Songfacts*. http://www.songfacts.com/detail.php?id=5649 (accessed: June 11, 2018).
16. Twitter, January 7, 2018. Atwood responded to my question about whether she knew of any relationship between her book and Mitchell's song: "I have never known that, but my poem sequence (inside the book and pub'd in a mag earlier than it) predated the song. I think more likely just coincidence tho."
17. One might consider this in relation to the ending of Virginia Woolf's final novel, *Between the Acts* (Oxford: Oxford World's Classics, 1998), in which an estranged couple who have not spoken to each other for the entire book, finally open their mouths to speak, in front of a barren landscape, seemingly disembodied in time: "Isa let her sewing drop. The great hooded chairs had become enormous. And Giles too. And Isa too against the window. The window was all sky without colour. The house had lost its shelter. It was night before roads were made, or houses. It was the night that dwellers in caves had watched from some high place among rocks. Then the curtain rose. They spoke" (Woolf 1998, 197).
18. Doug Fischer, "The Trouble She's Seen," *Ottawa Citizen*, October 8, 2006. http://jonimitchell.com/library/view.cfm?id=1459 (accessed: June 11, 2018), and Mercer (2009, 202).
19. I think of a recent inheritor of Joni's romantic sensibility, Lorde, whose song "The Louvre" contains a similar gesture when she claims that she and her lover are so awesome that they should hang them in the Louvre, "down the back, but so what? Still the Louvre." "The Louvre," *Melodrama* (New York: Universal, 2017).
20. Becky Ferriera, "The First Photographs of the Earth from the Moon Were Taken 50 Years Ago Today," Motherboard, August 23, 2016. https://motherboard.vice.com/en_us/article/bmvyzw/the-first-photographs-of-the-earth-from-the-moon-were-taken-50-years-ago-today (accessed: June 11, 2018).

Works Cited

Atwood, Margaret. "The Circle Game," in *The Circle Game*. Toronto: Contact Press, 1964.

Atwood, Margaret. *Surfacing*. Toronto: McClelland and Stewart Ltd., 1972.

Atwood, Margaret. *Survival: A Thematic Guide to Canadian Literature*. Toronto: House of Anansi Press, 1972.

Atwood, Margaret. *The Handmaid's Tale*. Toronto: McClelland and Stuart Ltd., 1985.

Atwood, Margaret. *Cat's Eye*. London: Virago, 1990.

Berlant, Lauren. *Cruel Optimism*. Durham: Duke University Press, 2011.

Dobrian, Joseph. "'Song for Sharon' Brings Back Memories," *Iowa City Press Citizen*, February 7, 2017. http://www.press-citizen.com/story/opinion/contributors/writers-group/2017/02/07/joni-mitchell-song-sharon-brings-back-memories/97296996/ (accessed: June 11, 2018).

Ferriera, Becky. "The First Photographs of the Earth from the Moon Were Taken 50 Years Ago Today," August 23, 2016. https://motherboard.vice.com/en_us/article/bmvyzw/the-first-photographs-of-the-earth-from-the-moon-were-taken-50-years-ago-today (accessed: June 11, 2018).

Fischer, Doug. "The Trouble She's Seen," *Ottawa Citizen*, October 8, 2006. http://jonimitchell.com/library/view.cfm?id=1459 (accessed: June 11, 2018).

Gunn, Frank. "Author Margaret Atwood, Left, and Singer Joni Mitchell Hug Each Other after Unveiling Their Stars on the Canada Walk of Fame in Toronto on Friday Oct. 19, 2001," *Baltimore Sun*, http://www.baltimoresun.com/la-et-ms-joni-mitchell-pictures-20150331-005-photo.html.

Lorde. *Melodrama*. New York: Universal, 2017.

Marom, Malka. *Joni Mitchell: Both Sides Now—Conversations with Malka Marom*. London: Omnibus Press, 2014.

McNamara, Mary. "Q and A: Margaret Atwood Answers the Question 'Is *The Handmaid's Tale* a Feminist Book?'" *Los Angeles Times*, April 24, 2017.

Mead, Rebecca. "Margaret Atwood: The Prophet of Dystopia," *New Yorker*, April 27, 2017. http://www.newyorker.com/magazine/2017/04/17/margaret-atwood-the-prophet-of-dystopia (accessed: June 11, 2017).

Mercer, Michelle. *Will You Take Me as I Am: Joni Mitchell's Blue Period*. Milwaukee: Backbeat Books, 2009.

Mitchell, Joni. *Ladies of the Canyon*. Hollywood: Reprise Records, 1970.

Mitchell, Joni. *Blue*. Hollywood: Reprise Records, 1971.

Mitchell, Joni. *Court and Spark*. Hollywood: Asylum Records, 1974.

Mitchell, Joni. *Hejira*. Hollywood: Asylum Records, 1976.

Mitchell, Joni. *Night Ride Home*. Hollywood: Geffen Records, 1991.

Mitchell, Joni. "'The Circle Game' by Joni Mitchell." *SongFacts*. http://www.songfacts.com/detail.php?id=5649 (accessed: July 13, 2017).

Weller, Sheila. *Girls Like Us: Carole King, Joni Mitchell, Carly Simon—and The Journey of a Generation*. New York: Atria Books, 2008.

Woolf, Virginia. *Between the Acts*. Oxford: Oxford World's Classics, 1998.

Hollow: "Cactus Tree" and the Signs of Freedom

Peter Coviello

In the midst of Henry James's magnificent heartbreak of a novel, *The Portrait of a Lady*, there is a curious turn of phrase—a phrase, you could say, for conjuring. Famously, *Portrait* is a novel about a young woman granted an almost unlimited freedom of action who is determined to live a life of bright and searching intensity and who, in part as a result of that very gift of freedom, brings herself to ruin. In the unspooling of this drama, one character pauses to wonder, of our tragic heroine Isabel Archer, "what queer temporal province she was annexing" (James 1983, 281).[1] In the small piece that follows, I want to take up James's offhand provocation. I want, I mean, to think a bit about young women, about freedom and its perils, and about some of the queerer temporal provinces to which we might be brought in our attentions to one track, one long-ago song in the expansive archive of songs by one of the most indispensable musicians of the twentieth century.

My work here clusters around a series of interlinked questions: Can a song written by a woman in her very early 1920s map out the arc of the nearly 50-year career trajectory that would follow it? When this happens—*if* this happens—what kind of folding are we in the presence of, what kind of anticipatory resonance or pop prolepsis? What is the proper name for the queer temporal provinces of pop idioms such as these or, for that matter, of the work of criticism as it encounters the time-folding magic of certain songs?

To answer these questions, and to think through some of their satellite implications, I want to address the closing track from Joni Mitchell's debut album *Song to a Seagull* (1968), "Cactus Tree," setting it in brief dialogue with another powerhouse work close to it in time and theme, Paula Fox's *Desperate Characters*. Now, "Cactus Tree," as Mitchell enthusiasts will be quick to tell you, was neither her first nor her most indelible hit from the 1960s; she had already written both "The Circle Game" and, even before that, "Both Sides, Now." All this is true enough. And yet "Cactus Tree" nevertheless holds something of a place of pride in Mitchell's body of work, singled out as it would be by one of Mitchell's own narrators. Nearly a decade later, in the closing track from the masterwork that was *Hejira* (1976), the speaker in Mitchell's "Amelia" would pause in her flight from romantic catastrophe and, memorably, spend the night at "the Cactus Tree Motel."[2] From the seeds of that little aside—what I take to be its backward-looking acknowledgment of *something*: be it achieved clarity, continuity, maybe a strong early attempt at an abiding set of preoccupations—the impulses of my argument here will grow.

My central claim, which I want to pursue by looking at some formal aspects of the lyrics and by framing them around the historical questions the song seems to pose about "the decade full of dreams" that is its subject, is both straightforward and counterfactual: it is that many, if not all, of what would come to be the signature conflicts of Mitchell's work, the most enlivening and also the most dismaying, are prefigured in this song. "Cactus Tree," I mean to suggest, brings to its first full expression less an idle embrace of "freedom," that keyword of the era, than a wrought, mistrusting, precisely calibrated *ambivalence* about the promises of that freedom, particularly as it had come to be routed through the gendered idioms of 60s-left cultural radicalism. A sub-claim here is that the exquisite, exemplary poise with which she holds the tensions of this ambivalence in balance, in a songwriter so young, about breaks your heart. But it offers us, too, a revelatory way into the pressures and contradictions, the tensions that refuse to resolve, at the defining center of Mitchell's career.

It's worth saying from the start: there are ways of not much liking this song. Were you to insist to me that "Cactus Tree" had no place whatsoever in your private pantheon of Mitchell tracks, and could not rightfully be compared to "River" or "A Case of You" or "Refuge of the Roads" or "Coyote" or any of the other likelier possibilities, I would not have a lot of heart to persuade you otherwise. The reasons are clear enough. If, for instance, you have any sort of allergy to what we might generously call Mitchell's youthful *poeticism*, "Cactus Tree" will be a song you might well find difficult to love. More precisely, you would not do well to take to this song any quick impatience you might harbor with respect to a certain hippieish indulgence in figures and phrases a little too easy, a little too artful, and altogether too delighted with themselves. When, at the outset, the singer speaks of a man "bearing beads from California / with their amber stones *and green*," the preciousness of that small reversal may well set your teeth on edge. A good deal more of this is to come, alas, as when the singer speaks of the man who has "climbed the scaly towers / of a forest tree"—with *towers* offered as a rhyme for, yes, inevitably, *flowers*.[3]

Let me say it directly: I understand the distaste for this sort of pat prettiness, I do. You do not need to persuade me that these are, each of them, figures unable to mask quite how pleased they are with their own poetic loveliness, or to overcome the atmosphere of coffeehouse confectedness they conjure around themselves. I get it. Nor, extending the claim, do you lose points with me either for identifying precisely that confection, so vivid in what is sometimes called Mitchell's "folk waif" period, with a familiar style of specifically countercultural affectedness.[4] We might specify such affectation with any number of expressions of high-flown hippie piety—"hey, if we think really hard maybe we can stop all this rain," to take the iconic example from Michael Hadleigh's 1970 film *Woodstock*—any one of which might help us clarify that style of quasi-political toothlessness it is difficult not to find, in its laxest moments, aggravating. This is, admittedly, an ungenerous accounting of the counterculture. But then anybody who grew up listening to punk rock, or just beguiled by the array of detonating refusals to be found there, will likely have a clear enough sense of what I mean, if only because so much of the eviscerating force of punk was aimed at, precisely, the played-out pieties of hippiedom, its neutering of the conflictual ugliness of politics, its unmaskable self-satisfaction. If you're the kind of listener for whom there hovers about the too blandly pretty lines of the song some faint trace of just those enervating pieties, then listen: love it though I do, I will not blame you too severely for consigning "Cactus Tree" to some playlist of worn-out period pieces not much in need of revival.

I would nevertheless want to insist, though, that, for all this, the song is in fact not truly in thrall to these figures, or not quite. Nor is it employing them as thoughtlessly, as unselfconsciously, as you might fear. To the contrary, what animates "Cactus Tree" is the way it ballasts these flights toward flower-child effusiveness with a language much more exacting, and unadorned, and resolutely quotidian. Indeed, the drama the song unfolds, the tension it works through by coiling and uncoiling, *is* that moment-to-moment counterbalancing. And, to anticipate some of my argument, this is precisely the style of rhetorical grace that will come to mark Mitchell's later work so significantly, and to give it much of its shape. And it is here, in "Cactus Tree," in early vivid form.

How does this work? In the song, it takes form chiefly as an agile counterweighting of what we might describe as poetic language with something nearer to the ordinariness of vernacular speech: the punctuation—though we might also say the puncturing—of flowery indulgence with plainspokenness. We have looked already at some of the moments of hippie over-prettiness. But think too of when Mitchell sings the following lines:

> There's a lady in the city
> and she thinks she loves them all
> There's the one who's thinking of her
> There's the one who sometimes calls.

There are so many small graces here—and they are, after a manner of speaking, *formal*, unfolding at the level of idiom, diction, the management of rhyme. Consider the closing phrase, "the one who sometimes calls," which is so *un*fanciful, so rooted in the workaday world; it is a phrase that sounds as it appears in the song, only more unfanciful, only more anchored in the rudiments of the quotidian, by virtue of being linked to the more elevated discursive precincts of a phrase like "she loves them all." But that freighting of particular words and phrases with the anchoring heft of the quotidian recurs elsewhere in the song too. "The one who sometimes calls," that is, answers back to similarly idiomatic lines that punctuate other verses. Some are small and offhand—lines like "he can miss her just the same." And some carry a special sort of punch, like "He writes, 'Wish you were beside me'"—a bit of reported speech that pierces with its truncated simplicity. The matter isn't only that such lines ring in a key only the more marked by plainspokenness as a result of being nested alongside the more high-flown phrases. That's true, but the counterweighting works in the other direction as well. These are the moments without which the later pivotal lines of the song would carry within them so much less gravity, so little a sense of being not merely abstractions but abstractions anchored in this way to the ordinary and unglowing human world.

This movement is perhaps nowhere more striking than in a verse nearing the end of the song:

> There's a man who writes her letters
> He is bleeding from the war
> There's a jouster and jester
> And a man who owns a store

I dissemble not at all when I say that, in the Introduction to Poetry classes I used to run back at the college where I worked, I taught this stanza. I taught it as an exemplification of the point made by modernist critics like Josephine Miles, John Hollander, and Mary Kinzie, about the extraordinary ligaturing work done by effective rhyme. Part of the function of rhyme, they remind us, is to fold together anticipation and surprise—you know *that* it's coming, inside the structure of a rhyming poem, but you do not know *what* is coming. This effect is heightened, they further remind us, by the yoking of words and phrases from contrasting rhetorical registers.[5] Here, in Mitchell's stanza, is about the finest materialization of this principle you're likely to find anywhere this side of Alexander Pope. The phrase "bleeding from the war" becomes more, not less, vivid, and in this more a condensed emblem of horror, by virtue of its swift conjoining with a phrase that could not speak more utterly of the homely, the unexceptional: *a man who owns a store*. The concision of that pairing, heightened by the rhyme, is jolting.

The point here is not finally to marvel at Mitchell's rhetorical poise—though I confess that, possessing as I do the heart of a formalist, I find it hard not to be moved by it. Nor is it even to note how that poise will work to similarly stirring effect in later works, though such moments are delectable. Think of the lines at the end of "Amelia"—think, I mean, of how "dreams, Amelia, dreams and false alarms" rings alongside the phrase, borrowed from an entirely other lexical universe, "747s over geometric farms." Or think of the heart-lifting wonderfulness of the moment in "Refuge of the Roads," where the narrator has a lover who has managed, in a winning way, to give her back herself "simplified." Ah, but then it all goes wrong. Said lover begins, as Pamela Thurschwell has remarked, in a phrase of deathless perfection, *mansplaining enlightenment*. He tells her, "Heart and humor and humility will lighten up your heavy load." Nothing exposes the windy paternal self-indulgence of the lover's phrases, his high-minded sententiousness, quite as killingly as the curt *simplified* quality of the narrator's prompt reply to all this: "I left him then." You can hear it a thousand times—most of you probably have—and still, as A. R. Ammons might say, it makes the heart move roomier.[6]

In "Cactus Tree," though, these formal moves do much besides. Above all, they make exquisitely clear the most substantive stakes of the song. With maximal fineness, they register the song's calibrated relation to its central preoccupations, which are of course "freedom" and the ways it circulates in what the song names, at the very outset, "a decade full of dreams." It is a relation that, for Mitchell, is not at all simple or self-evident. Indeed, it is precisely the wrought-up, articulate tension that the song nurtures and sustains in relation to an idea of "freedom" that makes it both the early-career powerhouse that it is, and something of a Rosetta stone for the whole of the career that was to follow. For Mitchell is of course invested in, attracted to, and not unbeguiled by prospects of freedom, even when they speak in idioms somewhat worryingly sententious; but in her persistent ironizing of those languages, her undercutting leaning *against* them, she registers as well a far-sighted misgiving about what "freedom" can and will mean in the contexts in which it circulates—especially for women.

Just as you might be excused for any knee-jerk recoil from its more indulgently hippieish turns of phrase, in a similar way you could be forgiven too for taking "Cactus Tree," at first blush, to be something of a second-wave anthem of liberation, of the sort that a book like *Girls Like Us* might be said to hail.[7] It seems very much to be the song of a young woman living in the enjoyment of the freedom proper to this decade full of dreams, and especially in the enjoyment of its *erotic* freedom—the freedom, say, to have just this heterogeneous array of lovers, taxonomized in their startling variety verse by verse. (Here they are, the great Whitmanian catalog of them: the sailor, the climber, the man in the office, the letter-writer, the veteran, the jouster, the jester, the man who owns the store . . .) And this is one way of describing the narrative of "Cactus Tree." The singer tells us over the course of the song that she will resist the calls they make, these many unlike and unlikely men, for contracts and pledges, abridgements of her field of action. The point could not be clearer—"they will lose her if they follow"—we are told, and that is that. And there is, too, a wonderful, winking, half-comic exhilaration—again, an erotic exhilaration—to be heard in lines like, "and who knows, there may be more." Here, then, is "freedom" figured as a liberation from outdated modes of female constraint and confinement. That freedom takes form for the singer as a putting away of a whole host of antiquated and specifically patriarchal proprieties, and "Cactus Tree" registers the blisses, many and not at all inconsiderable, that can be seen to follow from it.

There is much to this take from the song. We might hear in it, for instance, something of a thickening of those slacker, more vaporous countercultural versions of "freedom" that can be heard, however faintly, around the song's more quaintly poetic turns of idiom. To the degree that we take seriously the pleasures the song broadcasts, the possibilities taking form for the singer as a litany of trailing men, we do well not to dismiss the style of freedom the singer might be seen to embody. Again, though, as with the flights of poeticism that mark so many of the verses and lines, the song is not in the thrall of freedom so conceived. It is not, however richly it figures certain of the pleasures of what might be called "liberation," a cheerleading account of the freedoms opening in a decade full of dreams, though neither is it much interested in reactionary refusal or rebuke. What it finally expresses most pointedly is, instead, a fierce and finely calibrated *ambivalence* about freedom in exactly that construction—the mode of 60s-left cultural radicalism, say, as it moves through the porous outlands where sex, gender, and politics come into vexingly tight relation. All of this comes into focus in the compressed power of the song's ending:

> They will lose her if they follow
> And she only means to please them
> And her heart is full, and hollow
> Like a cactus tree

In part because of the clarity with which the song sees the joys of freedom, the genuine human delights, these final undercutting lines arriving a bit like a punch in the solar plexus. Again, this is a song not interested in dismissing freedom, and even less the erotic possibilities of freedom for young women at the end of the 1960s, and no just reading of the song can make it say that. But it is a song passionately invested in *mistrusting* that freedom, in worrying over the languages in which it gets articulated, the promises it makes, the falsities those languages mask.

In this articulate mistrust, expressed as an attunement to the hollowness of the proffered promises of freedom, particularly as they are shaped by and around the lives of women, Mitchell is of course not alone. Pamela Thurschwell, in an essay in this volume, describes Mitchell's especially spiky sort of wariness in relation to worlds shaped by patriarchal presumption—worlds of liberation and confinement both—as a strong iteration of a whole genre of critique, which she names "irritable feminism." For Thurschwell, Mitchell takes her place among other writers roughly contemporaneous to her—all of them white, feminist, Canadian—who are bound together by a style of anti-patriarchal intellectual comportment that is unconsoled by the easier liberal pieties of female *progress*, that is alive to the forms of micro- and macro-aggressivity and subjugation and violence that sleep within them, and that is keen to dwell in the forms of conflict that do not resolve with the satisfying definitiveness of, say, a pentatonic scale. Alice Munro and Margaret Atwood are, in their different idioms, the avatars of this style for Thurschwell, and her reading of Mitchell in relation to them is revelatory. What it reveals, among other things, is something of the *restlessness* that works itself out in Mitchell's corpus, an expansive and ill-satisfied rovingness that describes not simply an interest in roads and travel—those lines of flight from romance and its decaying enclosures that we see so vividly in a record like *Hejira*—but an intellectual, and political, and explicitly feminist disposition. (This is a "style" in the strong figuring Seamus Heaney gives us when he speaks about "technique," by which he means to signify an aesthetic, certainly, but also what he calls, winningly, a "stance toward life."[8])

In the interest of expanding the point and clarifying what I take to be at stake in the style of articulate mistrust we have been tracking in "Cactus Tree" and elsewhere, I want for a moment to set Mitchell alongside still another white feminist author working contemporaneously to her. Consider the example of Paula Fox and, in particular, her ferocious, compressed, and bleak novel *Desperate Characters*. Here is a novel that transpires over a few days in 1968—the season of the release of *Song to a Seagull*—though in a setting a good deal removed from the multiscenic "Cactus Tree," with its traversed open spaces and fleeting glimpses of office life. For the heroine at the center of *Desperate Characters*, 1968 feels, contrarily, claustrophobic—even if the scenes of her confinement are especially comfortable, sumptuous even. The novel opens upon a scene of unexceptional, but unmistakable, plenty, in the key of high-bourgeois American urbanity:

> Mr. and Mrs. Otto Brentwood drew out their chairs simultaneously. As he sat down, Otto regarded the straw basked which held slices of French bread, an earthenware casserole filled with sautéed chicken livers, peeled and sliced tomatoes on an oval willowware platter Sophie had found in a Brooklyn Heights antique shop, and *risotto* Milanese in a green ceramic bowl. A strong light, somewhat softened by the stained glass of a Tiffany shade, fell upon this repast. (Fox 1999, 21. Cited internally hereafter)

If there is an old-worldish insularity to this tableau—an antiquated formality that comes splendidly clear in the delicate deployment of a word like *repast*—it is soon enough interrupted. Disruption comes not from the as-yet-undisplaced neighbors in this rising Brooklyn neighborhood, these "slum people" (32) whose ragged windows can be seen from the Brentwood's back terrace. Or not only. The novel commences rather with a startling if tiny burst of violence, unleashed on the threshold between the Brentwood's tasteful interior and the wild outer world it keeps at bay. Sophie, in this first scene, is bitten on the hand by a feral cat that had been scratching around their back door and which, against Otto's wishes, she had gone out to feed: "It sank its teeth into the back of her left hand and hung from her flesh so that she nearly fell forward, stunned and horrified, yet conscious enough of Otto's presence to smother the cry that arose in her throat as she jerked her hand back" (25). Over the course of the rest of the novel, the wound festers. Sophie resists having it treated—that early note about Otto's chastening and censorious presence carries through the whole of the book—and because of this the possibility that she has been poisoned, that she has contracted a strain of rabies that even in the midst of all this cossetted security might actively be *killing her,* never dissipates from the novel. It is, throughout, alive with a corrosive menace.

The story the novel tells is of a period of stilled unhappiness, edging out toward crisis, in Sophie's marriage to Otto and, more broadly, in her life. Sophie and Otto are childless, and well-off; Sophie is a translator, though she has let her work lapse; Otto is a lawyer, and much of the local turmoil in the novel involves the fact that Otto's long-time partner, Charlie, has broken up their partnership, exasperated by what he understands to be Otto's stolidity, his conservatism, and above all his want of sympathy for Charlie's own burgeoning, essentially countercultural political commitments. Charlie understands himself to have been, in a basically domesticated way, *radicalized.* "You won't survive this," Charlie complains bitterly one night to Sophie, "what's happening now. People like you . . . stubborn and stupid and drearily enslaved to introspection while the foundation of their privilege is being blasted out from under them" (60). It's worth saying that no one in the novel is convinced by this, or convinced rather that in Charlie it expresses anything other than a dilettantish cocktail-party self-besottedness, a way of staging what Sophie aptly diagnoses as a sibling-like rivalry with Otto. (His disquisitions are coded by the novel, we might say, in exactly the way that "Refuge of the Roads" codes, and ultimately undercuts, those of the mansplainy "enlightened" lover.) But Charlie's crisis, and Otto's struggle with his partner's abandonment, however glancingly they both seem to touch the malaise of the world, open out onto the crisis that, for Sophie, *had* had a radical power, a capacity to shake her out of her accumulated habits of being, and into a newer, rawer relation to the world without. This was her affair some years earlier—undisclosed to Otto—with a man named Francis Early.

In the middle of the novel is a chapter in which Sophie recollects her affair, its initiation, its stages, its eventual nonclimactic dissolution. It is, without question, the scene of Sophie's most enlivening intensities, her least befogged passages of contact with the world, and the place where the resonances of the book, alongside Mitchell's song, are most clear. "But she had had her secret hoarding," we are told,

> seeing him as he searched for her in a bar where they met and where she, as usual, was early, watching him as he made coffee on the stove, noting with intense pleasure his long thin back, his slightly stooped shoulders, his sharply drawn profile as he turned from time to time to say something to her. (83)

Sophie will later realize that "her involvement with Francis had shoved her back violently into herself" (84), though this violent inwardness makes also for an outward attunement, a fine keenness of regard for the suddenly unblurred details of her life. She is vitalized, clarified, *galvanized*:

> She had never looked better; the whites of her eyes were as clear as a child's, her dark hair was especially lustrous, and although she didn't eat much, she seemed to be bursting out of her clothes, not because of added weight, so much as of galvanized energy. Strain, she thought, became her, tightened up her face which was overly plastic, lightened her rather sallow olive skin. She didn't have a moment of repose, thinking, thinking, thinking about him. (85)

If a sort of gendered conformity adheres to these passages—a new keenness of stance toward life acquired not in solitude but through immersive contact with a man—the force of Sophie's revelations, the breadth of their power to rework her relation not only to him but to herself and to the worlds she inhabits, mitigates at least something of this conventionality. There is a "Cactus Tree"-like achieved vividness of life here, a fierce and burning clarity that for a time unclouds Sophie, in a way that even the potentially lethal bite with which she is afflicted cannot.

And yet, here too, what's so striking about Sophie's retrospective account of her affair with Francis Early is the way that, while holding close to its expansive range of effects, she understands it to have been unavailing, its own kind of ruse—and *not* because it came to an end, failed to issue in some new scene of intimacy that might replace the airlessness of her relation to Otto with something larger and freer. In a way that might recall to us Mitchell's self-chastising narrator, Sophie seems rather to regard exactly that possibility, the all-but-narcotic promise of a liberation from the suffocations of domestic intimacy in a sex-driven *replacement* intimacy, as part of the ruse with which she must somehow contend, the humiliating lie that she recognizes but cannot, for all that, prevent herself becoming entangled in. Some of this, Sophie will tell herself, is surely recrimination. "Later," we are told, "during a time when there was no room in her thoughts for anything but remorseless obsessive recollection, a perverse desire to debase the tenderness she had felt for him led her to insist to herself that it had all been a kind of fatigued middle-aged prurience" (83). Revealingly, though, her sense of the inadequacy of whatever form of liberation Francis would present to her begins in fact, *before* she is well and truly embarked on their affair. After an exchanged, electric touch between them had sent them into a taxi, speeding to Francis's apartment, they enjoy a frozen moment together, in which Francis takes her hand, at which touch, "a tremor passed over her and her mouth went dry" (80). But then comes one of the most lacerating sentences of the whole novel: "She had, then," we are told, "an anguished foreknowledge that she would be a long time missing him" (80). Such foreknowledge, and the *anguish* that attends it, does not exhaust itself in the suspicion that what she is about to embark upon is mere "fatigued middle-aged prurience," a judgment that the novel does indeed mark as a sort of recriminatory wish, a falsifying story Sophie uses to comfort herself in the aftermath of loss. (It is as if, like Mitchell in "Amelia," she endeavors to console herself, not totally convincingly, with the idea these were all merely dreams, "dreams and false alarms.") The more unnerving possibility broached by *Desperate Characters* is that, without being in the grip of anything like cynicism or unconverted bourgeois conventionality or staid gender obedience, Sophie knows to *disbelieve* the promise of liberation that is shortly to arrive to her. Like Mitchell's narrator in "Cactus Tree," she will take its measure, and when she does it will be accounted as something richer in possibility, and less mired in self-deception, than Charlie's enthusiasms, or her husband's stolid resistance to them. But it will be insufficient nevertheless, unavailing, hollow.

All this gives, retrospectively, a stinging resonance to a scene that comes earlier in the novel (though *after* her affair), at a party on the night Sophie suffers her terrible bite. There she encounters "a couple in their early twenties" who are bedecked in countercultural markers—he has frizzy long hair and an army fatigue jacket covered in buttons, she hair to her waist and a "heavy bracelet around one of her ankles" (38)—and bristle at the *squareness* of the party. Their encounter ends thus:

> They looked at her as though they'd never seen her before, then they both padded softly out of the living room, looking neither left nor right. "That's a beautiful anklet!" Sophie called out. The girl looked back from the hall. For an instant, she seemed about to smile. "It hurts me to wear it," she shouted. "Every time I move, it hurts." (39)

When we first come upon it, the moment seems a bit of sharp observational comedy, mordant and undercutting. In the reflected light of Sophie's affair—the affair that was vivifying, clarifying, galvanizing, and unredeeming—it glows with a terrible inner darkness. The options for freedom, on either side of the generational divide marked out by 1968, are not without compelling force. They might even be beautiful. For the women, however, in and out of scenes of domestic confinement—in whatever proximity to the available idioms of liberation—they are also more and other than beautiful. They constrain. They *hurt*. They hurt with all the ache the protagonist of "Cactus Tree" avows, whose heart is full but unnourished: hollow.

We can, I think, read the novel's stirring conclusion in close relation to such submerged revelations as these. Here, Sophie thinks through her conviction that her phone will ring, that she will in fact be told that the cat that bit her was rabid, and wonders whether this "appalling certainty," this certainty of harm, "did not arise from reason or its systems, but was a fatal estimate of her true life?"

> "*God, if I am rabid, I am equal to what is outside*," she said out loud, and felt an extraordinary relief as though, at last, she'd discovered what it was that could create a balance between the quiet, rather vacant progression of the days she spent in this house, and those portents that lit up the dark at the edge of her own existence. (185, emphasis in the original)

Rabidity, for *Desperate Characters*, is the condition that adheres Sophie to the world: the heart's rabid desire for love even at the cost of steep self-deception;

the world's rabid malignancy, its narrowness of care and brutal, multiplying, deforming inequities. It is a novel that does not want for sympathy, a warm-blooded seriousness of regard, for anybody's hunger for some species of liberation, for a freedom that might crack open at least a little these narrownesses. But it is wedded no less committedly to its mistrust, an unwillingness to be beguiled by the languages in which those supposedly broadening freedoms are cast.

So when, in that beautiful moment in "Amelia," Mitchell stops at the Cactus Tree Motel, I take the moment to be a nod in the direction of the readings we are undertaking here. It is moment of several stacked recognitions. The song invites us to see that "Cactus Tree" is a shimmering distillation, less of Mitchell's youthful and ardent poeticism, than of her fierce and unsparing ambivalence: a testament, in all, to what would become for her, over many years and many records, a habitual resistance to "freedom" itself, in the offered registers, *especially* as they entangle the sexual and political. In ways that might recall to us the ferocity of vision we find in Fox—and recall to us as well Munro, and Atwood—Mitchell is a singer who mistrusts the available idioms of freedom, the languages that circulate around her and promise liberation from the toils of (say) being a woman. She does not dismiss them, nor she does present herself in the posture of someone unbeguiled by them. But she disrupts and disturbs them, with a mistrustfulness that's only the keener for being, also, beguiled.

As we know, that undercutting skepticism in regard to liberatory languages could calcify into unlovely forms—Mitchell's sometime racism, her sometime polemical antifeminism. "I was never a feminist," she says to Malka Marom in one of the interviews collected in *Joni Mitchell: In Her Own Words*. "I was in argument with them . . . And even though my problems were somewhat female, they were of no help to mine" (Marom 2014, 62).⁹ Fair to say, I think, that these are no one's favorite versions of Joni Mitchell. I would not want to dismiss them too hastily, though, or to contextualize them away. As a song like "Cactus Tree" shows, they are interwoven with the very aspects of artistry, the cultivated mistrust and vibrant ambivalence, that make her the particular kind of extraordinary that she is. "Cactus Tree" is a track where Mitchell's roving inquietude of mind, her often self-undermining refusal of complacencies no matter how steadying or pleasurable, expresses itself neither as dismissal nor embrace but a live wariness in relation to the hollowness of 'boomer utopianism, a hollowness vivid not solely to women but to women especially. Quite as much as the soprano radiance of her voice, the intricacy or thrumming insistence of her guitar, that exquisite self-confounding balance makes the song *sing*. And in its handful of minutes, and the queer temporal province we find ourselves in as it plays and replays, it maps out, too, in exquisite miniature, a whole future of songs, one that holds many of us even still.

Notes

1 The phrase, which comes early in chapter 28, appears in the New York edition, of 1907–1909.
2 Joni Mitchell, "Amelia," *Hejira* (Hollywood: Asylum, 1976).
3 Joni Mitchell, "Cactus Tree," *Song to a Seagull* (Hollywood: Reprise Records, 1968). All citation of "Cactus Tree" hereafter come from this recording.
4 See here for instance Luftig (2000), the second section of which is titled, "From Folk Waif to Rock and Roll Lady."
5 See especially Hollander (2001), and Miles (1976). On the "small and local movements" of style as a register of the distinctiveness of a given writer's disposition see Kinzie (1993, xii–xiii).
6 Joni Mitchell, "Refuge of the Roads," *Hejira* (Hollywood: Asylum, 1976). I've stolen the phrase "the heart moves roomier" from the closing of A. R. Ammons's poem "The City Limits." See Ammons (1986, 89).
7 *Girls Like Us* is a conjoint biography of Carole King, Joni Mitchell, and Carly Simon, that is long on boomer heroicization, largely in the key of second-wave liberation. See Weller (2009).
8 "Technique," Heaney writes, "involves not only a poet's way with words, his management of meter, rhythm, and verbal texture; it involves also his [sic] stance toward life." See "Feeling into Words," in Heaney (1980, 47).
9 It is here, too, that Mitchell narrates her own chronicled experiments in blackface (as on the cover of *Don Juan's Reckless Daughter*, from 1977). See especially 206–212.

Works Cited

Ammons, A. R. *The Selected Poems: Expanded Edition*. New York: Norton, 1986.
Fox, Paula. *Desperate Characters*. New York: Norton, 1999.

Heaney, Seamus. *Preoccupations: Selected Prose, 1968–1978*. New York: The Noonday Press, 1980.

Hollander, John. *Rhyme's Reason: A Guide to English Verse*. New Haven: Yale University Press, 2001.

James, Henry. *The Portrait of a Lady*. London: Dent, 1983.

Kinzie, Mary. *The Cure of Poetry in an Age of Prose: Moral Essays on the Poet's Calling*. Chicago: University of Chicago Press, 1993.

Luftig, Stacy. *The Joni Mitchell Companion: Four Decades of Commentary*. New York: Schirmer Books, 2000.

Marom, Malka. *Joni Mitchell: In Her Own Words—Conversations with Malka Marom*. Toronto: ECW Press, 2014.

Miles, Josephine. *Eras and Modes in English Poetry*. Westport: Greenwood Press, 1976.

Mitchell, Joni. *Song to a Seagull*. Hollywood: Reprise Records, 1968.

Mitchell, Joni. *Hejira*. Hollywood: Asylum Records, 1976.

Weller, Sheila. *Girls Like Us: Carole King, Joni Mitchell, Carly Simon, and the Journey of a Generation*. New York: Washington Square Press, 2009.

10

"The Only Thing That's Never Going Away": Still Listening to *Blue*

Ruth Charnock

In a 2009 *New Yorker* cartoon a couple sit opposite each other at a cafe. The man is balding, wearing glasses and a long, paisley scarf draped over an otherwise beige-looking outfit. The woman, also wearing glasses, is in a coat with elbow patches, a psychedelic patterned dress and lace-up knee boots. They have both come, in other words, partially dressed as the late 1960s or early 1970s, the time of their adolescence. The man appears to be speaking as the woman listens, smiling. The caption underneath reads: "The only thing that's never going away is Joni Mitchell."[1]

What does this cartoon mean? Is its caption a promise? A complaint? Or something else?

It could be a complaint. Maybe the man prefers other objects from his youth and doesn't understand the woman's continued investment in Joni Mitchell. "Joni Mitchell is never going away (but I wish she would)" in other words—a cruel reworking of "Big Yellow Taxi's" most famous line—which imagines Mitchell as a hanger-on, stubbornly present way past her time. In response, the woman smiles but also grips the table—angry, perhaps, at having Joni Mitchell dismissed and mansplained to her by someone wearing paisley.

The caption also tells us something about how sustained and sustaining an attachment to Joni Mitchell can be. She never goes away—outlasting times, places, friends, other loves—while also providing you with ways to bear these losses. Read as a consolation, the cartoon suggests that these other objects come and go but Joni is forever. We know, of course, that this is and isn't true, but the cartoon's promise is a salve, nevertheless.

The cartoon asks us to think about the complex ways that Joni Mitchell is, and isn't, associated with youth and youthful attachments, attachments that we might remain in an ambivalent and intense relationship to when we have "grown up." The recognition that an attachment to Joni Mitchell doesn't go away, and an interest in what that might mean, is what drives this chapter. In it, I will think particularly about the cultural positioning of *Blue* as the Joni Mitchell album that you're supposed to "move on" from. Under the canopy of Joni fandom, *Blue* arguably figures as the entry-level record, the Joni Mitchell that most people will own.² Culturally, it has appeared as a high school or early twenties album—the album that you leave behind when you exit this period of your life, which I'll be referring to as adolescence, here.³

Yet the figure of a sad, mostly middle-aged woman *still* listening to *Blue* is a recurrent image for this chapter, a signifier for longing and thwarted desire, desire for a time prior to the romantic disappointments of entrenched adulthood, especially those disappointments provided by hetero- and homonormative coupling. One of *Blue's* promises, a promise I'll explore by thinking about my own adolescent listening, is that, as a straight woman you can live happily outside of traditional heterosexual narratives. These promises are not what they seem, but nevertheless go some way toward explaining *Blue's* sustainability as an object for those of us still listening to it.

Just as the *New Yorker* cartoon can be read as, at least, two stories—one where a middle-aged man and woman are enjoying together their continued attachment to Joni Mitchell, and one where the man is criticizing the woman for her attachment—this chapter also thinks about how contemporary texts figure women's love for Joni Mitchell as embarrassing, irritating, anachronistic, and cruelly optimistic. The latter part of this chapter watches three contemporary scenes that cannot quite stomach women's (particularly middle-aged women's) feelings for Joni. These scenes index a broader cultural feeling about the late 1960s as a time of failed potential that doesn't seem to be going away.

In what's to come, I move between listening to *Blue* in 1971 (the year of its release), listening to it in 2003 (when I first heard it), listening to it as it appears in recent texts (where relationships with *Blue* are also figured as complexly temporal) and listening to it now. This structure plays out an interest in *Blue's* many incarnations, personal and cultural, and in seeing what happens when these incarnations are layered over each other, placed alongside each other, or interrupted by each other. But, more prosaically, this structure is shaped by my own self-interruptions. As I wrote this piece, I found it almost impossible to mute the earlier voices of my attachment to *Blue*, attachments that just prefigured my critical training which, in part, it turns out, is deeply wedded (pun intended) to linear, causal, reasoned thought modes. Of late, I have realized that these modes don't lend themselves to talking about things you love and have loved. As such, what follows is shaped by feelings, past and present, for *Blue*.

Blue's promises

Lauren Berlant observes that "when we talk about an object of desire, we are really talking about a cluster of promises we want someone or something to make to us and make possible for us" (2011, 23). Adolescence is a time, we might say, when the intensity of those promises is particularly felt. Here are the promises I heard in *Blue*, aged 21:

1. You can be romantically unattached, but not alone.
2. You can have a life with your own creativity at its center, not squeezed out by work—whether paid, domestic, or emotional.
3. You can have joyful encounters with men and leave without regret or other bad feelings.
4. You can vocalize your desires—in all their excessive, rambling, maybe sometimes narcissistic colors and no one will shut them down.
5. Life can be a series of absorbing scenes that you move through and make things from.
6. You do not have to "grow out of" or otherwise relinquish any of your attachments to these promises.

None of these were easy or necessarily attainable things for all (or even most) women in 1971, or in 2003—nor are they now. But certain songs on *Blue*—particularly "All I Want," "Carey," and "California"—suggest their ease and attainability and, relatedly, suggest that the 1960s free-love project has been genuinely liberating for women: or for Joni, at least. Aged 21, a lax reader of the 1960s, and a lax listener to *Blue*, as will become apparent, it was *Blue's* three free (sounding) love songs that I invested in the most.

"Carey," "California," and "All I Want" all evoke the agentic pleasures and possibilities of solo, female travel (Greece-maybe, Amsterdam-maybe, Rome; or Greece-Paris-Spain-maybe, California; dancing in dives! dancing on beaches! bitter wine!). Not all of these were scenes of desire I attached to in their specifics (I didn't really want to shampoo a man or knit him a sweater) but I passionately bequeathed myself to the force of their collection, and the freedom of their expression, driven by Joni's apparent sense of herself as a woman who had a *right* to her desires and their proliferation. All three songs keep desire in endless, joyful play, rather than treating it "as a problem to be solved," as Rebecca Solnit puts it (2005, 30).[4] What's more, they don't treat *female* desire as a problem to be solved—in opposition to the standard and prevailing Western pathologizing of female desire as in need of expedient fixing, pace Freud. While even the artsier cultural objects of 2003, objects such as Sofia Coppola's indie film *Lost in Translation*, presented women as (still) rendered unhappy and paralyzed by the amount of choices that they had,[5] listening to these songs on *Blue*, I had no sense that Joni was anything other than fully enthralled by her own capacity for desire and the choices before her.

Blue's capacity for desire is also one of the ways that it seems to avoid advancing down the well-trodden lifepaths of heterosexuality. "All I Want," "Carey," and "California," in particular, are much more energized by flirtation than by commitment. As Adam Phillips tells us, "The generosity of flirtation is in its implicit wish to sustain the life of desire" (2016, xviii). However, flirtation is also the thing that you are "supposed" to move beyond: "Our preference for progress narratives can make flirtation acceptable only as a means to a predictable end; flirting is fine but to be a flirt is not" (Phillips 2016, xvii). Flirtation disrupts heterosexuality's stories about moving forward (where moving forward means giving up on the desire for other possibilities and so means giving up on desire itself). And *Blue's* flirtiest songs are particularly tuneful retorts to the injunction that flirting is behavior a woman should grow out of.

When Joni isn't overtly flirting in *Blue*, she does still appear to avoid conventional looking forms of commitment. (Think of "My Old Man's" refrain—that a happy relationship needn't be a married one.) We can also see *Blue's* resistance to heteronorms in its track sequencing. For example, the album's opening triplet could, if you weren't listening very carefully, sound like a straight trajectory from desire to commitment to a baby. But we never know if Joni gets what she wants in "All I Want," marriage is deemed unnecessary in "My Old Man" (in ways that are more complex than the song admits to, as I'll discuss shortly), and, in "Little Green," the baby is a ghost: long absent, only felt in traces of what she might become, born to parents who are children themselves, and not a product either of "All I Want's" desire or "My Old Man's" (sometimes) domestic bliss. (Further disruption to the order of things: "Little Green," of course, was written before much of the rest of *Blue*.) Or, think about the way in which "The Last Time I Saw Richard" pictures an encounter with an old beau (purportedly Mitchell's ex-husband) that took place three years before *Blue*. The album *does* end with a marriage (two marriages, really—if you count Joni's marriage to Chuck Mitchell), but one has failed and the other sounds miserably bourgeois: Richard sits at home alone with only the dishwasher and the coffee percolator for company. By ending with "Richard," *Blue* undermines the marriage plot, where the wedding is the happy climax that needn't be imagined beyond.

In its disruptions to normative heterosexuality, its dwelling in moments of flight from romantic relationships, its attachment to scenes of potential and, especially, what felt like its relentless insistence on the primacy of female desire, choice and freedom, *Blue* sounded to my 21-year-old ears like a gorgeously promissory glimpse into what it must have been like, being Joni in 1971, and what it could be like for me in 2003, in love with my loving *and* my freedom (like Joni!). "All I Want," "Carey," and "California" provided especially promising scenes of untrammeled freedom and potential and made desiring sound like the best possible way a woman could spend her time. Suffice to say that, when I was 21 (which was a very good year), I loved flirting and I always skipped "Blue."

Skipping "Blue"

"Blue" dragged and held on too tight. "Blue" was fragile, wavering. "Blue" sounded exhausted and felt exhausting to listen to—so deflating after

"Carey's" flirty flights; such a cold-water shock. "Blue" made hard work out of desire. "Blue" did not make any promises, only tried to extract them from a man who didn't seem to be listening (we might hear the line "Hey Blue/ here is a song for you" as one of "Blue's" attempts to get Blue's attention and the song itself as a cri de coeur into an empty space). In "Blue's" drawn-out, melismatic lines, its use of the sustain pedal so that, even in its pauses you can still hear traces of what has been, I heard a roster of sticky and unpalatable feelings keeping Joni trapped, half-in and half-out of commitment, unable to move one way or another, becoming more enmeshed the more she tried to disentangle herself from the "no strings attached" relationship that was free love's proposition. As Mitchell herself put it, and as "Blue" makes manifest, free love "came with great strings attached. It was free for men, but not for women, same as it ever was."[6]

In response to the preceding run of "All I Want," "My Old Man," and "Carey," "Blue" offers two troubling thoughts: first, that Joni Mitchell wants to commit more than a man and; second, that the project of free love, which seemed to promise so much to women regarding the viability and importance of their own desire, was just a trick played by men who wanted "lots of ass/ [and] lots of laughs."[7] While "Blue" has "lots of laughs," it doesn't tell any jokes, unless you count the one it tells about the 1960s—which is not a funny one. Furthermore, in its sandwiching between "Carey" and "California's" fantasies of romantic nonattachment, "Blue" also suggests how "Carey" might really end and sends out a warning to "California's" enjoyment of its own mobility. In this way, "Blue" hears free love, a mode invested in the idea that men and women could and, indeed *should* dwell in endless flirtation, as a (pretty) lie, one told by men who turned their commitment phobia into a political manifesto.[8] In its obstruction to flirting (particularly within *Blue's* schema), "Blue" refuses the idea that flirtation could ever have been a viable political mode and suggests that men fetishized flirtation to make women feel bad about their (possible) desire for romantic commitment.

Free love made flirtation look hip and commitment look square, a thing, as Jenny Diski puts it "that we were supposed to have stopped caring about" (2010, 60). One can listen to many female artists' songs from the late 1960s and early 1970s and hear the emotional labor of women who clearly *do* still care and are trying to persuade errant men to commit to them. Think, for example, of the fierce desperation of Janis Joplin, who in "Cry Baby" tries relentlessly to draw her man (who's not hers, not really) back from his wanderings by promising him a shoulder to cry on. In Joplin's June 1970 interview with Dick Cavett (following a performance of "Move Over," another song about a man who won't stay or go), she remarks to Cavett that men "always hold up something more than they're prepared to give."[9] Or think of Laura Nyro's "Wedding Bell Blues" (1966) which sounds less urgent and labored in its delivery than "Cry Baby" but is no less frustrated by its man, the freewheeling "Bill," who refuses to marry his girlfriend. "Blue" belongs to this category of songs of women frustrated by men more in love with their freedom than their loving.

The song directs its bad feeling not only at free love, but at the 1960s counterculture as a whole. In the line, "acid, booze and ass/needles, guns and grass/lots of laughs, lots of laughs," Mitchell sticks a pin in "Woodstock"/ Woodstock deflating its airy utopian dreams with pointed, pragmatic precision. "Blue" seems to make light work of both song and event and any reading of it as a political or cultural zeitgeist. Quick work too, because, the 1960s were barely over by the time Mitchell wrote "Blue."[10] The latter plays out the counterculture's commitment issues, in its attempts to minimize and shake off "Woodstock's" hazy, under-conceptualized dreams of what the counterculture might achieve[11] and in its suspicions that men benefit from free love while women suffer, not free at all.

Yet, though they are fading and looked upon with disappointment, the dreams of happier past scenes still persist, faintly, in "Blue" as a "sigh/a foggy lullaby." Despite its disavowals of the counterculture's utopian dreams, its heaviness, and its moments of lyrical and melodic drag, it does not fully commit to cynicism and despair. As Lloyd Whitesell identifies, the song has moments of "rhythmic release" and "uplift" (2008, 136) that interrupt its leaden descent. While I heard "Blue" as an unwelcome intrusion into what I perceived as *Blue*'s mostly hopeful modes, Whitesell insightfully points to the way these modes also lighten up "Blue's" heavy load. Speaking specifically here about the end of the line "Blue, I love you," Whitesell notices that "the harmonies seem to spin off into a new key altogether":

> This momentary sidetrack is patently wishful, its gestures somehow not fully integrated into the song's fabric. And in fact the piano cadences in these four measures do represent a kind of intrusion, constituting as they do any almost exact quotation of a passage from another love song on the album—the introduction to "My Old Man." They thus [. . .] capture and import the brief memory of a happier time and a different outcome. (2008, 137)

"My Old Man," lest we forget, is also a song about romantic commitment but one which treats it with a light touch—sure, Joni and her old man aren't married but they don't need to be to commit to each other and, sure, he might go away (where *does* he go?) but he'll always come back again to share her bed and eat her food. Rendered this way, of course, "My Old Man" looks like another song where Mitchell is consoling herself about a man who won't stick around; where free love turns out to be a woman keeping house for a man while he goes out and loves *his* freedom and she mourns a too-big bed. It's not necessarily the case, then, that "My Old Man" represents a "happier time and a different outcome," as Whitesell puts it (137). That said, in "Blue," "My Old Man" appears as a foggy lullaby, one about how free love might have kept women's blues away—even if "My Old Man" doesn't quite believe its own bedtime stories.

In her fantastic consideration of queer time and the objects it shapes, *Time Binds: Queer Temporalities, Queer Histories*, Elizabeth Freeman describes the 1960s and 1970s as composed of "a series of failed revolutions [. . .]—political programs not only as yet incompletely realized but also impossible to realize in their original mode." Here, Freeman is talking of the failure of "class revolution [. . .] of second-wave feminism's lost possibilities; the unfinished mutually intertwined projects of black emancipation and gay freedom." The texts that Freeman deals with all index this period as a moment of failed potential that cannot, yet, be fully disavowed by the contemporary, precisely because the politically revolutionary work of the decade remains undone. Within her corpus "[the 1970s] glimmer forth as an embarrassment, as something that remains to be thought, as [. . .] indigestible material" (Freeman 2010, xiv).

Aged 21, I heard "Blue" as *Blue's* indigestible material—the song I rejected because it got in the way of my sense of *Blue* as an album about how great free love was for women. Coming between the airy mobility of "Carey" and "California," both songs that appear to make flighty work of romantic attachment (literally, in that both imagine leaving relationships by air), "Blue" drops like an anchor. It looks back on the objects of the late 1960s, particularly free love and the utopian dreams of "Woodstock," with a kind of embarrassment that fails to fully vanquish the feeling that these objects still have potential.[12]

The contemporary texts that I'll turn to now suggest that there's something *unincorporable* (to borrow Freeman's language) about *Blue* and Joni, that they cannot be absorbed into these texts' narratives, and that they cause uncomfortable scenes. These texts are also fascinated by the fact that, as in the cartoon, Joni hasn't gone away. Furthermore, these texts index Joni Mitchell and *Blue* as troubling clues to who these women were, what they might have been, what they became and what they might, still, become.

Blue's stretched-out adolescence

In *Love Actually*, an episode of *New Girl*,[13] and in *The Kids Are All Right*, women time travel by listening to Joni Mitchell, going back to their adolescence and, especially, modes of adolescent listening: listening on repeat, listening closely, listening in the bedroom, and listening while singing along. Adolescence shimmers in these texts as a time of potentiality, of pleasured and extended absorption in objects of desire, particularly *Blue*, a time of learning how to feel—where many of these feelings were learnt by listening to Joni Mitchell.

One of the things *Blue* promises, then, is what J. Jack Halberstam calls a "stretched-out adolescence":

> The notion of a stretched-out adolescence [. . .] challenges the conventional binary formulation of a life narrative divided by a clear break between youth and adulthood; this life narrative charts an obvious transition out of childish dependency through marriage and into adult responsibility through adulthood. (2005, 153)

The stretched-out adolescence refuses the temporal markers of heteronormativity (babies, marriage, monogamy), and instead, according to Jana Funke and Ben Davies: "insist[s] on expanded moments lived with heightened intensity and urgency" (2011, 7). As I've already delineated, there are several ways *Blue* insists on such "expanded moments," even if there remains a question as to whether Joni always loves her freedom as much as certain songs seem to proclaim. In this way, *Blue* languishes in a stretched-out adolescence, predicated on what Jenny Diski describes as the counterculture's intention "to live out Peter Pan's imperative never [...] grow up." (Diski 2010, 3) *Blue* is often also marked as the album of the neophyte listener, the amateur who has not yet matured enough to move on to Joni's "harder" albums, who keeps going back to *Blue*.

Backslide/still listening

An episode of the TV series *New Girl* entitled, aptly, "Backslide" (2012) indexes *Blue* as the album that stretched-out adolescents are sad to. The series is premised on disappointed and interrupted heteronormativity; the first episode sees protagonist, Jess, a woman in her late twenties, moving into an all-male houseshare when she breaks up with her boyfriend. "Backslide" opens with Jess listening to "River" on repeat in states of unravelling melancholia over one day—represented in the first few moments by a series of shots: we see Jess on her bed, crying to "River," fetal on the floor, crying to "River," then sitting in her closet with her best friend, crying to "River." In these moments, Jess appears adolescent: she cries in her room, she doesn't seem to have to go to work, she has time to listen to "River" on loop, and she gets on everyone's nerves.[14]

The episode plays out a series of scenarios where its central characters (particularly Jess and romantic lead, Nick) go back to ex-partners. Backsliding, both in the romantic terms that the program employs and, more broadly, is culturally coded as a bad move (although those of us who lean to the queer might rather like it); associated with regression, relapse, and going astray. "Backslide" recognizes the temptations of straying off the path of straightforward relationality but also presents its characters' sallies back into the past as wrong-footed, a wrong-footedness that, in Jess's case, is mapped onto her retro and repetitive listening to "River." In this way, the episode reads Jess's attachment to "River" as an *over*-attachment to a past that will not reward her. She ends up sleeping with her ex, an "ugly crier," who happens to be in a relationship. Listening too much to "River," the program imagines, will lead to you being uncomfortably saddled (albeit temporarily in the episode) with a man whose abject emotionality trumps your own. As such, Joni Mitchell's music is presented as a bad object Jess needs to move on from, if she is to move forward.

As Joanne Winning has discussed, the film *Love Actually* (2003) also figures Karen's relationship to Joni Mitchell initially, through "River" (here, in its guise as sad Christmas song—prefiguring Karen's own sad Christmas to come) which plays in the background as odious husband Harry remarks "I can't believe you still listen to Joni Mitchell." "True love lasts a lifetime"[15] Karen responds, suggesting both the durability of an attachment to Joni Mitchell (Joni Mitchell is never going away) but also prefiguring the masochistic structures of heterosexual romance played out by Karen's later response to Harry's infidelity: the film implies that she will not leave him, although he might leave her, for a while.[16] In an unarticulated but implied triangulation, *Love Actually* also implies that Karen's lifelong attachment to Joni Mitchell is one of the reasons why she *will* stay with Harry: the lesson she has learnt from Joni Mitchell is to feel deeply for a man who doesn't deserve her depth of feeling. (Another of heteronormativity's cruelties in *Love Actually*: you might wind up saddled with a man who does not like Joni Mitchell and cheats on you with someone who prefers the Sugababes.)

Initially, it appears to Karen (although not to the viewer) that her articulation of her love for Joni Mitchell might reap surprising gifts. She finds a jewelry box, a heart-shaped necklace, in Harry's coat pocket, a Christmas gift that, she presumes, is for her and a promising change from the boring scarves he has been buying for most of their marriage. While *we* know that this gift is for Harry's secretary, not for Karen, she doesn't know this yet. As such, the film indirectly associates Karen's articulation of her lifelong love for Joni Mitchell with her husband suddenly seeing her as a desirable love object again.

Yet when Karen unwraps her gift from Harry, it is a copy of Joni Mitchell's 2000 album *Both Sides Now* that she finds. In this way, Karen's attachment to Joni Mitchell both works as the object that allows her to imagine that her husband still finds her desirable and the object that confirms he does not. "To continue your emotional education," says Harry, as he hands her the box. This is undoubtedly the film's most misogynistic moment: with its message that middle-aged women need to be educated out of hoping that their husbands could ever want them again. Joni Mitchell is tooled, here, to deliver that gift and to provide consolation, on receipt. Upon receiving the album, Karen goes into the marital bedroom, puts on the record and paces in circles, fighting back tears, while Mitchell's 2000 version of "Both Sides, Now" plays in the background. The film ultimately diminishes Joni Mitchell and the woman who loves her by showing Karen minimizing, squashing down, and sublimating her feelings about this betrayal, while listening to "Both Sides, Now"—a song, inevitably, about romantic disappointment and the (female) hope that produces it.

Harry's observation that Karen "still listens" to Joni Mitchell—like Jess's housemates' growing irritation as she listens to "River" on repeat—positions Mitchell and, particularly, *Blue* as an object from the past that women cannot let go of. These texts read Jess's and Karen's attachment to Joni Mitchell as an adolescent and retarding desire threatening their ability to move forward (Jess supine in her room, listening to "River" on repeat; Karen in the marital bedroom, pacing the floor to "Both Sides, Now"). Insofar as either *New Girl* or *Love Actually* have negative feelings about heteronormativity, these texts play out these feelings via Joni Mitchell and the women who (still) listen to her. Both texts also employ minimizing strategies to try and contain *Blue's* threat to heteronormative narratives. In *New Girl*, Jess's listening is figured first as a joke, then as an irritation, then as a thing that she needs to be relieved and distracted from. *Love Actually* presents Karen's love for Joni Mitchell as an anachronism (why is she *still* listening?), thus also interpellating Karen as a love object from the past who will be traded in for someone new. There's an uncanny twisting of the marriage rite old/new/borrowed/blue/*Blue* to this.

"All I Want"

Another scene, from the queer family drama *The Kids Are All Right*,[17] picks up the same troping of Joni Mitchell as the musician women are unhappily glommed to, but with a difference in that this scene proffers more fully the possibility that this attachment might be an energizing and sustaining one. Part of the way through the film, we see Nic, an uptight, possibly alcoholic middle-aged woman contemplate a copy of *Blue* as her assembled family—featuring wife, Jules, their children Laser and Joni,[18] and sperm donor Paul, who is having an affair with Jules (but Nic doesn't know this yet)—happily prepare dinner behind her. Nic is excluded from this scene of hetero-worldmaking; her (re)discovery of *Blue* presages a brief, unadulterated moment of pleasure, despite this exclusion.[19]

Nic brings up the subject of Joni Mitchell at the table, as the family are assembled, eating. "'Hey, I noticed your record collection,'" Nic says to Paul before asking him what his favorite Joni album is. "*Blue*," replies Paul. "Ohhhh," sighs Nic—reaching to high-five him across the table—to which Paul replies—in a snaky moment of disingenuous connection, when placed against Nic's real vulnerability in this scene, not to mention evidence of the film's insidiously conservative gender politics[20]—"my brother from another mother." In response, mercifully sidestepping Paul's interpellation, Nic invokes a time before she was a woman at a family dinner trying to bond with the sperm donor who happened also to be fucking her wife: "Listen—I spent half of high school in my room crying to that album. That record? It kills me."

Nic then launches into an earnest, vulnerable, tuneless, and arrhythmical performance of "All I Want" as her family (with the exception of Paul who is a fellow, if less ardently vocal Joni fan) watch in varying states of discomfort, states which deepen the longer that Nic performs. We see Nic move into a kind of rapture: her eyes close, her head tilts back, she is lost in music; she is, posturally, an uncanny if more-butch reiteration of Joni on the cover of *Blue*, a reiteration that suggests the rightness of her attachment to the album, while also never letting the viewer forget her distance from Joni's straight femininity.

But Nic is also at a painful series of removes from the song's original which plays, extra-diegetically, throughout the scene. Her alto might, at a stretch, invoke the deepening of Mitchell's voice to come but here it stands in stark contrast to Mitchell's young soprano. And Nic's timing and tuning are out: she stretches words Mitchell doesn't; she falls in and out of the original key (mostly out). She's singing along but isn't—both because she can't hear the original and because she isn't rendering it faithfully. This makes sense, viewed in one way: after all, "All I Want" is a song, on its top layer, about straight desire—that Nic cannot sync up or sing in tune with its melody (it is a tricky one too, to be fair) is one of the film's only true queer moments.

Nic's attachment to *Blue* and her rendering of this attachment through "All I Want" isn't nostalgic, or not in any simple way, at least. As Elizabeth Freeman argues, simple nostalgia suggests that "a given form has a stable referent, a prior wholeness locatable in a time and place we ought to "get back to"" (2011, 31). However, Nic's attachment to *Blue* is a thing of the present, happening now, as well as then. We see this in her description of *Blue* as an album that she cried to in high school, and that kills her now, still; one of the understandings that dawns across this scene is that the way *Blue* kills you in high school might be very different from the ways it kills you in middle age. "All I Want" may sound like pure hope to an adolescent, practicing desiring and being desired, but by the time you have collected a few relationships, there might be something exhausting about its endless oscillations between loving and hating, desiring another and wanting your freedom. The scene unfolds this knowledge via a series of awkward (in)congruences: between Nic and the rest of her family and between Nic's voice and Joni Mitchell's voice.[21]

By the overlaying of Nic's voice onto Joni's in this scene we are made to confront the disjuncts between what Nic wants (the desire, freedom and potentiality that are suggested as romantic love's possibilities in "All I Want") and what she has (a wife who is cheating on her with the sperm donor; a drinking problem). We might think, then, of Nic's as a bad cover version of "All I Want"—bad, in its explicit mapping against the original in this scene; bad, in that Nic's rendition results in her family's embarrassment and bad, in that Nic's pleasured, loosening absorption in *Blue* loosens her up to the point that she goes to the bathroom, whereupon she discovers her wife Jules's hair in Paul's hairbrush, then in his bathroom bin, then by his bed.

In *New Girl*, *Love Actually*, and *The Kids Are All Right*, listening (and sometimes singing) to Joni Mitchell evokes the promises of a stretched-out adolescence. Yet each text also punctures these promises in a series of horrible, "educative" moves where female characters are shown that they can never get back to their adolescent potential and that their adult lives are also worsened by their sustained attachment to Joni. In this way, these texts present attaching to Joni Mitchell beyond adolescence as an exercise in cruel optimism. "A relation of cruel optimism exists," as Lauren Berlant tells us, "when something you desire is actually an obstacle to your flourishing" (2011, 10). All of the women in these texts want Joni Mitchell, in complex ways, and all of them are punished for this desire. What Karen and Nic want, particularly, as middle-aged women is to feel endlessly desirable and desiring, feelings that they associate with being young, and listening to Joni Mitchell. But more expansively, these women desire the same things that *Blue* desires but also cannot make happen for itself: namely, sustained and sustainable ways of being a woman outside of the misogynistic, deterministic, heteronormative and constrictive narratives of the patriarchy. As a dear friend and contributor to this volume put it to me: "Not even Joni could be Joni. *Blue* [. . .] with all its contradictions, kind of shows that."[22]

Conclusion

"The real problem with adolescence," writes Adam Phillips, "is that most people can't sustain it." (2016, 169) This is one of the sadnesses of listening to *Blue* once deep into adulthood: there are ways in which it reminds us of things we have failed to sustain, of things we thought were endlessly sustainable which we now feel are not, of feelings/people/scenes/dreams we have forgotten or moved away from which we did not think we ever would. Some of these are *Blue's* feelings, too.

Maybe the thing that's most painful about listening to *Blue* in adulthood is that it takes you back to a time before you had quite realized, as a woman, how certain cultural stories were waiting to close around you, that you would be implicated, either way, by your relationship to these stories, and that your sense of yourself, aged 21, as endlessly desiring, desirable, possible, porous, and suspended joyfully in your utter, utter *Blue* rapture would not last. I'm not saying that, aged 21, I hadn't experienced misogyny, or other forms of gendered injustice, or that I didn't have a feminist politics. I am saying that I didn't yet know how much of my time would be taken up by thinking about and in resistance to these stories about being a woman, stories about who I was, should be, could be, would be.

> Instead, I spent my time listening to *Blue* (but not "Blue")—dreaming of all I wanted.

Coda

Our unlived lives—the lives we live in fantasy, the wished-for-lives are often more important to us than our so-called lived lives. (Phillips 2016, xvi)

It is 2003 in Norwich and I have missed my 21st-birthday party twice: first, by sneaking out to a nearby park to drink wine on the swings with a man I am in love with who has a girlfriend, second because, on my return to a worryingly quiet house, I get so stoned that my friends have to put me to bed, whereupon, so I'm told, the party happens without me. The next morning, at 6.00 a.m., I awake to the sounds of "Hi-Ho Silver Lining" belting from my neighbor's kitchen. He is an ex-policeman; he has been kept awake all night; he smelled the drugs. Abject and frightened, I apologize before going back home to clean up after a party I missed. That afternoon, tired already of being 21, wishing I was anywhere but there, feeling too old and too young, a friend gives me my birthday present: a ripped copy of Joni Mitchell's *Blue*. "This will sort you out," he says.

> And for a long time and still, sometimes, it does.

Notes

1. Victoria Roberts, "The Only Thing That's Never Going Away is Joni Mitchell," *New Yorker* (March 16, 2009). http://jonimitchell.com/library/cr_miscellaneous.cfm?id=336 (accessed: June 11, 2018).
2. In her essay on Joni Mitchell, Zadie Smith describes *Blue* as "the album pretty much every fool owns." See Smith, "Some Notes on Attunement: A Voyage around Joni Mitchell," *New Yorker* (December 17, 2012). https://www.newyorker.com/magazine/2012/12/17/some-notes-on-attunement (accessed: June 2, 2018).
3. Recent research suggests adolescence now extends into early twenties. See, for example, Lucy Pasha-Robinson, "Adolescence Now Lasts from 10 to 24, Say Scientists," *The Independent* (January 9, 2018). https://www.independent.co.uk/news/health/adolescence-puberty-10-24-teenager-scientists-report-lancet-a8168481.html (accessed: June 11, 2018).
4. Solnit is not talking explicitly of *Blue*, here but she is talking about blue—specifically the desire one might feel when looking towards the blue of a horizon.
5. Postfeminist ideology reigned throughout this period. For an account of this ideology, see Angela McRobbie, "Post-feminism and Popular Culture," *Feminist Media Studies*, 4.3 (2004): 255–264.
6. Quoted in Judy Kutulas, " 'That's the Way I've Always Heard It Should Be': Baby Boomers, 1970s Singer-Songwriters, and Romantic Relationships," *Journal of American History*, 97.3 (2010): 682–702. [Actual source unknown].
7. Joni Mitchell, "Blue," *Blue* (Hollywood: Reprise Records, 1971).
8. Sean Nelson makes a similar point, with regards "Little Green" in his *Court and Spark* (New York: Continuum, 2007), 29–30.
9. Janis Joplin and Dick Cavett, *The Dick Cavett Show* (June 25, 1970). https://www.youtube.com/watch?v=Z-QBjZF4e4o (accessed: June 2, 2018).
10. As Michelle Mercer puts it: "In retrospect, everyone can see how the '60s went bad. But Mitchell's time frame for hindsight was always much tighter than most people's. What take most of us a few years to realize seemed to take her only a few months" (Mercer 2012, 175).
11. Let's not forget, though, that "Woodstock" was already nostalgic for Woodstock, an event which Mitchell did not, herself, attend.
12. "California" has similar feelings to "Blue" but tries not to look at them as closely.
13. "Backslide," *New Girl*, dir. Nanette Burstein (2012).
14. It should be clear from this that the episode presents Jess's listening in highly gendered ways.
15. *Love Actually*, dir. Richard Curtis (2003).

16 There is much to hate about *Love Actually*'s treatment of Karen.
17 *The Kids Are All Right,* dir. Lisa Cholodenko (2010).
18 Jules and Nic's naming of their teenage daughter after Joni Mitchell is another way that the film associates the singer with figures of adolescence.
19 And maybe also because of it—something I don't have the space to discuss here.
20 For more on these, see Jack Halberstam, "The Kids Aren't All Right!" *Bully Bloggers* (July 15, 2010). https://bullybloggers.wordpress.com/2010/07/15/the-kids-arent-alright/ (accessed: June 11, 2018).
21 There's a further incongruence in the combination of Paul and Nic's voices in this scene—they start by singing together—that is another of its complex layers.
22 Conversation with Pam Thurschwell, private correspondence, May 2018.

Works Cited

Berlant, Lauren. *Cruel Optimism*. Durham and London: Duke University Press, 2011.
Burstein, Nanette. Dir. "Backslide," *New Girl*. 2012.
Cholodenko, Lisa. Dir. *The Kids Are All Right*. 2010.
Curtis, Richard. Dir. *Love Actually*. 2003.
Diski, Jenny. *The Sixties*. London: Profile Books, 2010.
Freeman, Elizabeth. *Time Binds: Queer Temporalities, Queer Histories*. Durham & London: Duke University Press, 2010.
Freeman, Elizabeth. "Still After," in *After Sex: On Writing Since Queer Theory*, ed. Janet Halley and Andrew Parker. Durham and London: Duke University Press, 2011.27–34.
Funke, Jana, and Ben Davies, eds. *Sex, Gender and Time in Fiction and Culture*. London: Palgrave, 2011.
Halberstam, Jack. "The Kids Aren't All Right!" *Bully Bloggers*, July, 2010. https://bullybloggers.wordpress.com/2010/07/15/the-kids-arent-alright/ (accessed: June 13, 2018).
Halberstam, J. Jack. *In a Queer Time and Place: Transgender Bodies, Subcultural Lives*. New York: New York University Press, 2005.
Joplin, Janis, and Dick Cavett. *The Dick Cavett Show*. June 25, 1970. https://www.youtube.com/watch?v=Z-QBjZF4e4o (accessed: June 2, 2018).
Kutulas, Judy. "'That's the Way I've Always Heard It Should Be': Baby Boomers, 1970s Singer-Songwriters, and Romantic Relationships." *Journal of American History*, 97.3 (2010): 682–702.

Mercer, Michelle. *Will You Take Me as I Am: Joni Mitchell's Blue Period*. Milwaukee: Backbeat Books, 2012.

Mitchell, Joni. *Blue*. Hollywood: Reprise Records, 1971.

Nelson, Sean. *Court and Spark (33 1/3)*. New York: Continuum, 2007.

Pasha-Robinson, Lucy. "Adolescence Now Lasts from 10 to 24, Say Scientists," *The Independent*, January 9, 2018. /www.independent.co.uk/news/health/adolescence-puberty-10-24-teenager-scientists-report-lancet-a8168481.html (accessed: June 11, 2018).

Phillips, Adam. *On Flirtation*. Cambridge: Harvard University Press, 1996.

Phillips, Adam. *Missing Out: In Praise of the Unlived Life*. London: Penguin, 2016.

Roberts, Victoria. "The Only Thing That's Never Going Away is Joni Mitchell," *New Yorker*. March 16, 2009.

Smith, Zadie. "Some Notes on Attunement: A Voyage around Joni Mitchell," *New Yorker*. December 17, 2012. https://www.newyorker.com/magazine/2012/12/17/some-notes-on-attunement (accessed: June 2, 2018).

Solnit, Rebecca. *A Field Guide to Getting Lost*. Edinburgh: Canongate, 2005.

Whitesell, Lloyd. *The Music of Joni Mitchell*. New York: Oxford University Press, 2008.

Contributors

Emily Baker is a third-year PhD student at the University of Liverpool, UK. Her thesis explores the aesthetic of age in popular music, in particular how ageing voices engender a "temporal shudder" when we listen to them. This gendered phenomenon pulls on the discourses of voice, cultural studies perspectives on age and ageing processes as well as phenomenological, feminist, and queer perspectives on identity more broadly. Funded by the AHRC, in practice this means that she spends equal amounts of time reading Barthes, Foucault, and Halberstam as she does listening to Dolly Parton, Aretha Franklin and, of course, Joni Mitchell.

Ruth Charnock is the editor of this collection and a senior lecturer in English Literature at the University of Lincoln, UK. She writes about contemporary culture, feminism, music, affect, and sex. Her monograph *Anaïs Nin: Bad Sex, Shame and Contemporary Culture* is forthcoming in 2020. If you want her, she'll be in the bar.

Peter Coviello is Professor of English at the University of Illinois, Chicago, USA. He has written about Walt Whitman, Steely Dan, step-parenthood, the history of sexuality, queer children, American literature, Chance the Rapper, polygamy, and Prince. His newest book is *Long Players: A Love Story in Eighteen Songs*, published in the spring of 2018.

Anne Hilker is a doctoral candidate at Bard Graduate Center, New York, and a long-time admirer of Joni Mitchell's music. She thanks Ruth Charnock for her tireless and thoughtful editing.

Matthew J. Jones received a doctorate in Critical and Comparative Studies of Music from the University of Virginia, USA, in 2014. Since then, he has held visiting lectureships and professorships at the University of Georgia and Miami University. His work explores the intersections of American music with queerness, disability, illness, and social justice activism. His work appears in *The Journal of Popular Music Studies*, *Women & Music*, and *The Oxford Handbook of Music and Queerness*, and his essay in *The Journal of the Society for American Music* won the prestigious ASCAP Deems Taylor/ Virgil Thomson concert music criticism article prize in 2017. While continuing his search for a tenure-track position, Matt lives in Ohio with his cat, Joan Clawford.

Eric Lott teaches American Studies at the Graduate Center of the City University of New York, USA, where he currently chairs the English Program. He is the author of *Love and Theft: Blackface Minstrelsy and the American Working Class* (1993; twentieth-anniversary ed., 2013), from which Bob Dylan took the title for his 2001 album *Love and Theft*; *The Disappearing Liberal Intellectual* (2006); and *Black Mirror: The Cultural Contradictions of American Racism* (2017), a study of race, culture, and fantasy across the long twentieth century.

Gustavus Stadler is Associate Professor of English at Haverford College, USA. He is the author of *Troubling Minds: The Cultural Politics of Genius in the U. S. 1840–1890* (2006) and numerous articles on American literature and aural cultures of the nineteenth and twentieth centuries. His book *Woody Guthrie and the Intimate Life of the Left* is forthcoming.

Pamela Thurschwell is a Reader in English at the University of Sussex, UK. She has written *Literature, Technology and Magical Thinking, 1880–1920* (2001) and the Routledge Critical Thinkers, *Sigmund Freud* (2009), and edited *Quadrophenia and Mod(ern) Culture* (2017), and has published widely on Henry James and pop music. She is currently working on a book called *Keep your Back to the Future: Adolescent Time Travel across the 20th Century*.

Howard Wilde is lecturer in music at the University of Hull, UK, where he teaches music analysis, rock/pop musicology, and songwriting. He has published reviews and essays on popular music and is currently working on a chapter on Dylan and Shakespeare for Oxford University Press.

Joanne Winning has research interests in twentieth-century and twenty-first-century literatures, culture, theory, and practice. Her specific interests include: modernisms, especially female and lesbian modernism; critical and cultural theory in the twentieth century; theories of gender and sexuality; lesbian subjectivities and cultural production; psychoanalysis and its theories; relations between illness, language and the clinical encounter; medical humanities and the interface between critical theory in the humanities and clinical practice in medicine.

Index

adolescence 1–7, 201–4, 209–10, 215
album covers. *See under* individual albums
aleatoric music 77–8
Alias, Don 124, 130–1, 134–5, 137
Altamont 103, 109, 124. See also *Gimme Shelter*
Arc Iris x–xiii, 7
Art Nouveau/Claude the Pimp. See under *Don Juan's Reckless Daughter*
Atwood, Margaret 12, 14, 167–79
    and *Cat's Eye* 167, 169–73
    and *The Circle Game* 175–6
    and feminism 167–70
    and *The Handmaid's Tale* 168–9

Baez, Joan 106, 129–30, 143, 146, 148
Band, The 12, 104–17. *See also* Rick Danko, Bob Dylan, Robbie Robertson, Levon Helm, Richard Manuel, *The Last Waltz*
Barthes, Roland. *See under* voice and the grain
Bartók, Béla 32, 154
Beatles, The 87, 127, 148, 158
Benjamin, Jessica. *See under* "Both Sides, Now" and thirdness
Berlant, Lauren 4, 168, 203, 215
Black Cat in the Black Mouse Socks, The 12, 123
Bloom, Harold 143, 145–6, 158
Bonenfant, Yvon 55, 79
Bowie, David 146
Brahms, Johannes 48
Browne, Jackson 123, 127, 136

Canada, images of 170–9, 192. *See also* Margaret Atwood, feminism
Carter, Rubin 130–1. *See also* "Hurricane" (Bob Dylan)
chords of inquiry 29, 85, 93, 115. *See also* tunings

Clapton, Eric 114
Claude the Pimp. See under *Don Juan's Reckless Daughter*
Cohen, Leonard 143, 146, 151, 155
Collins, Judy 66, 86–7, 148
compulsory heterosexuality. *See under* heteronormativity
cover versions x–xiii, 47, 66, 86–7, 124, 135, 141, 146, 148, 157, 175, 214–15
cripping 13, 21–37. *See also* polio and PPS
    and harmony 28–31
    and technique 31–6. *See also* tunings
    and virtuosity 21–8, 31, 36–7
critics, relationships with 14
crooner, the 43, 55–6
Crosby, David 1, 6, 114, 123
Crosby, Stills & Nash 127
Crosby, Stills, Nash & Young 86–7
Curtis, Richard 69–71, 79. *See also Love Actually*

Danko, Rick 12, 105–7, 111–17. *See also* The Band, *The Last Waltz*
    and "Sip the Wine" 116–17
Daum, Meghan 3–5
deep listening/detailed listening 8–9, 50
Desperate Characters 12, 186, 193–8
detailed listening. *See under* deep listening/detailed listening
DiFranco, Ani 149
Diltz, Henry 122
Doors, The 103, 127
Douglas, Mary 12, 91
Dylan, Bob 8, 12–13, 14, 106–8, 115, 129, 141–58
    and The Band 106–7
    and *The Basement Tapes* 107, 116, 147
    and canonization 142–3, 148
    and comparisons with Joni Mitchell 14, 141–58

and cover versions 146, 148, 157
and Mitchell's discussions of 141, 147
and *Renaldo and Clara* 108, 129
and the Rolling Thunder Revue 106–8, 112, 129–30
and the sermonic mode 142, 149–50, 157
albums
  Blood on the Tracks 156
  Nashville Skyline 144, 147
  Slow Train Coming 157
songs
  "Ballad of a Thin Man" 144
  "Every Grain of Sand" 151
  "Gotta Serve Somebody" 151
  "Hard Rain's A-Gonna Fall, The" 151
  "Highway 51" 147
  "Hurricane" 130, 150
  "I Shall Be Released" 115
  "It Ain't Me, Babe" 144
  "Maggie's Farm" 144
  "Not Dark Yet" 151
  "Positively Fourth Street" 147
  "Talkin' World War III Blues" 151
  "Tangled up in Blue" 150, 155–6
  "Tempest" 151
  "This Wheel's on Fire" 107, 116 *See also* Rick Danko
  "Thunder on the Mountain" 147

Eagles, The 127, 136

feminism 2, 7, 12, 14, 22, 25, 125, 133, 135, 143–4, 146, 167–83, 192–3, 198, 208, 216. *See also* gender, heterosexuality, heteronormativity, patriarchy, queerness, sexuality
Fox, Paula. See under *Desperate Characters*
Freeman, Elizabeth x, 11, 208–9, 214
Freud, Sigmund 83, 92, 158, 204

Geffen, David 106, 128, 133
gender 4–7, 14, 22, 25, 29, 45, 54–5, 107, 111–12, 114, 129, 131–2, 135, 142, 149, 169–73, 186, 191, 195–6, 213, 216. *See also* feminism, heterosexuality, queerness, sexuality

and aging 13, 44–8, 51–7
and crooning 55–6
and listening 3–7
and the music industry 7, 13, 44, 46, 51, 122, 125, 133
Gimme Shelter 103–5
Guerin, John 128

Halberstam, Judith/Jack 209–10
Hancock, Herbie. See under *River: The Joni Letters*
harmony 22, 28–30, 153. *See also* cripping
Hawkins, Ronnie 108, 129
Helm, Levon 108, 112. *See also* The Band
Hendrix, Jimi 6, 103, 108–10
heterosexuality 18, 168, 170, 204–5
heteronormativity 25, 54–5, 170, 204–5, 210–12
Hoskyns, Barney 3, 6, 126, 128

Irvin, Les 32

James, Henry 12, 185
Jazz 11, 21, 24, 27–8, 34–5, 43, 45, 48–50, 53, 73, 76, 87, 123–4, 128, 130, 132–4, 142, 146, 148, 150, 153, 155. See also *Both Sides Now*, "Both Sides, Now," *Mingus*, *Travelogue*
Joplin, Janis 108, 110, 207

Karppinen, Anne 6
Kelly, John 7, 44
Kids Are All Right, The 209, 213–15
King, Carole 123
Klein, Larry 46, 72–3, 76–7

LA Express 128
Last Waltz, The 11–13, 103–17
  and Rick Danko 12–13, 107, 114–15
  and Bob Dylan 108
  and Joni Mitchell 12–13, 107, 111, 114–15
  and Robbie Robertson 108, 111, 117
Laurel Canyon 2, 6, 104, 123–4, 126–8, 136, 173
Lennon, John 148

Lerner, Murray. See under *Message to Love: The Isle of Wight Festival 1970* 103–5
Levinson, Barry. See under *The Black Cat in the Black Mouse Socks*
Los Angeles 3, 124–8, 132
Love Actually 69–71, 78, 209, 211–12, 215. See also "Both Sides, Now," "River"
Lynyrd Skynyrd 154

Manuel, Richard 107, 111. See also The Band, *The Last Waltz*
Marling, Laura 157
Marom, Malka 2–3, 53–4, 67, 80, 84–6, 113–15, 122, 168, 171, 173, 198
melancholy 12–13, 53, 83–93
  and *Blue* 84–5
  and lyrics 83–9
  and melody 83–93
  and setting 88–93
  and suspended chords 85–7. See also chords of inquiry, tunings
Mendoza, Vince 43–4, 48–50, 54, 56, 76–7
Mercer, Michelle 2–5, 172–3, 217
Metheny, Pat 76, 92, 135
Mingus, Charles 24, 123–4, 132–5. See also *Mingus* (album)
Mitchell, Chuck 114, 133, 205
Mitchell, Joni (works)
  albums
    Blue 2–4, 6, 13–4, 45, 84–5, 90, 123, 143, 145–6, 148, 150, 152, 156, 158, 201–16
    Both Sides Now 11, 43, 51–3, 66, 70 (for Malka Marom's book of the same title, *see under* Malka Marom)
    Clouds 66, 72, 146
    Court and Spark 2–3, 8, 45, 106, 123, 128, 153, 157
    Don Juan's Reckless Daughter 12, 121–37
      and Art Nouveau/Claude the Pimp 12–13, 121–37
      cover art 123, 131
    Fiddle and the Drum, The 11
    For the Roses 123, 128

Hejira 1, 45, 105–7, 109–10
  meaning of, 115, 123, 124, 129, 146, 153, 155, 157, 192
  cover art 1, 124
Hissing of Summer Lawns, The 123, 128, 132, 146
  cover art 132
Ladies of the Canyon 45, 123, 131, 148, 175
Love Has Many Faces: A Quartet, A Ballet, Waiting to Be Danced 11
Miles of Aisles 88
Mingus 4, 10, 24, 123–4, 134–5. See also Mingus, Charles
Self Portrait 146
Shadows and Light
  Album 92
  Film 123
  Tour 3, 130, 137
Shine 10–11, 54
Song to a Seagull 2, 193
Songs of a Prairie Girl 1
Taming the Tiger 10, 36
Travelogue 11–13, 43–9, 51–7, 76
  and cover art 43, 57
Turbulent Indigo 45–6, 48, 53, 56
Wild Things Run Fast 11
songs
  "All I Want" 84, 89, 204–6, 213–15
  "Amelia" 12–13, 33, 83, 89–93, 110, 186, 190, 196, 198
    and Amelia Earhart 91–2, 110
    and the Cactus Tree Motel 12, 91–2, 186, 198
    and tuning 33
  "Barangrill" 35
  "Beat of Black Wings, The" 87
  "Big Yellow Taxi" 11, 24, 104, 123–4, 131, 201
    performance at Woodstock 104
  "Black Crow" 109
  "Blue" 12, 156, 205–9, 216
    and free love 206–9
    and Woodstock festival 207–8
  "Blue Motel Room" 129
  "Boho Dance, The" 124, 128–9
  "Borderline" 45–7, 49–54, 56–7
    and the *paso doble* 49–50, 54, 57

"Both Sides, Now" 13, 44, 65–80, 86, 92, 123, 135, 186
  and covers of 66
  and inspiration for 66–7
  and *Love Actually* 69–71, 211–12
  and Mitchell's versions of 52–3, 65–7, 69–73, 75–7
  and tuning 33
  and thirdness 11, 65, 67–9, 71, 75, 77
"Cactus Tree" 3, 12, 90, 92, 185–99
  and ideas of freedom 185–6, 190–2, 197–8
  and lyrical structure 3, 187–90
  and tunings 33, 35, 90
"California" 150–1, 203–6, 209
"Carey" 84, 90, 156, 203–6, 209
"Case of You, A" 11, 43, 66, 90, 149, 152, 156, 186
  Prince's cover of 124
"Chair in the Sky, A" 24, 134
"Chelsea Morning" 35
"Cherokee Louise" 33
"Chinese Café/Unchained Melody" 11, 85, 89
"Circle Game, The" 87, 123, 175–6
  as a response to "Sugar Mountain" 176
  and tuning 33
"Cold Blue Steel and Sweet Fire" 1, 32, 87, 89
"Come in from the Cold" 40, 88, 167, 170, 177
"Court and Spark" 132
"Coyote" 12–13, 107, 109–10, 116, 129, 186
  and *The Last Waltz* 105–6, 111–13, 115, 129
  and tuning 33, 113–15
"Dancin' Clown" 10
"Dawntreader, The" 34
"Dog Eat Dog" 24
"Don Juan's Reckless Daughter" 10
"Down to You" 170
"Dreamland" 121, 124
"Edith and the Kingpin"
"For Free" 131
"For the Roses" 137

"Free Man in Paris" 106, 128, 133
"Funeral" 10
"Furry Sings the Blues" 24, 123–4, 129
"Goodbye Pork Pie Hat" 134
"Harlem in Havana" 35
"Harry's House/Centerpiece" 8, 12, 128
"Hejira" 1, 84, 88, 92, 116, 176
  and tuning 33
"Help Me" 2, 130
"Hissing of Summer Lawns, The" 1
"In France They Kiss on Main Street" 128
"Jungle Line, The" 124, 128
"Just Like This Train"
  and tuning 33, 35
"Last Time I Saw Richard, The" x–xi, 84–6, 152–7, 205
  live performance on *Miles of Aisles* 88
"Little Green" 84, 156, 205
  and tuning 33
"Love" 87
"Magdalene Laundries" 87, 149
"Moon at the Window" 33
"My Old Man" 12, 103, 205–6, 208
"Nathan La Franeer" 24, 90
"Night Ride Home" 33
"Nothing Can Be Done" 84–5
"Otis and Marlena" 33
"Paprika Plains" 88
"Pirate of Penance, The" 90
"Priest, The" 34
"Raised on Robbery" 106
"Refuge of the Road" 116, 167, 177–9, 186, 190, 194
"River" 1, 134, 186
  and *Love Actually* 69, 211–12
  and *New Girl* 210–12
"Roses Blue" 90
"Same Situation, The" 174
"Sex Kills" 24
  and tuning 33
"Shades of Scarlett Conquering" 128
"Shadows and Light" 88, 136
"Sire of Sorrow, The (Job's Sad Song)" 85
"Slouching Towards Bethlehem" 87
  and tuning 33
"Song for Sharon" 167, 172

"Sweet Sucker Dance" 134
"Sunny Sunday" 34
"That Song About the Midway" 89
"This Place" 24
"Twisted" 128
"Underneath the Streetlight" 33
"Wolf that Lives in Lindsay, The" 32
   and tuning 34
"Woodstock" 86, 89, 123, 131, 176, 207, 209. *See also* Woodstock festival
   and CSNY cover 86–7
Monk, Katherine 2–3, 52, 54, 141
Monterey Pop 105
Morissette, Alanis 152, 157
Morrissey 141
Munro, Alice 174–5, 192, 198

Nelson, Sean 2–3, 124, 217
New Girl. See also "River" 209–10, 212, 215
Nico 148
Nietzsche, Friedrich 2, 25, 72–3, 77
Nyro, Laura 123, 207

paranoid and reparative reading 9
Pastorius, Jaco 135, 137
patriarchy 54–5, 142, 167, 170, 215. *See also* feminism, gender, heterosexuality, queerness, sexuality
Phillips, Adam 204, 215–16
polio and PPS 11, 13, 21–4, 29, 35–7. *See also* cripping
Pop music 5, 24, 28, 48–51, 123–7, 131, 143, 145–9, 152, 154, 178, 185
poptimism vs. rockism debates 5
Powers, Ann 6
Prince 5, 124, 128

queerness 3, 7, 13, 44–5, 54–7, 185, 199, 210, 213–14
   and cripping 25–6
   and the fretboard 21–2, 36
   and time x–xii, 208, 214. *See also* Elizabeth Freeman, Judith/Jack Halberstam

   and the voice 45, 50–1, 54–7

race 22, 25, 45, 51, 122–37. *See also* Art Nouveau/Claude the Pimp
   and Watts riots 124–7
Reagan, Ronald 126, 136
River: The Joni Letters 124
Robertson, Robbie 104–12, 114–17. *See also* The Band, Rick Danko, *The Last Waltz*
Rodgers, Jeffrey Pepper 30–2, 34–5
Rolling Stones, The 103, 127
Rolling Thunder Logbook 122. *See also* Sam Shepard
Ronstadt, Linda 127, 136

Schubert, Franz 22, 152
Schumann, Robert 152
Scorsese, Martin 104–5, 107–9, 111, 115–17
Sedgwick, Eve Kosofsky 7, 9, 18
Seth, Vikram 65
sexuality 2, 7, 22, 25, 46, 51, 54, 88, 110–11, 114, 130–5, 178, 191, 196, 198, 202, 204–5, 211. *See also* feminism, gender, heterosexuality, queerness
   and race 130–1, 135
Shepard, Sam 8, 106–7, 110, 129
Shorter, Wayne 78
Simon, Carly 123
Simon, Paul 148
sixties, the 14, 24, 103–5, 126–7, 131–3, 135, 152, 157, 172, 175–6, 178, 186, 191–2, 201–4, 206–9
   and the counterculture 14, 187, 207, 210
   and free love 206–9
   and protest songs 159
smoking. *See under* voice
Souther, J. D. 121
Sprechstimme. See under voice
Stills, Stephen 127
Stravinsky, Igor 48, 74, 146, 154–5
suspended chords. 85–6, 88, 90, 92, 113–15. *See also* chords of inquiry, tunings
Swerving. *See under* Harold Bloom

teenagers. *See under* adolescence
thirdness, concept of 11, 67–8, 71, 75, 77.
    See also "Both Sides, Now"
tunings 22, 24, 29–36, 46, 90, 111, 113,
    145–6, 214. *See also* Joni
    Mitchell, songs by title and
    chords of inquiry

Vazquez, Alexandra T. 8
Vietnam War, the 87, 127
Virtuoso, the. *See under* cripping and
    virtuosity
voice 50–7, 68, 77, 86–8, 111, 154, 199, 214
    and affect 65–6, 70, 74, 78–80
    and aging 13, 45, 47, 51–7, 65, 72–3, 76–
        7, 80. *See also* gender and aging
    and the grain 50–1, 55, 75
    and queerness. *See under* queerness
    and race 129, 134
    and smoking 1, 53–4, 71, 75
    and *Sprechstimme* 66, 74–5

Wainwright III, Loudon 146
Wainwright, Rufus 157
Weller, Sheila 121, 190
Whiteley, Shelia 6–7
Whitesell, Lloyd 2–3, 7–8, 12, 29, 85, 89,
    90, 124, 147, 153–4, 207–8
Who, The 103
Wilson, Carl 22
Winehouse, Amy 122
Wolfe, Tom 128, 13
Woodstock festival 1, 103, 132, 207. *For
    song see* "Woodstock"
    film 105, 187

Yaffe, David 2–3, 84, 124, 132
Yogi Joe 103–4. *See also* Woodstock festival
Young, Neil 57, 106, 111, 123, 127,
    173, 176

Zehme, Albertine. See under *Sprechstimme*